SO-ART-975

A MASTER SPEAKS

Articles from *Share International*

THIRD EDITION

SHARE INTERNATIONAL FOUNDATION

Amsterdam, London, Los Angeles

First published in the Netherlands
by Share International Foundation
PO Box 41877, 1009 DB, Amsterdam
All rights reserved
Copyright: © 1985 Benjamin Creme, London
ISBN 90-71484-01-7
© Second edition, 1994 Benjamin Creme, London
ISBN 90-71484-10-6
© Third edition, 2004 Benjamin Creme, London
ISBN 90-71484-29-7

Manufactured in the United States of America

First edition, December 1985
Second, expanded edition, January 1994
Third, expanded edition, April 2004

*The cover picture is reproduced from a painting by Benjamin Creme: **Aspiration**, 1964. The golden ball of fire represents the soul to which, through aspiration and meditation, the personality is linked by the connecting channel of light, the antahkarana.*

Contents

Preface

In every age, major and lesser spiritual teachers have guided humanity. We know them, among others, as Hercules, Hermes, Rama, Mithra, Vyasa, Shankaracharya, Krishna, Buddha, the Christ and Mohammed. They are the custodians of a Plan for the evolution of humanity and the other kingdoms of nature. This Plan works out through the agency of the esoteric Hierarchy of Masters of Wisdom.

The Masters are those members of the human family Who have made the evolutionary journey ahead of us; Who, having perfected Themselves — by the same steps by which we advance — have accepted the responsibility of guiding the rest of us to that same achievement. They have stood behind the whole evolutionary process, guiding and helping us, through a gradual expansion of consciousness, to become, like Them, perfected and illumined.

The majority of the Masters live in the remote mountain and desert areas of the world, contacting the world but seldom, and doing Their work through Their disciples, mainly by telepathic communication. It is through this means that I have the privilege of being in contact with one of the Masters. For various reasons His identity may not be revealed for the time being, but I may say that He is one of the senior members of the Hierarchy, Whose name is well known to esotericists in the West.

His information, training and stimulus have enabled me to do the work I am engaged in: making known that Maitreya, the Christ, the supreme head of the Hierarchy of Masters, is in the world. He has been in London since July 1977. There He lives and works as a modern man, concerned with modern problems — political, economic and social. He is a spiritual but not a religious teacher, an educator in the broadest sense of the word, showing the way out of the present world crisis.

One of the means by which my co-workers and I spread this information is the monthly magazine *Share International*. Since its beginning, in January 1982, my Master has been kind enough to write an article for every issue, and, as far as I know, this makes *Share International* the only magazine in the world to number one of the Masters among its contributors.

The articles contain a wealth of wisdom, insight and information, and to make it easier to reread them, as many *Share International* readers often do, we have collected them in one volume, under the title *A Master Speaks*. I hope you will find His words inspiring and relevant. His name will be known after Maitreya the Christ has come to the fore and has made His public appeal to humanity — an event which we believe is now near.

Benjamin Creme, January 1994

Editor's Note:
The third edition has been expanded to include articles appearing in *Share International* from January 1994 to December 2003.

A New Age concept of time

A much needed change in the life of humanity will come about when the concept of Time has undergone a transformation. Today, most people think of Time as an ongoing process, linking moments of action, whereas, in truth, Time is not a process but a state of mind. When we see this, we will transform our lives and enter into an altogether closer understanding of reality; a wonderful new freedom will become man's, and, no longer dogged by the limitation of Time, he will soar into his birthright.

How is this to be achieved? At present, most of us are confined within the rigid framework of our daily activities: the means of living has to be earned, decisions have to be taken in relation to others' needs, a constant battle goes on against the clock and the remorseless 'passage of time'. There is little hope within our present modes of living of any fundamental shift in our understanding of Time. Now, for the first time in history, the possibility arises for a completely new experience of that phenomenon, and social transformation is the key to this desirable happening. When humanity is One, in fact and in truth, Time will disappear. When man approaches life from the inner, creative standpoint, Time will lose its hold over our minds and thus free us from its tyranny. All of this requires a new assessment of man's place in the Universe and the establishment of a truer rapport with the Source of our Being.

It has become customary to speak of Time as a passing sequence of events. A new and more correct view of Time becomes possible when man takes the steps to align himself with his higher Self. This achieved, the way is opened for a truer understanding of cyclic activity and non-activity, and thus of Time.

Such a correct understanding is inherent in a correct relationship to our fellow men, for only when the sense of separateness no longer exists can a true realization of cyclic activity come about. A new world order, political and economic, is the essential prerequisite for this truer vision, for the required sense of Oneness can be achieved only when harmony and justice prevail. What this means in practical terms is the creation of structures — political, economic and social — which will bring men together and create the sense of Oneness on all planes and in every field. When men see this, they will take the measures to implement the necessary changes and pave the way for the establishment of correct human relations. From that new relationship between men will emerge the conditions on which a new sense of Time depends.

From the Master's viewpoint, Time exists only in the sense of cyclic waves of activity, followed by non-activity, repeated infinitely. He is completely unconditioned by Time as sensed in the three worlds of human experience, and must make constant adjustments when dealing with His disciples, for instance, in order to accommodate His meaning and intentions to the state of consciousness of those still ensnared by Time.

Already, signs are appearing that men's minds are beginning to realize the inadequacy of their approach to Time, and it will not be long before an intellectual appreciation of this fact becomes more general. Inherent in many of the discoveries of present-day science is the assumption that Time is dual, and, more and more, this will condition men's perception of reality; but only as a result of man's direct awareness of himself as part of an integral Whole will a true realization of Time be his. When man creates around himself the forms and structures, based on unity and brotherhood, essential for that integration to take place, he will stand on the threshold of an entirely new experience of reality from which will flow a steady stream of creativity unlike aught seen before in this world.

January 1982

Sharing

In this coming Age, mankind will evolve several methods of dealing with the problems involved in implementing the Principle of Sharing. Each stage in the unfoldment of this precious principle will bring man closer to his Source. Gradually, a new humanity will be seen, manifesting more and more of its divine potential.

In the first stage, redistribution will be the keynote, each nation making available to the common pool those resources which it has beyond its needs. Through a sophisticated form of barter, the world's goods will be shared until such time as man's inner divinity awakens in him a desire for a simpler method of structuring his economic life.

Then will follow the stage of emancipation of humanity from the drudgery of needless work. Machines will gradually take over from man the tasks of manufacture. All the artefacts of our daily lives will one day be created in this way. This will lead to a self-sufficiency unthinkable today, so great are the differences in development and resources among the nations. These machines will liberate man for the exploration of his own inner nature and guarantee his progress towards divinity. In time, these machines will be created by an act of will. By the power of his illumined mind, man will bring together an aggregate of forces, and call into being these instruments and devices through which all his needs will be met.

Then that which is shared will be the resources and fruits of the spirit. A creativity unlike aught seen before will transform man's life, and in this new livingness and beauty all will share. Thus will men demonstrate themselves as Gods.

All of this is conditional on man's right choices now: his ability to make the necessary sacrifices for the good of all. This achieved, the way is opened for the deliverance of man from those self-imposed limitations which now have him in thrall.

From Our viewpoint, these conditions are being met. Already, the signs are becoming apparent that humanity is daily growing in awareness that the time available in which to make the needed changes is short indeed.

Before long, there will emerge a new sense of Oneness, of belonging to one family of brothers and sisters. A new and better direction will fashion men's lives, and together, in growing harmony, the steps will be taken which will ensure their progress. A growing realization of man's destiny and purpose will carry him forward and enlighten his path.

Thus the stages of sharing will be implemented, expressing at each stage some further aspect of man's divine nature, revealing in ever growing radiance the glory of that nature. Much there is to do in this coming time to seize the opportunities now being presented to humanity to evolve in an altogether heightened rhythm. Never before, in such potency, have the energies been available for this. The time is thus unique. Unique, also, is the Presence *in your midst* of the Prince of Peace, the Herald of the New Dawn, and a growing number of His Disciples. Under Our wise guidance man will come to realize his true stature and fulfil his destiny.

February 1982

A new approach to social living

An entirely new possibility of social relationship opens up for humanity. As man stands on the threshold of the Aquarian experience, altogether new levels of awareness will manifest themselves in this coming time. This will lead to the creation of new forms through which man can express his growing sense of the interrelatedness of all things.

At first, these new structures will be slow to form as man carefully finds his way out of the present morass; but, gradually, a fresh impetus to change will be given by the Masters forming the first group of the externalizing Hierarchy. New ideas will sweep across the world, relating men to each other in a new way, and a new approach to social living will begin.

Here it is necessary to digress for a moment to underline the inadequacy of the present social structures, now fast decaying. Today, large numbers of people live deeply unfulfilled lives, dedicated only to 'earning a living', contributing little of a truly creative nature to the general fund of knowledge and experience. Through no fault of their own they remain passive onlookers of a life which passes them by. Bereft of any real joy and meaning in their lives, they await in growing resentment their day of revenge. This constitutes a major world problem. On all sides today can be seen bafflement, confusion and anger.

Into the midst of this confusion has come the Christ. His is the task to point the way into the new structures which will allow man's growing sense of himself as a divine being to be expressed. Only the Masters and the Christ Himself know the enormity of His task. Nevertheless, We await, with confidence, humanity's response.

To begin with, massive aid for the poorer areas of the world must be given the highest priority to alleviate the suffering of many millions. The redistribution of the world's resources according to need should then proceed until a more equitable balance is achieved. This will take two to three years to implement. Concurrently, a far-reaching programme of education must be inaugurated to deal with the growing problems of unemployment and the ever-increasing demands for a correct and more creative use of leisure. A gradual restructuring of society will take place with the minimum of cleavage; men's hopes of a society based on sharing and love will gradually be fulfilled, and the new era will guarantee to each his rightful place.

These new forms will lead to the expression of as yet dimly sensed attributes in man. The awakening of powers of perception and reception hitherto unrealized will quicken his understanding of the spiritual basis of life, and more and more, in mounting rhythm, his inner divinity will become manifest. His social forms will mirror his sense of the interconnectedness of all creation and will lead to the establishment of correct relationships to all the kingdoms. Once again, man will realize the sacredness of all life and will take the necessary steps to protect that life from harm. A creative interchange between all groups will flow and will ensure a steady realization of man's human — and divine — potential.

Freed by machines from the burden of unnecessary work, millions will find within themselves a creativity absent until now, and will contribute their share to the glowing tapestry of joyful living which will become the hallmark of the New Age.

March 1982

The return of the Christ

Today, the world stands ready to receive into its midst the Teacher, the Avatar, the Forerunner of the New Age. On all sides, a high expectancy is becoming manifest; on every hand, people are becoming aware, however dimly, that the destined hour has struck. Cleavages abound, but, more and more, the nations are realizing their interdependence and the need for concerted action in solving their problems. Global consciousness is growing, slowly but surely, and humanity today stands in better readiness for the Christ's return than ever before in its history.

Many are the ways in which He is awaited today. Many are the hopes He is expected to fulfil. Manifold are the tasks that await His wise concern and dutiful care. The Christ, Maitreya, is poised to assume the role of Teacher to a world longing for Truth. Lost in the labyrinth, mankind struggles to free itself from the shackles of ignorance and greed, and seeks a saner, simpler life in which to work out its destiny. Into this turmoil has come the Christ, answering man's call for succour. How will He proceed? What will be His first tasks as He confronts the world's problems and begins His mission?

The solution to the problem of hunger and starvation in the midst of plenty will be His aim, giving voice therefore to the aspirations of millions for a better, more just world. Thereafter, His plans concern the stabilization of the world's political imbalances; the restructuring of the economic order along more rational lines.

With all of this He must contend, showing men the way, step by step, to restructure their lives. Under His inspiration and guidance, humanity will transform itself and its structures, opening the way, therefore, for a deeper understanding and expression of that Reality of which it is a part.

The immediate task is the galvanizing of world public opinion. Otherwise, His call for justice would go unimplemented. When the alternatives before the race — peace through sharing; or war and self-destruction — are clearly understood, millions will align themselves with the advocacy of the Christ, and call for an end to injustice, misery and war. The task before the Christ will be so to guide this mounting cry for freedom, sharing and peace that the minimum cleavage results.

Half the world's population now lives in poverty; enormous gaps exist between the rich and poor. Inherent in the tensions thus engendered is great danger for mankind. The Christ will point the way forward, reducing step by step these inequalities and tensions, so ensuring a relatively tranquil transition to the New Age. All has been carefully planned beforehand. Nothing has been left to chance; but humanity itself will determine the speed of implementation of the needed changes, for mankind's free will may never be infringed.

Those who read these words have, now, the choice: to aid the Christ in His work and help to awaken mankind to the needs of the time, thus serving the race in a most potent fashion, or to await events in passive inaction, so rejecting an opportunity for growth seldom given to any generation.

April 1982

The gift of life

Towards the end of this century, a new understanding of the meaning and purpose of life will dawn upon humanity; a new approach to living will prevail, and a fresh outlook on all relationships will take place, leading to a complete transformation of man's sense of himself and his destiny. This will come when man has achieved that social integration which is his immediate task, when, through the sharing of resources, justice and harmony reign.

With this new-found harmony will come a new sense of responsibility, a new experience of belonging to one great family of brothers and sisters for whose needs each must care. A fresh impetus will be given to evolution, and, under the guidance of the Masters, man will begin his climb to Divinity.

For this new advance new energies are needed and these will be available in ever-increasing potency. The Waters of Life of Aquarius will enter man's life on all levels, and from this stimulus a new man will be born, reflecting more and more his innate divinity.

This Gift of Life the Christ will bestow, revealing Himself as the Water Carrier, the emancipator of all men, bringing 'Life more abundantly', as He long ago foretold. With this 'life more abundantly' will come a new creativity. From men will flow a rich stream of ideas and discoveries, surpassing all that has gone before, and this in accordance with Cosmic Law. Nature will yield her secrets, the universe will submit to man's enquiring mind, and the knowledge thus acquired, placed at the service of the General Good, will beautify and enrich all life on Earth.

Thus will it be. And thus will men become Gods, acting as agents of the Divine Will, leading all creatures forward on the path of evolution in accordance with the Divine Plan. There will come a time when man will know God in an altogether new and more vivid way, not as a vague and distant idea but as an ever-present Reality, informing all life and expressing Itself through all forms. Then man will become a co-creator with the Divine and take his destined place in the evolutionary scheme.

Moreover, as this advance on the part of man takes place, so too will the planet itself evolve; all proceeds together, as an integral Whole. Man stands now on the verge of great achievements, and this time not alone. His Elder Brothers, the Masters and Initiates, stand ready now to aid and guide. Under Their wise supervision all will be accomplished. Returning to the outer world They will show men the ways of God and the Path to God. With the Christ at Their head, They will nurture and protect, teach and train, galvanizing all those capable of response into unprecedented activity. Thus will the work be done. Thus will the New Age bring to men the gift of renewed life, and thus, in response to that new life, will man achieve his true stature.

May 1982

A new era dawns

Within months from now a new era will have begun. Almost imperceptibly, over the last few years, great changes have been taking place in the world which herald a new dawn, a gradual transformation of society and its structures on a scale hitherto unknown. Soon, the first outlines of the new structures will be seen. Before long, there will be set in place the initial ground-plan on which the new civilization will be built.

All of this depends on the acceptance by humanity of the principles of sharing and justice, brotherhood and love. Without such acceptance naught can save this world. For this reason, Maitreya has named these principles as the foundation of all progress for man. When you see Him, He will call for the implementation of these basic and divine concepts so that all men may live in harmony and justice for the first time. Soon, men will see that there is no alternative to sharing, that all else has failed, and with united voice will call for the restructuring of the world along more just lines. Thus will it be.

Initially, of course, there will be those who will resist the changes for which this transformation calls, seeking to cling to their ancient privileges and power. Not all men are at the same point of readiness for change. But, as the need for change becomes more and more self-evident, they will find it increasingly difficult to influence events and, in gathering momentum, all will be remade.

It will take time to reorganize, totally, all world structures, but a start can soon be made, a foothold in the New won, and a significant step taken in the new direction in which humanity must go.

Clearly, many hands will be needed in the creation of the new society. Many are the tasks to be performed. Many are the adjustments which must be made. All who wish to serve will hear the call to service ringing in their hearts and from the heart will they respond. The united voice of the people of all lands calling for justice and sharing will set up an invocation which nothing can resist. Thus will the world be transformed. Thus, gradually, will the new forms be created, the new relationships forged, a new and happier era dawn for humanity under the guidance of the Christ and the Masters.

Today, as never before, to those who would travel more quickly along the evolutionary path is proffered an unique opportunity to serve and grow. Taking upon themselves the task of transformation and thus serving the Plan and the world, they can set new standards by which spiritual progress is measured and speed the process for humanity as a whole. This is the challenge of this time. Disciples today have the opportunity to quicken the evolutionary process for all those who will follow, thus serving the Plan of the Logos in a most potent fashion. Serve and grow. Serve and grow. That is the key to progress on the path.

July 1982

The new civilization

At the beginning of this New Age which is dawning it is difficult for many to imagine the kind of civilization and culture which will grace the succeeding centuries. Most attempts to do so remain enmeshed in a materialistic vision; seldom does one see the effort made to embody the aspiration of mankind for a life of spiritual meaning and expression.

Let us try to envisage the future in terms of the new civilization and culture. Soon, the first steps will be taken in the direction of the new dispensation. Soon, the new signposts will be set, indicating the way ahead for humanity. At first, the changes will be gradual but eventually, in quickening momentum, all will be refashioned.

Let us consider the nature of the elements which will make up the new civilization. The outstanding attitude of the new time will be the attempt to create right relationships, to express goodwill. A massive shift in emphasis from the individual to the group will reorientate humanity along more fruitful lines, and will reflect itself in the creation of structures more in keeping with the Plan of God. A further characteristic of the future time will be the desire to know better the nature of God and to come into closer relationship with that Divinity. From being peripheral to men's lives, as is the case today, this aim will become paramount in the lives of millions. Accompanying this new approach to God will be a new reverence for all manifestations of life, thus bringing men into better alignment with the subhuman kingdoms. This new sense of responsibility for the lower kingdoms will speed their evolution and so serve the Plan.

_ Before long, a new approach to science will open the way for a complete readjustment in men's attitude to the Reality in which we live. The new science will show humanity that all is One, that each fragmented part of which we are aware is intimately connected with all others, that that relationship is governed by certain laws, mathematically determined, and that within each fragment is the potential of the Whole. This new knowledge will transform men's experience of the world and of each other and confirm for them the truth that God and man are One. Thus, the new science will demonstrate man's divinity and will lead to the establishment of the New World Religion. The ancient schism between religion and science will be healed and a new impulse given to man's spiritual growth.

In this fertile climate, the hidden psychic powers of man will unfold naturally and the vast potential of the human mind will conquer space and time and control the energies of the universe itself. The resources of the human spirit are unlimited. In a crescendo of revelation, the glory of the unseen worlds will be revealed to man's astonished gaze and the full magnitude of the divine creation will be realized.

All this awaits man as he stands on the verge of the Aquarian experience. The waters of life of Aquarius, channelled to him by the Christ, will awaken in him his dormant divine consciousness and show him to be the God he is. Under the wise guidance of the Christ and His Brothers, man will attain the full stature of revealed divinity which is his birthright, did he but know it.

Stage by stage, century following century, man will build a civilization which will demonstrate his growing manifestation of divinity; a culture in which the beauty of the divine creation will be expressed in all its aspects, a mirror in which the Divine Idea will be reflected in all its glory.

Thus will man take his true place in the scheme of things under the Divine Plan. Thus, under the inspiration of the Christ, will he transform this world — separated by fear, dogma and hate — into that in which the Law of Love governs, in which all men are brothers, in which all that pertains to the divine nature engages man's attention and controls his life. Thus will man's dreams of divinity be realized, his potential be achieved, his destiny fulfilled.

August 1982

Reason and intuition

We are entering an age in which reason will gradually be replaced by the higher faculty of intuition. That which constitutes the reasoning faculty in man, and of which he is justly proud, will one day drop beneath the threshold of consciousness and become as instinctive as breathing or moving is today. There lies ahead of man an immense increase in awareness through the unfolding of his intuition, an awareness of states of Being as yet altogether unknown to him but which lie ready to be perceived by his awakened mind.

All expansions of consciousness are preceded by periods of tension, and this time of conflict and difficulty through which mankind is now passing will be succeeded by one of tranquility and poise, which will set the stage for the gradual flowering of the intuition. When that happens, man will know directly, past all gainsaying, his true nature as a soul created in the image of God.

Through the awakened intuition, man will discover the secrets of nature, and learn to play his part in the Plan of evolution for all the kingdoms. He will discover within himself faculties and knowledge beyond his ability to dream; all he needs to know will come readily to his illumined mind.

The next step in the flowering of the race will be the advent of those souls in whom the intuitive faculty is already active and potent. Those souls are now being gathered on the inner planes of life and soon will make their appearance. They will constitute the next (6th) sub-race of the present 5th root race and will lead humanity out of the darkness of the limited rational mind into the light of the intuition. All things will become possible for man. The light of the soul will play upon man's problems and simultaneously show the solution to these problems. By straight knowledge, man will move unerringly to his goal.

That which we call reason has played its part and has brought man to the threshold of divinity, preparing him for its own replacement by the faculties of the higher mind. Strictly speaking, that which is normally called intuition stems from the manasic level of consciousness whereas true intuition has its origin in the higher, buddhic, level. It is essentially loving understanding or true wisdom. Separateness is unknown when the intuition functions; the Oneness of all things is directly perceived. The illusions of the rational mind are transcended and Reality is known.

In the light of the intuition, man will rebuild his world and tread the Path of God, following the steps of all Those who have gone before and realized Themselves as Sons of God. Our task, when living and working among you, will be to stimulate wherever possible this higher faculty of mind and lead you forward on the Way.

Even now, the doors of perception are being opened and many are finding themselves possessors of intuitive truths. Soul-alignment has opened the channels and much light descends. A clearer perception of Reality becomes possible for the race in its hour of greatest need and augurs well for the future. As the intuition unfolds, so do the separative tendencies of the rationalizing mind diminish and a healthier climate for all relationships is the beneficent result.

The task ahead is clear: open the windows of the soul and let the soul's light illumine your lives. Through the awakened intuition allow the soul's knowledge and purpose to be expressed. Know the meaning of compassion and spread that love abroad. Allow your soul's wisdom to banish all illusion and become a light for your brothers. That is the task of all who would tread the Path of Light. Awaken the intuition and see clearly the Plan; awaken the intuition and dissolve the darkness; awaken the intuition and cast out all fear.

September 1982

Health and healing (part 1)

Everywhere, today, are to be found groups whose main concern is to further the idea of healthy living and to foster the interest of the public in achieving greater vitality and freedom from disease. On all sides, books are appearing offering dietary and other regimes — some new and unproved, others based on ancient lore — which claim to cure all bodily ills from overweight to the deadliest scourges to which humanity is prone. A new impetus has been given to research into the causes and nature of disease and to its prevention and cure.

As yet, the true cause of disease is quite unknown. Buried deep in man's past, it is largely karmic, and is transmitted by heredity. In this karma, all of humanity shares. Ancient transgressions of the Laws of Life have left this unwelcome heritage and only a profound reconstruction of our ways of thinking and living will transform this situation and, gradually, bring balance. That such balance will come is inevitable; but it will take time to eradicate certain age-old diseases and to cleanse the soil of the planet itself. In particular, the traditional forms of burial, widespread today, must give way to cremation, the only sanitary method of disposal of the body after death.

Everywhere, now, are to be found enclaves of research into the newer healing methods; much experimentation is proceeding along reasonably correct lines and the doors of knowledge are opening one by one. Soon, a flood of new insights will sweep the world, leading to an entirely new approach to disease and its cause and treatment.

Behind all of this activity stands Hierarchy, watching and guiding from behind the scenes of life, seeking, wherever possible, to stimulate research and experiment. This stimulus flows along two main lines: to galvanize far-seeing men into exploration of man's constitution and structure, on the knowledge of which an understanding of the mechanism of disease depends; and to stimulate the various means, curative, ameliorative and preventative, old and new, orthodox and unorthodox, which seek to control disease today.

One of the outstanding happenings of the present time has been the rise into prominence of so-called spiritual or faith healers of various kinds. There has been a marked shift in public acceptance of their role and gifts and this on a worldwide scale.

A new interest in the ancient healing methods of the East has widened the technical resources and understanding of Western practitioners, while prevention of disease — the creation of conditions of health and vitality — is gradually gaining a major role.

All of this portends well for the future, a future in which we shall see the gradual conquering of the ills which so beset mankind. The first step will be to eradicate the *fear* of disease and, from an understanding of its cause, inculcate a more correct approach to its control.

The transformation of social structures will do much to improve the health of humanity, removing much of the chronic stress and anxiety which is the experience of millions today. Greater leisure and recreation will play their part while sounder agricultural methods will ensure the production of food whose vitality is adequate to man's needs.

When mankind realizes the true nature of its constitution — as a soul reflecting itself through mental, emotional and twofold physical (etheric and dense) bodies, the first step in the conquering of disease will be taken. Until now, man's attention has been focused on the dense-physical plane while the causes of disease are to be found in the misappropriation of the energies flowing through the subtler bodies.

Man is on the verge of a great discovery: that disease is the result of imbalance; that correct balance is maintained by correct thought and action and that such correct thought and action involves his brothers and sisters everywhere. If man would end disease he must first end separation.

October 1982

Health and healing (part 2)

Every few years, a further advance is made in the understanding and control of disease, as we call that state of disequilibrium of mind and body which so troubles mankind. Each new advance pushes back a little the limits of man's knowledge of himself, and opens the door to further illumination. As we stand on the threshold of a new era, humanity is poised, as never before, to receive new light. Quickened by the stimulus of the Christ and His Masters, man is ready to discover the truths of his existence which, eventually, will free him totally from disease.

The first step in the eradication of any disease must be an understanding of its cause. Hitherto, the cause of most disease has eluded man's search, so ignorant has he been of the nature of his constitution and the laws under which he functions. From now on, as man proceeds along a more correct course and grasps the necessity of right relationship, this will begin to be remedied. Disease is ultimately the result of wrong relationship: to our higher self, the soul; to our brothers and sisters throughout the world; and to the Whole of which we are a part. By the misuse of soul energy we set in motion the causation. By wrong relationship to our fellows we bring about disequilibrium and disharmony, and illness of all kinds. Through our sense of separation we cut ourselves off from the healing potencies which everywhere surround us.

A mighty task awaits humanity at this turning-point in its life: to cleanse the world of the age-old habits of wrong thinking and living; to change entirely its manner of social living in such a way as to make possible a new freedom from fear: fear of want, of war, of disease and death. An enormous task, indeed, but one worth all the effort involved, for it will lead to a new livingness, a new and sweeter relationship between men, and to a world governed by the principles of justice and brotherhood, sharing and love. What finer goal could there be for humanity than to create such a world? No one can gainsay the benefits that such a transformation would bring, and We, the Masters, will help you in your task, revealing to you the best paths and possibilities.

Science, today, stands poised to contribute its share to the conquering of disease. The etheric planes of matter await man's exploration and study. Therein will be found the origin of that disequilibrium of forces which manifests itself as the body's ills. The treatment of disease will take on a new dimension when the function of the force centres (chakras) as receivers and dispensers of energy is understood and when their connection with the major glands of the endocrine system is known. Already, of course, there are those few practitioners who know this and who do valuable work, but not until this knowledge is general shall we see much advance in the understanding of the mechanism of disease.

It will not be long until this research into the etheric fields begins in earnest. When it does it will transform the therapeutic situation. The new psychology, the coming science of the soul, will throw much light on the nature and cause of disease and point the way to its prevention. In time, man will learn to approach and work with the deva (or angelic) evolution, many aspects of which are deeply engaged in the healing process.

Thus, stage by stage, disease will be eradicated from the world, to be replaced by a vitality and well-being seldom seen today but which is man's birthright, did he but know it. The stage is being set for this transformation. The Masters, on Their return, will point the way, and under Their wise guidance all shall be made new.

November 1982

Political forms in the New Age

Present-day political structures are of three main types, reflecting, however imperfectly, three separate aspects of the Divine intention. To these three forms we give the names of Democracy, Communism and Fascism. However distortedly, each embodies a divine idea; however corruptly, each is the expression of a divine energy, and each is related to a major planetary centre.

That which we call Democracy is a reflection, albeit inadequate today, of the love nature of God, exemplified by the Spiritual Hierarchy, the centre where the Love of God is expressed. That to which we give the name of Communism is an expression, as yet imperfect, of the Intelligence of God, centred in humanity itself; while Fascism, today in a totally distorted manner, reflects the energy of Will from Shamballa, the centre where the Will of God is known.

Each of these three forms of organization and relationship is in a state of transition, more or less, and in their gradual transformation into a fuller expression of the divine idea behind them lies the hope of future peaceful co-operation.

Each of these forms today is characterized by a spirit of intense rivalry and exclusiveness. The followers of each are convinced that they alone have the answers to man's need for structure and organization and are ready, if need be, to plunge the world into catastrophic war to uphold their particular system.

What of the future? How can we ensure that these apparently disparate and opposing modes of political thought do not overwhelm humanity? Very little foresight is needed to see that without a change of direction mankind faces terrible dangers. There is no need to elaborate; the nuclear threat is clear to all.

An immediate first step is the realization that humanity is One, its needs are the same, everywhere, however varied and apparently conflicting the outer forms. The enormous discrepancies in living standards between the rich and poor countries make mockery of this essential Oneness, and have within them the seeds of war.

The answer therefore is simple: the implementation of the principle of sharing provides the solution to the divisions in our planetary life. Nothing less will do. Sharing is divine, part of God's Plan for His children, and must one day become manifest.

And when men share, the divisions will grow together, the separations will be healed; and through the three major political structures the Love, the Will and the Intelligence of God will find a truer reflection. A true Democracy in which all men participate will take the place of the present sham. A new spirit of freedom will invest the Communist ideal with warmth and love. A truly spiritual hierarchy embodying the beneficent Will of God will one day replace the present authoritarian regimes.

Thus will it be. Thus will the outer forms reflect the inner divine life and purpose and so present to men new modes of expression and relationship through which their growing sense of the nature of God can be realized.

All awaits the acceptance of sharing — the key to justice and peace.

December 1982

The creation of new structures

Poised as man is on the threshold of the New Age, it is essential to give some thought to the forms into which the present inadequate structures should grow. To ensure that the changes proceed in the desired direction of greater social justice and eventual brotherhood, we would do well to look closely at the means whereby these conditions may be achieved.

It is obvious that the present structures no longer serve man's need for peace and co-operation on a national or international level; the opposite holds true. Were man to continue in the present mode, annihilation would be inevitable. Fortunately, there are those who see this and work for change.

Structures are required which, at the same time, give the greatest freedom and tolerance to individual needs yet deny to the individual the right to exploit his brothers. While preserving the enterprising spirit of the talented individual, they must also ensure the rights of the community as a whole.

Structures must be sought which take advantage of man's natural desire to participate in all that affects his life. This will make for greater social cohesion and sense of shared responsibility. The present political party systems are clearly inadequate to provide for this participation and must give way to other forms of representation. This holds as true for the Democratic West as for the Communistic East.

Envisage a process whereby, more and more, each man or woman becomes engaged in the making of decisions on the level of community affairs. Calling on the untapped potential of millions, a transformation of social life can quickly take place in an orderly and responsible manner. Participation is the keynote, for only through such participation can each one identify with, and work wholeheartedly for, the communal goal. In this way, social and group responsibility will be inculcated; the present unhealthy, anti-social attitudes, born of a fragmented and unjust society, will fade away like mist before the heat of the sun.

That some such process already exists in certain countries is true but as yet it is confined mainly to rural communities whose social structures are still relatively homogeneous. The task ahead will be to create conditions on a worldwide scale whereby all men will have a voice in creating the future society. Only thus will the present divisions be resolved. This is not as difficult as it might seem, for the key rests in man's hands. The key, as always, is the principle of sharing. Once implemented, this principle will remove the obstructions which prevent co-operation between different social and national groups and will thus prepare the way for more harmonious forms through which humanity can express itself.

Leisure, available for the first time to millions, will provide the opportunity, hitherto denied them, for a close involvement in community and national life and organization. When men have the leisure to participate, they will find within themselves the answers to the problems which now beset them: the problems of sectarian hatred and division, of injustice and poverty, crime and war.

Not all men will welcome, at first, the changes which must take place but, in growing numbers, they will come to see the wisdom of justice and shared responsibility, the only guarantee of harmony and peace, communal, national and international.

Many now are active in their communities, seeking to impress their vision on society, and much of worth is taking place; but humanity awaits the key which will unlock the door of the future and assure them of new and fuller life — the divine principle of sharing.

January 1983

Life in the New Age

Much has been written about life in the future; much fictional writing is devoted to a description, imaginatively conceived, of the life ahead for humanity. Almost without exception, these writings describe a life and environment dominated by technology and scientifically organized systems. A chilling, mechanistic view of the future is held before the reader who could be forgiven for preferring the present, with all its uncertainties and dangers, to such an inhospitable prospect.

However, the future need not be so bleak and barren of human warmth as that presented by writers of fiction. That science and technology will flourish, there is no doubt; we are entering an age in which the mysteries of life will be revealed, and the energies of the universe will be controlled, through the discoveries of science. Our technology, too, will become ever more sophisticated as it adapts to the challenges posed by these discoveries. We must ensure that a proper balance is maintained, and that the achievements and resources of science are channelled along lines that serve, rather than are served by, mankind.

We will help you to do this. Ours will be the task to oversee the development of the new society along paths that preserve correct balance, and naught that infringes human need will receive Our recommendation. Beauty and sense of fittingness will be the touchstone. All that is ugly, mechanical, and harmful to the human spirit will be eschewed. The aim will be to maintain, in full freedom and harmony, a right relationship between man and his environment; to ensure that every technological and scientific advance is seen as serving better man's needs and knowing better the nature of Reality.

In this way, you may be sure, the needed safeguards will be built into the new structures. All that pertains to the enhancement of life and the beautifying of its forms will know Our blessing; every manifestation which serves the common weal will gain Our support.

The time is coming when man will develop a new relation to his environment. In keeping with his sense that man, nature and God are One, he will build forms which allow him to manifest that truth. The closest contact and free interchange between all aspects of the Whole will be achieved; a sure knowledge of the meaning and purpose of life will replace the present confusion and lead to a demonstration of beauty hitherto unknown. The true, the good and the beautiful will become a reality in men's lives.

All of this presupposes, and depends on, a change in direction from the present chaos. Naught of good can emerge without a fundamental restructuring of social forms along lines more compatible with human needs. Were man to realize how much of his God-given potential is sacrificed to the present unholy order, he would delay not one moment in making the needed changes. Were he to sense but an inkling of the glory of that potential, naught would be allowed to bar his way to its achievement. The future calls man to his finest efforts, his noblest aspiration, his grandest vision.

Let man build a future in which his sacrifice is not of his divinity but of his separated self. Let him embrace his brothers in love and make himself whole.

February 1983

The future beckons

From time to time, I have spoken of the need to inculcate the spirit of sharing whereby the world's resources can be more equitably distributed. This would lead to a reduction of tension and of incalculable human suffering. It would also bring about a revitalization of the life and of the economies of the already developed nations. The life-blood of the planet must circulate. The stagnant economies of the richer nations can only be galvanized into motion through the recognition that the poorer nations, too, have a right to live and to enjoy a reasonable standard of life. Only sharing can make this so.

Daily, the evidence mounts to show men that the world is One, that humanity is an organism whose well-being depends on the health of every part, and that to ignore the signs of danger and of disease is no longer possible or wise. Many now see this and call for justice but only the cry of awakened humanity will suffice to shift the Powers from their positions of greed.

Soon, the world will know for certain that men must share or perish. Maitreya will lose no time in bringing home to all, this truth. He will show men that the world belongs to everyone — rich and poor, powerful and dispossessed, white and coloured. He will make clear the need for concerted action to solve the problems which confront man today, and will point the way to their solution. Calling upon all men to accept the need for change, He will quicken the aspiration and focus the will of men everywhere to see justice done. Thus will He unite all those who seek the establishment of better forms through which the divinity of man can be expressed; and from that multitude will rise a cry unlike aught heard before on this Earth, a cry for justice and truth, freedom and peace.

Then will the leaders respond and, in growing momentum, this world will be transformed. Thus will it be; thus will

Maitreya lay the foundations of the new civilization based on sharing and love.

Can you not feel the new rhythm which is entering your lives? Who can ignore the new impulse which quickens men to action? All will be remade, and soon the darkness will give way to revealing light.

All who can respond to the needs of the time will find a place. This the Law of Service guarantees. No one who longs to serve need fear lack of work or purpose nor the willing guidance of experienced hands. We shall help you to restore this world to health and shall work as brothers at your side, clearing away the debris of the past.

Soon the world will see great changes taking place and will know that the New Age has begun. The old is passing away and the future beckons mankind. No one need fear that future for it holds for man the promise of his divine heritage, and the establishment everywhere of the Will of God.

Serve, and realize that future for yourselves and your brothers. Serve, and know you are working in unison with God's Will. Serve gladly and wisely, and enter into freedom and joy.

March 1983

A time of change

Almost without exception, the nations of the world are experiencing profound changes, both internally and in relation to each other. This process is the direct result of the energetic stimulus now pervading the planet as a whole, and will lead eventually to a complete transformation of the existing structures. To quicken these changes is Our desire and wish, but so great today are the tensions that We must proceed with care; too much pressure here or there could have disastrous consequences for large sections of the world. Hence Our cautious approach to the problems which face man today. Change must proceed in an orderly fashion or chaos will result.

Many there are who fear change and who see the breakdown of the old as a profound loss of much-loved forms. Many reject these changes as a threat to their privileges and prestige. Many mistake the legitimate aspirations of peoples for freedom and justice for the threat of anarchy from within. At the same time, there are those who would sweep away all that humanity has garnered of the beautiful and the true. Impatient for the new forms, they fail to see the necessity of gradual progress and discount much that is of value in the past.

Our problem, as Guardians of the race, is to steer a course between these two extremes, applying the curb and the spur as We sense the need. Always, Our aim is the achievement of ordered change with the minimum of cleavage. Look, therefore, for Our hand in world events and judge them wisely. Much that takes place is fashioned by Us and must eventuate in a better world. When you see Us, you will know that this world is in safe keeping.

Listen to Our counsel and act. Heed Our advice and refashion the world in stages which are possible and sure. Take care that your brothers' needs are met and you will not err. If you are asked: "In which direction should we go?", answer with joy: "To serve the greatest need; to Brotherhood."

To rebuild the fabric of your lives, new materials and new skills will be necessary. Replace the outworn forms with the new energies now available, and learn to create in relationships forged in joy and love. Temper your lives in the fire of service and contribute your share to the work of change.

With Us as guides, all is possible. All will be remade in beauty and truth. Willing hands will be there to help you and naught can delay the New Beginning. When you see Us you will know that the Brothers are men like yourselves but whose love is manifest. We will teach you the secret of love. In joy shall We take you to the farther shore and shall place you before the Keeper of the Gates.

All change is preceded by tension and tension brings fear. However, fear has no place in the heart activated by service and love. Don, then, the armour of service and envisage the future with joy. Welcome gladly the changes which must ensue and create together the Dispensation of Love.

April 1983

We are not discouraged

Many are aware, today, of a definite change which is taking place in what might be called the 'atmosphere' of the world; not the physical but the psychic atmosphere. This change is due to the inflow of entirely new energies, of great potency, to which mankind is making response. With deliberate intent, the Hierarchy of Masters, led by the Christ, is seeking to bring about a shift in consciousness on a worldwide scale; to inspire a transformation in thought and action which will lead inevitably to the reconstruction of the world along more spiritual lines.

We, the Guardians of the race, have the task of guiding and controlling, so far as We may without infringing free will, each evolutionary step made by man on his upward climb to divinity. In accordance with this responsibility, We lay down the guidelines for man to follow, We apply the needed stimulus, then watch and wait.

The results are not discouraging. Despite the many signs of cleavage, much that is happening is for the better. Many are the gains being made along a truer path. Manifold are the tasks ahead but real progress is taking place.

Seen from Our viewpoint, the Earth stands ready to undergo the changes without which there would be no future for man. When men see this, they will welcome these changes as the guarantee of continuity and of an advance into divinity unlike aught made before. We watch and wait and are not discouraged.

Soon, it will become apparent that man is not alone. Never, in all its long history, has humanity lacked guidance from Those Who have gone before and Who have mapped the route for man to follow. Now, as the spiral turns, We take Our places once more among you and offer to you the benefits of Our achievements. Regard Us as brothers, eager to help. Look on Us as guides to the future, for We know well the way. With Our

Brotherhood behind you, you cannot fail. Our inspiration will be yours, and from that source of strength will flow the knowledge and the power with which to fulfil your dreams.

Heretofore, Our guidance has been limited to the inner planes of life and progress has been necessarily slow. Henceforth, with Our presence in your midst, a new and dynamic rhythm of change will manifest itself and will speed the creation of the new civilization. Our task will be to present to you the possibilities and thus to help you realize your potential.

Clearly, all future progress is dependent on humanity's ability to respond to Our stimulus; each step of the way must be taken, and each stone of the new structure must be laid, by man himself. Only thus will you grow and attain your full stature.

That you will reach this goal We have no doubt; the timing alone of this achievement rests in your hands. Hold this goal before you as the New Age dawns — the attainment of divinity and the fulfilment of God's Plan.

May 1983

A better future for all

A new order is being fashioned, and by man himself. Out of the chaos of the present time is emerging a new direction for man to follow. Under the impress of the new forces entering their lives, men everywhere are seeking solutions to the various problems which beset them, and, blindly and falteringly as it may seem, are finding pointers to a better future for all.

Thus will be built the new civilization; out of the old and decaying forms of the age now ending will grow new and sturdier shoots, better rooted in man's spiritual reality and better able to express his innate divinity.

It will take time for these new growths to flourish and consolidate, but, even so, vast changes can be looked for in a relatively short period, and much is already taking place that encourages this belief.

Each new cycle brings into manifestation new energies and new groups of souls with the equipment to respond to and express the qualities of these energies. Entering our planetary life now, and in increasing numbers as the centuries slip by, are members of certain advanced groups of souls who for long have awaited this opportunity for service. Their achievements of the past will be placed at the service of the race, and from their long contact with the world of meaning will come a new understanding of man's purpose and a deeper appreciation of the true value of life. From them will flow a wisdom hitherto lacking in man's affairs, and in the light of that wisdom all will be transformed.

Each evolutionary step made by man needs long periods of preparation, and what is happening now, and that which we are about to witness, is the result of centuries of planned activity on the part of Hierarchy. From Our work in all areas and directions is growing a new synthesis. Seen from Our viewpoint, humanity stands better prepared than ever before to inherit its birthright and to realize from within itself its full, divine potential.

The first step is to grasp the meaning and necessity of sharing. Sharing is the key to the solution of all man's problems, and has behind it the potency of God's Will, for sharing is the outcome of the manifestation of God's Love and Will. Maitreya has said: "When you share you recognize the God in your brother." This is verily so. Without sharing, there is a denial of God, immanent in all Beings. Without sharing, there is endless separation from God and your brothers. Sharing alone confers on men the dignity of true men.

Sadly, not all governments recognize the need for sharing as the only guarantee of peace, and no effort should be spared in making known this truth. However, more and more, the leaders of the world are trying to reorganize their relationships in the light of this knowledge, and are grasping more coherently their mistakes and the vision of a new order.

There is much to do before that vision is embodied in action, but already the way is being cleared, the signposts set, and a new realism is entering the deliberations of nations as they seek to solve their problems.

To help speed this process, Maitreya has come earlier than planned. Daily, His energies promote goodwill and justice. Hourly, His love saturates the world. From His point of focus, streams of love and light and power encircle the Earth, awakening it to the New Dawn.

June 1983

The need for synthesis

It is strange that, despite the lip-service paid to the ideas of unity and brotherly love, so few of the groups involved with New Age concepts do in reality demonstrate an inclusive attitude. Far from doing so, they tend rather in the opposite direction and are among the most separative and exclusive of all the groups engaged in the education of mankind.

Their role is to hold before the peoples the vision of a better world in which separatism has no place, in which each is seen as contributing something essential to the Whole — and of equal value. Yet, almost everywhere, the accent is on the superiority of a particular teaching or point of view. Rare indeed is it to find the *actions* of co-operation and mutual understanding which hold so proud a place in their vocabulary.

An ancient rhythm still dominates the thinking of these groups, and much needs to be learned and changed if they would truly represent the ideals of the coming time. That such changes will come is inevitable but for many the process will be difficult and long. Many see the need but cannot find within themselves the ability to relate to others on equal terms, so deeply ingrained is the habit of competition and exclusiveness. Furthermore, for some, the need to be seen as leaders of thought is a dominant factor; with them, the glamour of personal ambition has a powerful hold.

Such is the situation today, yet the need is for a growing sense of identity with one another, an apprehension of the underlying synthesis which unites the endeavours of all such groups. Moreover, it is only when that synthesis is grasped and presented to the general public that the educational role of these groups can be fulfilled. At the moment, the average seeker is confused and baffled by the competing claims for his attention and allegiance.

Soon, the world will know that the many teachings and formulations of truth stem from one source; that the same divine stimulus flows through all; that the varied interpretations result from the fact that mankind has diverse needs and stands at many stages on the ladder of ascent. Not for nothing has Hierarchy worked to present the needed teachings and ideas on the broadest front, on many different levels and in a multitude of ways.

The synthesis of ideas underlying Our multifarious presentation springs from Our sense of the unity of all things, from Our constant awareness of the Whole and of the indivisibility of that Reality. When men share this experience all things will become possible.

When men see the Christ and His Disciples, the Masters of Wisdom, they will come to understand how needed are the many presentations of truth, for they will come to realize how old is man, how varied his experience and expectations down the ages, and how different are the ways in which men absorb ideas. They will come to grasp, too, something of the inherent unity behind the outer diversity.

Men will see for themselves that behind the ideas and teachings stands a Plan; that every teaching is the formulation of but one fragment of the Plan; that the Plan is the expression of the creative Will of God and as such is in process of constant change. How then could one group, society, or institution embody the Truth for all time?

Many, of course, believe that even now they work for synthesis and unity, but this is largely an illusion. Little credit should be taken for forming links with those of like mind; that is useful but relatively simple. More difficult is it by far to link arms across a sea of differences and to embrace as equals those with whom you disagree.

Seek that which unites in your brother's presentation. Know that behind all stands the Christ and His Disciples. Remember that the one Truth informs all approaches and that naught divides but the minds of men.

July 1983

The joy of living

Each winter, the sun sets earlier and earlier until, on the shortest day, we see it, if at all, for but a few brief hours. Such is the reality of our planetary life. However, experience has taught us that, without fail, the days will gradually lengthen and the blossom of spring and the warmth of summer will return once more, bringing us renewed hope and joy in living.

When one considers this, when one sees how inevitable is change, one sees also how unnecessary is despair. Despair strikes at the heart of truth, for the truth is that nothing remains the same for ever, not even the darkest-seeming fate.

Since this is so, what is to be gained by fruitless despair? Better it is, by far, when the blows of karma seem difficult to bear, to await calmly the appointed hour of change in the sure knowledge that it will come. True joy in living can be ours only when we learn to accept with equanimity the blows and the gifts of life.

Such a one is a disciple. Such a one knows that naught in this universe stands still; all is in movement, constantly changing and assuming new forms. Consider, then, how vain it is to expect the present to persist. This insight engenders freedom; from that freedom spontaneously arises joy.

Joy must be understood to be the natural state, underlying happiness and sorrow alike. When uncovered, it radiates its light — the light of the Soul — on all around and makes manifest the love which is the nature of God. Love and joy coexist in the heart which is pure, unclouded by fear, hate or the anguish of despair. Remove fear from your heart and know joy. Release yourselves from hate and know the meaning of love. Cast from you dark despair and stand in your true light. Thus can you enter the Kingdom of Souls and become a saviour of the world.

Many approach the future with fear, knowing little of the glory which awaits them. For them, naught beckons but bleak destruction. Show them that the future for man will be wonderful to behold, holding as it does the promise of revealed divinity. Trust is not easily engendered but the light of joy will prove the best ambassador. Teach the young to express the joy which is their birthright and place not upon tender hearts the weight of guilt and fear. Thus will be born a generation of joyous servers of the race.

Take Us, your Elder Brothers, as your example; the radiance of Our joy is Our hallmark. Emulate Us, and spread abroad joy's light.

Conquer fear and uphold the hope of others; fear and joy are equally infectious. Demonstrate love and joy and close firmly for ever the door upon despair. Do this and you will aid mankind more than you could know.

September 1983

The art of living

Before long, a great change will take place in our approach to life. Out of the chaos of the present time will emerge a new understanding of the meaning underlying our existence and every effort will be made to express our awareness of that meaning in our daily lives. This will bring about a complete transformation of society: a new livingness will characterize our relationships and institutions; a new freedom and sense of joy will replace the present fear. Above all else, mankind will come to realize that living is an art, based on certain laws, requiring the function of the intuition for correct expression.

Harmlessness is the key to the new beauty in relationship which will emerge. A new sense of responsibility for actions and thoughts will guide each one in every situation; an understanding of the Law of Cause and Effect will transform men's approach to each other. A new and more harmonious interaction between men and nations will supplant the present competition and distrust. Gradually, mankind will learn the art of living, bringing to each moment the experience of the new. No longer will men live in fear — of the future and of each other. No longer will millions starve or carry the burden of labour for their brothers.

Each one has a part to play in the complex pattern being woven by humanity. Each contribution is uniquely valuable and necessary to the whole. However dim as yet the spark, there is no one in whom the fire of creativity cannot be lit. The art of living is the art of giving expression to that creative fire and so revealing the nature of men as potential Gods.

It is essential that all men share in this experience and learn the art of living. Until now, a truly creative life has been the privilege of the few. In this coming time the untapped creativity of millions will add a new lustre to the achievements of man. Emerging from the darkness of exploitation and fear, in true and correct relationship, each man will find within himself the purpose and the joy of living.

The presence of the Christ and the Masters will speed this process, inspiring humanity to saner and safer methods of advance. A new simplicity will distinguish the coming civilization under the guidance of these Knowers of God.

Already, there is a growing sense that all is not well in man's estate. More and more, men are becoming aware of the limitations of their lives and search for something better. They question the modes and structures which inhibit participation in the fullness of life and long for meaning and purpose in all that they do.

Shortly, new energies will enter our lives and inspire men to creative action. A new and harmonious stimulus will be given to art and the art of living. A beauty not seen before will transform the ways of men and illumine for all time the nature of God.

Man stands now ready for Revelation. His heart and mind poised and turned to the future, he awaits the glory which, by readiness, he has invoked.

October 1983

The turning-point

At each turning-point in human history, a new energy (or combination of energies) has entered our lives and evoked response. In this way, man's evolution has been quickened and new strides have been taken on the long path to perfection. Thus has it always been and thus will it continue until, in the fullness of time, the Plan of the Logos of our planetary scheme is complete.

Today we stand at such a turning-point. Throughout the world, there is a growing sense that events that will change the pattern of existence are on their way, moving in which direction no one can be sure: into a future of unending progress and betterment, or towards oblivion. Many are the views put forward in describing that future, but shared by most is the understanding that naught will remain the same; that the world will change utterly, for better or for worse.

The changes which will and must take place stem from the inflow of streams of force which cyclically make their presence felt in our world, together with certain energies reaching us for the first time and in great potency. As they impinge on the hearts and minds of men, these energies provoke new attitudes and relationships and galvanize large sections of humanity to action. When their impact reaches a critical point, change is inevitable.

Today, the energies of major note are those which are drawing mankind together, producing, for the first time, a fused synthesis. A mighty Avatar has been invoked from Whose Being flows a powerful stream of blending Will. Behind the Christ He stands, this Mighty One, supporting the Lord of Love in all He does.

From Shamballa flows the Will-to-good, evoking in mankind response to the Plan of God. The Ray of Ritual, waxing daily, slowly imposes its ordered rhythm on our lives.

Thus the Plan proceeds, bringing man finally to the feet of God. Despite all appearances to the contrary, very real progress is being made. Could you but see events from Our standpoint much of your fear would melt away.

When the Christ begins His outward mission, in full view of all, it is as the Water Carrier that He will work, dispensing to each the Waters of Life. From far Aquarius this New Life flows, bringing the promise of a new livingness for men.

Even now, through Him, another mighty Avatar bestows His grace on this world. By the transmutation, under Law, of violence and hate, He lays in store for man the blessings of harmony and peace.

Thus does Maitreya work for the benefit of all. The Great Service has called Him, once again, into the arena of everyday life and gladly has He answered that call. Serve with Him and change the world. Not alone by Him can it be done; His hands, as He has said, are tied by Law.

His emergence, when complete, will act as a signal to galvanize into action those now waiting in the wings. Across the world His words will flow, encouraging all to stake their claim to life and to abandon for ever the separation of the past.

Stand, now, with Him, in the vanguard of change and add your voice to the clamour for justice and truth.

November 1983

Let there be light

Each century brings man closer to his goal: the demonstration, in all its perfection, of the Light of God. In this way man becomes what he potentially is — a living God. Each incarnation marks a step cut in the mountain of ascent. With each such experience man adds to his vehicles a modicum of light, subtly changing thereby the vibration of his bodies. When all his bodies are thus vibrating to the frequency of light, the task is completed, the journey ended. From the point of view of man, the journey is over; from the point of view of Those Who have achieved, the journey has but begun.

Thus each man and woman makes the metamorphosis from man to God. Out of the chrysalis of matter, with all its limitations, emerges the liberated Master, radiating the Light of God.

Across the vastness of the universe, this Light persists; through all dimensions and planes it expresses its nature, conditioned only by the forms in which it shows itself. These forms give access to the Light to those whose consciousness rests in the world of matter, but essentially Light is formless, needing no structure to sustain its Being.

Deep within each one of us dwells such a light, awaiting the opportunity to shine forth. Within each glows the potential of all Cosmos. Within each, too, is the will to bring forth that light and thus make manifest the nature of God. That light and that will pertain to the soul and come into activity as a result of soul alignment. Seek, therefore, alignment with the soul and bring into manifestation the purpose of God. Search within and find the source of all knowledge and love. Reveal to the world the Light of the soul and join the ranks of those who serve.

The world stands ready for more light. The peoples everywhere are thirsty for new knowledge of themselves and of

God. Because of this readiness, the Masters have prepared Themselves to inaugurate a new era of Light. Limitless opportunities for progress will be offered to mankind: man will marvel at the discoveries which will open the door to mastery of natural forces; he will stand amazed by the wonder and beauty thus revealed; he will know for certain the fact of God and his relation to that divinity, and will enter willingly into co-operation with the Divine Plan.

All of this awaits humanity as it stands at the threshold of the Aquarian Age. This will be an age in which the Divine Plan will flourish once again, bringing man at last into conscious acceptance of his destiny.

Many today would doubt this, as they survey a world of cleavage and tension. The problems seem too complex, the divisions too extreme. But precisely then, at the moment of greatest need, comes the Teacher, ready to bring new Light. Such a One is now among you, waiting in the wings, patiently, for the invitation to serve.

Release the Light that He brings and enfold all things in holiness. Embrace His Teachings and bring succour to all in need. Manifest His Light and create anew this world.

December 1983

Victory is assured

It is becoming increasingly clear that the conflict between Good and Evil is being won by the Forces of Light. Gradually the Good is gaining the upper hand in this age-old struggle for the minds and hearts of men. To some, this may seem an astonishing statement to make in the light of the tensions and cleavages which exist in the world. Yet such is the case, and were you to see the world and events as do We, the Elder Brothers, you would see a world undergoing an extraordinary transformation. On all sides there is evidence that the old order is crumbling. Ancient hatreds divide the peoples and lawlessness abounds, but everywhere there are signs that a new spirit is awakening in man, a new sense of responsibility and a renewed reverence for life in all its forms.

Many are the manifestations of this new beauty; many and marvellous are the visions of the future opening up before mankind. Man stands as yet at the threshold, only, of a new beginning, yet already the signs of progress are there for those who have eyes to see.

We are witnessing now a polarization which is forcing humanity to choose. So fearsome are the dangers in the present modes of living that the spirit in man revolts and searches for the new. In this way is man brought to the recognition of the Will of God. Behind all stands the Plan, embodying that Will, and, knowingly or not, men are now ready to implement that Plan.

Groups of men are forming themselves on every hand to manifest the new. Inspired by love and the spirit of necessity they envisage a simpler and a saner world. They see that from the imbalances and tensions of the present must grow justice and harmony. They know that they are divine and can perform miracles of change. They sense the needs of the time and dedicate themselves to service. They represent the Good in every land.

Many are the ways to God but the quickest and the surest is the path of Service. No other path so fully embodies the nature of God. Take your place on this path and carry out the dictates of your soul. Follow the promptings of your heart and awaken to the needs of the world. Know that as you enter on the path of Service you accept your place within the Plan, and find yourself well set upon the path to God.

Ready, then, will be the response from Us, your Elder Brothers. Quickly shall We seize the opportunity to help you on your way through stimulus and proffered fields of service. Thus can you join Us and aid Us in Our work. Make this your aim and join the ranks of the Servers of the world. Take your place at Our side and work with the Forces of Light. Victory is assured but must be fought for and won.

Be not afraid in the midst of the chaos and tension. Fear has no place in the present situation; rather, see it as a challenge to your faith.

February 1984

A major opportunity

Each year, as the Spring months approach, Hierarchy makes preparation for the three Spring Festivals of April, May and June. Every year, as the time draws near, plans are set in motion to enable those who seek the Light and wish to serve to do so more fully and more effectively. During this Spring We intend to make a major manifestation. Throughout these months, energies of enormous potency will flow outwards to the world. Their heightened power will facilitate certain *rapprochements* much needed today, and great efforts will be made to canalize the goodwill of millions. In this way it is hoped to effect great changes in human affairs, and to prevent a further slide into chaos and war.

This time of heightened activity We call a Spiritual Push, and during this period *all* spiritual activity will be potentized many-fold. Spiritual action of all kinds, stemming from whatever tradition or belief, will find enhancement during these months, and much can be achieved if full use is made of this opportunity. It behoves all those who desire to serve and to better the world to contact and use these forces and so make them manifest in their lives.

We seek to establish among men a new sense of shared responsibility. We seek to awaken in them a taste for concerted action. We endeavour to create the conditions in which these two can manifest together and thus lead to change. All is energy; energy alone exists. Through the impact of these higher energies on the Centre, humanity, We seek to engender a new atmosphere in the world. Help Us to create conditions of trust and so bring renewed hope to the world. Sow the seeds of love and trust and watch them blossom as hope and joy.

Everyone can do something to ease the pain of his brothers. Take stock of where you stand and see what you should do.

Pledge, now, your support for every act of sacrifice and contribute your share thereto. Make this time a time of giving; let your will to serve have full expression. Know that as you serve you work towards the Light and align more correctly with the purpose of your soul.

Take your stand with Us and allow the dreams of men to come true. Take your stand with Us and be assured of Our stimulus and help. Take your stand at Our side and perform deeds you thought impossible to achieve.

When you see Maitreya you will know that the moment of decision for the world has come. He will call for action from all who would save the world. Join the ranks of those who act and serve, and enter the mainstream of the Great Current of life.

The time has come, as never before, to act in accordance with your professed ideals, and to make manifest the vision enshrined in your heart. Know that you are not alone; that millions embrace these same ideals. Join hands with all who seek to serve and spin a web of light around the world. Remember that you are in the world to serve and that only through service can you grow. Remember that you are your brother's keeper and accept responsibility for your brother's needs. Present yourselves, as never before, as channels through whom We may work, as transformers of the mighty potencies which will shortly flow to you.

In this way can you set the seal of service on this life and in due course join the ranks of those Who have gone before you.

March 1984

Glamour

Of all the problems which beset humanity there is none greater than the problem of glamour. It provides the basis for all our difficulties and dangers, and holds the vast majority of humanity in thrall. It is at the root of every division and cleavage and the source of every dimension of pain and suffering. It has its roots in the ancient past of mankind and all but a very few are held under its sway.

Essentially, glamour originates in man's sensuous, feeling apparatus — the emotional or astral body — and in man's identification with its action. Through wrong identification with his feelings and emotions — his desire nature — he has surrounded himself with, and lost himself in, thick fogs of illusion and unreality. This constitutes the glamour in which most people live out their lives. Glamour is illusion on the plane of the emotions and provides the greatest obstacle to progress, for the individual and for the race. It throws a multitude of misconceptions across the path of the unwary, and the loftiest idealist is no freer from its influence (nay, he is frequently more prone) than the hardened cynic.

To come to grips with glamour, humanity must recognize its mechanism, by which means the central heresy — that we are separate — is created and maintained. All that tends to reinforce the sense of separateness is the result of the action of glamour, and all that seeks to undermine that heresy works for its destruction. Glamour resides in the notion that man's desires are real, that they have their own intrinsic validity and purpose, whereas, in truth, they are the cause of all unhappiness; no more real, no less transient, than the mirage of the desert.

The well-meaning aspirant clouds his action with desire for achievement; the idealist looks upon his as the only possible ideal that right-thinking people could hold; often do we see the absurdities of national pride lead nations into actions against the interest of their peoples. These, the actions of glamour, are the product of desire: for power and the fulfilment of ambition. The light of science has rid the world of certain ancient glamours but created others in their stead: the glamour of possessions enthralls half the world while the other half go hungry and die in misery and want.

Eventually, humanity will work through this phase and establish a truer perception of reality. The myriad glamours which beset the race today will one day dissolve in the light of man's soul, invoked into manifestation as the New Age proceeds. But the present is a time in which new types of energy are making their impact on men's lives and creating conditions of bewilderment and confusion. The heightened tension of the time fosters the glamours of fear and destruction, erupting into violence of all kinds.

What can be done to free humanity from this ancient thralldom, in part innate in the nature of substance itself? How can man free himself from wrong identification and the tyranny of his self-created thoughtforms? The answer lies in a shift of focus, from the self to the group; in a truer identification with the soul and its relation to all souls. The light of the soul, through the agency of mind, is the great dissipator of glamour, and long ago the Buddha taught the conquering of desire: the Noble Middle Path between the pairs of opposites. In the light of the soul the essential unity is seen, the astral waves subside and the aspirant finds himself at initiation's gate.

April 1984

Justice is divine

Justice is divine. Longed for by millions bereft of its sacred balance, justice brings to the world of men the harmony of God. As a looking-glass reflects the image of man, so does justice reflect the nature of the divine. The measure of the lawlessness of the time is known by the degree of injustice in the world, and today, injustice stalks the poor on every hand.

Legally, justice rules the field of social regulation, of crime and punishment, but fundamentally justice has to do with the laws of God, which work towards harmony and correct relationship. Every injustice, however small, brings disharmony to the whole. Today, so great are the areas of injustice in every land that extraordinary measures are required to prevent total chaos.

Injustice is a denial of man's divine potential; it separates man from man and humanity from God. Throughout the world, many are struggling to free themselves from age-long injustice, exploitation and tyranny; to set down at last the yoke carried by their forebears. We, the watching Hierarchy, commend their struggle, for We see it as the expression of the Divine Spark in all men, yearning for freedom and justice. We give them Our Hand as We gaze with compassion on their plight.

There are those who would deny that all men have equal rights to a share of God's providence. Those who argue thus have listened only to the voice of the separated self, forgetting that naught that they have and hold but comes to them from God. When men take heed of the voice of God within them they find in sharing and justice the only answer to man's ills.

Today, more and more, that voice of the inner God is being heard. On all sides are arising spokesmen for the dispossessed. The clamour for justice is growing and soon will swell into a crescendo of sound, drowning out the cries for caution which issue from the representatives of the past.

How can there be two worlds when the world is One? How can there be division when the law is the same for all men? Presently, men will understand that the suffering of the many is the illness of the whole, and that justice alone will provide the cure.

Aid provides but half the answer, though aid is essential now. Justice must blossom fully in the garden of men's hearts and so set all men free.

Justice creates the conditions in which man can know himself as God. Linked to his brother by love, he can take boldly in his hands his future and fashion it according to the blueprint of God. Many desire that future now, blessed as they are with the vision of the whole, yet naught but work and effort will bring it into being, through the manifestation of justice, love and joy.

Remember as you move towards the future that no one takes these steps alone. As brothers, all, must men proceed along the pathway that leads directly to the Source. From that very Source does justice emanate, relating men in harmony and love.

May 1984

The Son of Man

Many people await the return of the Christ with trepidation and fear. They sense that His appearance will promote great changes in all departments of life. His values, they rightly assume, will necessarily alter their ways of thinking and living and they blanch at such a prospect. Besides, so mystical has been the view of the Christ presented down the centuries by the churches, that many fear His judgement and omnipotent power; they await Him as God come to punish the wicked and reward the faithful.

It is sadly to be regretted that such a distorted vision of the Christ should so have permeated human consciousness. No such being exists. In order to understand the true nature of the Christ it is necessary to see Him as one among equal Sons of God, each endowed with full divine potential, differing only in the degree of manifestation of that divinity.

That He has achieved the fullness of that divinity is His Glory, and well may we stand in reverence at this achievement. That this same achievement is rare indeed is also indisputably true. But the wonder of the Christ for men is that He was one of them. Naught there is, in the trials and sufferings of men, but He did know it. Each step of the path that men still tread has He painfully trodden. Nothing is there, in the whole panorama of human experience, that He has not shared. Thus truly is He the Son of Man.

There can be little doubt that were He to appear unannounced in our midst few would recognize Him. So far from the general notion is He that He would pass unnoticed in the crowd. Thus it is today among His brothers as He awaits man's invitation to begin His mission. Many who see Him daily know Him not. Others recognize Him but are afraid to speak. Still others wait and pray, hopeful that He may be the One for

53

Whom they dare not hope. Only His Declaration before the world will establish Him in the sight and hearts of men.

While we await that Day of Days, let us clarify in our minds the reasons for His return. Let us understand the nature of the task which He has set Himself. To establish in our midst the fact of God, has He come. To recreate the Divine Mysteries, is He here. To teach men how to love, and love again, is He among us. To establish man's brotherhood does He walk the Earth once more. To keep faith with the Father and with man does He accept this burden. To usher in the New Age has He returned. To consolidate the treasure of the past, to inspire the marvels of the future, to glorify God and man has He descended from His high mountain.

Let us look at His priorities: the establishment of peace; the inauguration of the system of sharing; the removal of guilt and fear — the cleansing of the hearts and minds of men; the education of mankind in the laws of life and love; an introduction to the Mysteries; the beautification of our cities; the removal of barriers to travel and interchange of peoples; the creation of a pool of knowledge accessible to all.

That such a task is not an easy one, not even for the Son of Man, is clear. Ancient habits of division and separation have strong roots, while fear and superstition cast their spell over millions of mankind. But never before, in the history of the world, has a Teacher come better equipped for His task. Maitreya has come to do battle with ignorance and fear, division and want. His weapons are spiritual understanding, knowledge and love; His shining armour is Truth Itself.

June 1984

Human rights

The question of human rights is at the centre of modern man's problems. In the past, the social structures dominated the lives of the individual and set up a hierarchical series of relationships in which everyone knew his place: the wife obeyed the husband; the man obeyed his lord; the lord obeyed and carried out the will of the king; while the clergy acted as intermediaries between God and man. These relationships, while artificial and imposed, served the needs of societies struggling to find their identities and place in the world.

Today, all of this is changed. Apart from a few areas in which the ruling groups cling to the old forms, often at the cost of civil dissension and war, the peoples have asserted their right to self-determination. They have taken upon themselves the responsibility for just government and by various procedures of representation can make their wills known. More than ever before, the peoples are calling for a closer participation in the decisions affecting their lives.

This new freedom has set up a number of tensions which await resolution. Everywhere, the cry for more freedom sounds forth — answered by an equally strident call for order and the rule of law from the groups concerned with maintaining the existing structures. Altogether new approaches are required to harmonize the aims of these opposing groups. That such harmony may be slow and difficult to attain must be accepted. That many conflicting viewpoints must be reconciled is self-evident. Yet while we await the solution of these problems it might be advisable to set down some basic principles, some guidelines, without which the problems may appear to be intractable.

The first consideration is that the laws governing society should be fair and applicable to everyone. Without such basic justice and impartiality no one can be expected to observe the law. Frequently, today, there is "one law for the rich and another for the poor" — a certain recipe for social strife. A further need is for the laws to be known and understood and couched in language accessible to all. Too often are men held prisoner, and judged to be guilty of breaching laws long outmoded and known only to specialists.

The greatest need is for an ever closer identity of interest between the individual and society; only thus can the freedom of one and the stability of the other be preserved. How can this best be achieved?

The United Nations Organization has formulated a code of human rights which, if implemented, would go far to resolve the existing social tensions, and to provide the basis for a just and stable society. So far, this Universal Declaration of Human Rights remains but a dream for millions of dispossessed and disfranchised people in every country in the world. The aim must be to establish, with all possible speed, these basic rights in all nations.

With the acceptance of the principle of sharing this becomes possible. No longer need men fight for the right to work, to feed their families, for a measure of control over their destinies. At a stroke, the acceptance of sharing will heal the divisions, end the confrontations and cure the malady of the present situation, leading men out of the morass in which they have foundered. Make sharing then the goal of your endeavour. Show that the world now needs, more than ever in its history, the establishment of this just and basic principle, through the acceptance of which alone man will find and demonstrate his divinity.

July 1984

The need for unity

Unity must be sought for with all diligence. In unity there is not only strength but beauty. Cultivate unity as a wise gardener cultivates his garden, tending carefully each new bud and shoot. Unity follows every true manifestation of love and graces each achievement of the Spirit.

Take unity as your banner and walk the way of power. Unity makes all things possible. Without unity nothing is certain; the finest possibilities come to dust. Achievement lies in the right use of the given capacities; lacking unity, the highest potential may be wasted.

Unity is a manifestation of Spirit, for the true nature of humanity is One. All that leads to unity benefits the race and lends wings to the journey. Unity is invincible; the dark ones beat on the shield of unity in vain. The time is coming when unity will be achieved but the first steps in that direction must be taken now. Useless it is to wait for others to start; the move towards unity must be made by each one. Nothing so pierces the web of unity as criticism. A thousand possibilities are lost in this way. Keep silent the tongue of criticism and protect the precious fabric so carefully spun.

Each in his own way knows the power of unity; each seeks from his neighbour approval and consent, but mechanical conformity of thought here has no place. Each move in the direction of unity adds power to the whole and lightens the task of the Toilers behind the scenes. Create unity and know the true nature of man. Preserve unity and allow the Spirit of man to flourish. Teach unity and unleash the love in your brother's heart.

If humanity would know peace it must see itself as One. Nothing less will take it to that blessed state. Peace will be established when justice rules and the poor no longer beg for mercy. Without justice, unity is unthinkable and would for ever evade man's grasp. Establish, then, the rule of justice and bring unity and peace to this anguished world.

Through sharing alone will justice be confirmed. Sharing alone will bring the peace desired by all the nations. When men share and destroy the walls of separation, they will know at last the truth of their existence and flood the world with brotherhood and love.

Take sharing as your guide into the future. Release your brothers from the grip of poverty and pain. Open yourselves to the impulses of the soul and establish in your midst the Will of God.

God's Will, We affirm, will be established. Through unity and love men will come to share. Through sacrifice and reason men will find the way to justice and peace. Freedom and brotherhood await man's action. All can be achieved.

Together, men can perform all manner of mighty deeds. Limitless are the possibilities of change, but men must act together to create the new world. Through unity alone will men conquer. The strength of unity will open all gates. Hold fast to the ideal of brotherhood and cease to mock your brother's efforts. Know that he, too, faces the storm and struggles in the dark.

Since man was, man has fought. Always have the cleavages been known. Today there enters a new light into the lives of men to cleanse the world of bigotry and war. Help to spread the light of sanity and peace. Help to create the ways of justice and freedom. Work to build the unity which will see men through and gather them together under the banner of the Christ.

The future must be won. All hands are needed for the work. Let the inner union manifest and join hands together for the task.

September 1984

The Masters in the world

When the Masters establish Their presence in full view of the world, a great change will take place in the relationship existing between humanity and Them. Whereas, until now, They have been remote and removed from close contact with all but a few disciples, in the immediate future the Guides of the Race will foster a deeper and more continuous form of co-operation with mankind. This process, known as the Externalization of the Hierarchy, has already begun and several Masters have established contact with groups on the physical plane. So far, this contact has been restricted to groups working in the fields of economics, administration and science, and to a lesser extent in education, but the time will come when Their inspiration and guidance will be given freely to all the groups working to rehabilitate the world.

From that time onwards, an entirely new system of communication will be established between the Inspirers and humanity. For the most part, telepathy will continue to be the mode of contact, especially where disciples are concerned, but where necessary, the Masters, Who have undergone special training for this purpose, will use the ordinary modes of speech. This will bring within the orbit of Their influence many who otherwise would not receive this stimulus.

Then the true training of humanity will begin. Firstly, colleges will be established where the most promising students will be taught the elementary levels of the new sciences, including the science of the soul. These new sciences, it will be found, will cover all aspects of the natural environment of man, both the seen and the unseen, from the subatomic to the cosmic. In this way, a new vision of the glory of the unseen worlds will be given to man; a spirit of co-operation between different disciplines will be fostered and a new, broader, more inclusive outlook will replace the present fragmentation. Thus will the

Masters work, stimulating and strengthening the minds of men, inspiring them to new heights of enquiry and achievement.

In due course, the stage will be set for the Restoration of the Mysteries. Schools for advanced students will be opened at various sites, both ancient and modern, in several countries. Eventually, there will be found, stretching across the world, a network of these training centres for initiation into the Mysteries. The Mysteries are the mysteries of man's origin and purpose, and hold hidden the key to controlling the forces of the universe. With time, a very large number of men will pass through these schools, entering thereby, stage by stage, into the mind of the creating Logos. In this way, the Masters will oversee the evolutionary process, outwardly and openly in the world. For long have They prepared Themselves for this purpose, awaiting the day of Their emergence. That day has been signalled by the Christ; He leads His Brothers into the world. They are the Exemplars and the guarantee of man's future achievement. Their work will open up for men a new vision of their potential.

All of this presupposes the acceptance of the Christ and His proposals for the well-being of humanity: the implementation of the principle of sharing and the restructuring of the world along more just and more rational lines. We await, with confidence, man's decision.

October 1984

Co-workers with God

Looked at from Our vantage point, the present situation of the world is not without its problems and dangers, but nevertheless carries within it the seeds of change and hope for the future. What that future precisely will be depends on man himself and his readiness for a radical transformation of his attitudes and actions.

Without doubt, were man to stumble forward blindly, alone, his cause were as good as lost, for he lacks as yet the wisdom to restrain his power; he lacks the will to implement his higher aspirations; he lacks, above all, the love for his brother which would end for ever much of the misery in the world.

Happily for the world, man is not alone. Behind him stand, and have always stood, the Elder Brothers of the race, ready to succour Our ailing younger brethren when the call for help rises to Us. Once again that call has come and We respond with joy. Without Our help, man's plight would be sorry indeed. So far has he strayed from the Path of Truth that even the least wise see the dangers. The foolhardy, however, ignoring the quicksands, continue to play their game of chance.

When you see Us, you will see men Who have made before you the journey back to God. You will recognize in Us divine characteristics potential in yourselves. Thus will you know your future glory. Out of the present chaos shall We inspire a new order; from the hatreds and divisions shall we create harmony and peace, while from doubt and fear shall We engender meaning, faith and joy.

We come to serve, to teach and to work together with you. We know your problems and We know, too, the solutions to these problems. We can see, and hold in reverence, the inner divinity of men, and await, with confidence, its manifestation when evoked by Us.

This will lead to a new situation on the Earth. God, through Us, and man will come together. From that divine at-one-ment will flow the new civilization, and into man's hands will be placed the power of the Creator. Man will find himself a co-worker with God.

Presently, the world will know of Our existence. For long have We prepared to come before you and do so now in a spirit of joy. Know that there is naught that you suffer that We have not suffered; there is no pain or humiliation which We have not known; your failures have been Our failures, your faltering steps Ours. On the self-same path have We achieved and offer you the fruits of that achievement. We are the forerunners, the Pointers on the Way.

Now is approaching the time of regeneration. Now commences the Era of Truth. First, Maitreya. Then We shall be seen.

The present is a time of crisis and promise. The New struggles to find form. The Old strives to survive amidst the destined change. Humanity is ready for the next step; the long sleep is ending; the sleepers awake. The call to freedom and joy echoes in the hearts of the peoples and stirs them to action.

Little time there is now to prepare. Soon the face of Maitreya will be seen. He alone can bridge the divisions among the nations and bring them, trusting, to each other's aid.

November 1984

Co-operation

Humanity today stands poised for a great leap into the future, a future in which man's essentially divine nature will demonstrate. Little though he may know this, man has passed and is passing the tests which will allow him, in full adulthood, to become the recipient of knowledge and powers with which to fashion that future.

At present, only to the inner vision of the Guides of the Race may this reality be clear, but such it is, and portends well for the coming time. Wherever men gather today, can be seen and felt a new urgency, a new sense of commitment to the well-being of the planet and its kingdoms.

Only now, after aeons spent in the struggle for existence and progress, can man be said to have reached maturity, a maturity discernible to Us, albeit well hidden from man himself.

The opportunity arises now for a major advance in human progress, outstripping by far, in speed and accomplishment, all previous advances. Whereas, until now, a slow and steady progress was desirable, and even preferable, a new, dynamic rhythm is being created whose momentum will sweep humanity into the future on a wave of global change. So great are the tensions in today's divided world that only a rapid change of direction will prevent catastrophe. This rapid change, there is no doubt, will present problems of adjustment to many, but many more, by far, will welcome these changes as the opportunity for new life.

We, the Toilers behind the scenes, have every confidence that humanity will set in motion this radical transformation of its structures. They no longer serve man's needs and block the emergence of the new. We watch and guide, overseeing all.

Little by little, a new consciousness is awakening humanity to its inner needs. The old, competitive spirit dies hard, but nevertheless a new spirit of co-operation is likewise to be seen. This augurs well for the future, for it is by co-operation alone that mankind will survive; by co-operation alone that the new civilization will be built; by co-operation only that men can know and demonstrate the inner truth of their divinity.

Co-operation is the natural result of right relationship. Right relationship likewise follows wise co-operation. Co-operation holds the key to all successful group effort and is a manifestation of divine goodwill. Without co-operation nothing lasting can be achieved, for co-operation brings into synthesis many diverse points of view.

Co-operation is another word for Unity. Unity and co-operation are the springboards to the future and the guarantee of achievement for all men. Great reservoirs of power lie untapped within humanity, waiting for the magic of co-operation to unleash.

Competition strains the natural order; co-operation liberates the goodwill in men. Competition cares only for the self, whereas co-operation works for the highest good of all.

Competition leads to separation, the origin of all sin; co-operation seeks to blend and fuse the many-coloured strands of the one divine life.

Competition has led man to the precipice; co-operation alone will help him find the path.

The old and backward-looking love competition; the new embrace with joy divine co-operation.

The people of the world can be divided into two kinds: those who compete, and those who co-operate.

Cleanse the heart of the stain of competition; open the heart to joyful co-operation.

December 1984

The Law of Rebirth

Great confusion reigns in man's understanding of the laws governing rebirth. This confusion is reflected in the variety of teachings and interpretations which exist, and which serve to deepen further man's ignorance and fear.

For untold ages in the Orient, the idea of successive lives governed by an immutable law of karma has seldom been in doubt. The result has been the ready acceptance of the circumstances of the present, however degrading and inhuman they might be. In the Occident, on the other hand, the concepts of repeated incarnations has lain dormant, engaging the attention only of the few since its exclusion from the Church's teachings in the 6th century at the instigation of the Emperor Justinius. Had the teachings of Origen remained within the body of Christian belief, an altogether different approach to the facts of life and death would pertain in the West.

That great Initiate knew and taught the truth of incarnational cycles, inaugurated by the Lord of the World, proceeding under the impulse of the Law of Sacrifice, and governed by the Law of Cause and Effect. The deletion of this truth from the Church's teachings has resulted in the ignorance and fear so much in evidence today. Where interest in reincarnation has survived, it has, for the most part, taken the form of an almost exclusive interest in the supposed personal details of previous lives.

In the coming cycle of Aquarius, an entirely new approach to the Law of Rebirth will be taken. No longer will the old, fatalistic acceptance of all that happens as the inexorable hand of karma hold sway in the East, condemning millions to lives of drudgery and pain; no longer, in the West, will men ignore the fundamental laws of their existence and the personal responsibility which the working of these laws confers. Men will know that they themselves create, through thought and action, the circumstances of their lives; but also that by the working of these same laws they can transform and change for the better their natures and conditions.

This will lead to a revaluation of life's meaning and purpose and a healthier approach to the fact of death. An understanding of the continuity of all life, incarnate or not, will replace the present fear; the old phobia of death as the end of everything will vanish in the new light which will illumine the minds of men. Into the darkest corners of superstition and ignorance this new light will shine, awakening men to an awareness of their divinity as immortal souls.

The true understanding of the maxim of the Christ, that what we sow we reap, will transform human existence in all its aspects. Tolerance and harmlessness not known before will replace the present separation, as men recognize the justice and the logic of the Law.

The new era will bring new insights and man will approach life as the adventure it is, a journey of discovery — the discovery of the fact that God and man are one; that naught divides but the limited vision of the seeker; that all men chart a different course to the same goal, and that the goal of all our striving is the realization of the divinity which awaits our recognition.

Under the great Law of Rebirth we undertake that journey again and yet again, until at last we enter into the Light of our own understanding as self-perfected Sons of God.

January 1985

The Knowers return

Seldom in the world's history has there been a time like the present, a time of such convulsive change and promise for man. Once again, in the turning of the Great Wheel, man is about to discover a new meaning and purpose behind the outer manifestations of his life, and to renew contact with the source of all his wisdom and inspiration. After long and due preparation, the ancient Body of Knowers, the Spiritual Hierarchy, is returning to the world of men, ready to implant there the seeds of knowledge and truth which will take men to the heights from which the Gods smile down.

In the immediate time ahead, men will come to know the Masters of Wisdom as their friends and allies on the long path of evolution, as their guides and mentors in an expanding awareness of the Plan They serve, and as their guarantee of future, and like achievement.

At the present time, the Masters are gathering Their forces for the onslaught on tyranny and greed, exploitation and want. They know that not all men are ready for the changes which must ensue but they know, too, that most men, by far, desire a new dimension of life, and are ready for the deeds and sacrifices which will bring it into being. They will not be slow to respond to the counsel of the Great Ones. Make ready to see Them and to answer Their call. Make ready to act and to aid Them in Their task. Make ready, too, for the stream of new light, new life and new knowledge which will flow from Them into the world.

Thus will all be changed. Thus will the old be swept away and a new era begin. Thus will the Teachers revitalize men's lives and create the conditions for the emergence of a new man.

The new man will demonstrate his allegiance to the truth that humanity is One, held together by the force of Love Itself; by his tolerance and harmlessness, his correct relation to all the kingdoms. The new man will be known by his capacity for right action, intuitively understood; by his ability to interpret rightly the Will of God. Thus will gradually emerge the God Who sits within the heart of all men, potential, waiting to be called into manifestation by the actions of man himself.

The key to this development lies in a growing working relationship between the Masters and men. From this will grow a bond so deep that naught can sever it, creating thus a channel for the gifts of wisdom, love and knowledge which are the Masters' to bestow. Their divinity will call forth the divine in man, and men will discover they have been, for ever, Gods.

All of this will not happen in a day, but slowly and surely the divine in men will respond to the fire of divine love and wisdom which radiates from the Masters. They will gather round that fire and find among the flames the reflection of their future. So will it be, for so it has been decreed by the Lord of Life Himself.

Shortly, now, the Masters will be seen and known for what They are — the Guides and Teachers of the race of men, the Elder Brothers of humanity, the Knowers in whose hands lies the destiny of the world. Welcome Them into your midst and be prepared to serve with Them. Be generous with your offering of service and become Their co-workers. Know that They know the Way and will take you with Them to the Gates of Freedom.

March 1985

The future

There are many roads to the future. Many possibilities await the exploring minds of men. Manifold are the tasks that lie before those who would create a future worthy of man. Manifold are the experiments through which men can discover the modes which suit them best. Also, for the first time in countless millennia, the senior members of the Spiritual Hierarchy will be at hand to counsel and guide. In this way, men can be saved much heartache and years of wasted effort.

Progress at first may be slow, but gradually the momentum will quicken until, in a crescendo of discovery, a new world of meaning will open before man's astonished eyes.

Heretofore, progress for man proceeded in piecemeal fashion. While vast areas of the world remained in isolation, long ages were required to inculcate the smallest change. Today, all is different. Communications have set before humanity the wherewithal of quickened evolution, and everywhere there are the signs of ferment and transformation. The blueprint of the future is descending, and the sensitive minds of the race are responding to the new vision. Never before, in the history of the world, has such an opportunity as now exists been presented to men. From the chaos of the past can order be created; into the darkest ignorance can new light shine. Together, for the first time as brothers, can men establish the rule of divine law, and enter into right relation with their Source.

Now, as we enter the time of renewal, men should understand the principles on which a correct advance can be made. Brotherhood, itself a fact in nature, must more and more determine the nature of the new forms. All that is awakened to the fact of brotherhood will find itself in the centre of the path to the future. All that pertains to brotherhood will find the quickening energy of Hierarchy flowing to its cause. Peace will be established on the idea of brotherhood, ridding the world for ever of the canker of war.

Co-operation is the key to the new relationships. When co-operation reigns, the iniquities and inequalities of the past will cease. The fires of competition, fanned by selfishness and greed, will die down, enabling men to live in harmony and trust. So will it be. And so will the Plan, which is the Purpose of God embodied, be fulfilled. Many are the steps which must be taken towards that blessed state, but already men's minds are turning hopefully in that direction.

Sharing is the key of keys. Through sharing men will come to know the meaning of God's love. Without sharing there can be no future for man, for the time has come to manifest God's love — or die. Sharing provides the answer to all man's problems and a sure entry into the New Age. Through sharing, peace will prevail. Through sharing, justice will be won. Through sharing and co-operation, brotherhood will flourish, and a new and glorious future open for man.

April 1985

Initiation

The purpose of Hierarchy is to implement the Plan of God. In this endeavour, They utilize all means open to Them. Among the many procedures of which They make use, that known as *Initiation* is the most important. It takes precedence over all other measures, and contains within it the requirements for all progress on this planet. Each initiation confers on the initiate a deeper understanding of the meaning and purpose behind God's Plan, a fuller awareness of his part within that Plan, and an increasing ability to work consciously and intelligently towards its fulfilment. There is no process on this Earth that can take a man so swiftly and so surely to the mountain top of Liberation.

The process of Initiation is of ancient origin. For millions of years, it has been the main stimulus behind man's evolution, and, for those ready to accept its rigours and disciplines, has provided a sure path of unfoldment of the inner divinity. Many today press close to the doors of initiation, and for humanity as a whole this fact is of great moment. It represents an enormous step forward in the slow advance towards a full expression of that divinity, it is a guarantee that the Plan is working out, and is the sign that the methods used by Hierarchy for millennia are successful and are bearing fruit.

Perhaps a slight digression here would be in order. Over the centuries, it has been the habit of Hierarchy to work from behind the scenes; seldom has a Master functioned openly in the world. Through Their disciples alone has the main task of stimulus been made. Now, all is changing. More and more, the Senior Members of the Hierarchy will take Their places among you and give you the benefit of Their wisdom and experience. Thus will be brought to bear on humanity an enormous spiritual stimulus which will sweep through the Gates of Initiation millions now treading the first steps of the Path. To help prepare the way for this time, much information has been released about the requirements for each initiatory experience, and aspirants should acquaint themselves with the details of the various stages and grades. It is not for nothing that this information has been given and much may be learned of this deeply esoteric process by careful study and reflection.

The Christ stands ready to begin His work. As the Hierophant of the first and second initiations His task will be to perform the esoteric practices and ceremonials connected with this ancient science and to reveal to the astonished eyes of the initiate the secrets hidden therein. This He performs today on the inner planes, but from this time forth He will gather together in groups all who are ready to receive the 'fire of the Rod' on the physical plane, and thus set the seal on their achievement. In this way, humanity will merge with Hierarchy and in the fullness of time these two centres will become one. Thus will be completed the task of the Christ: the outer manifestation of the Kingdom of God. Thus will He be enabled to contemplate His handiwork and be satisfied.

May 1985

Maitreya's mission

It is not long until the world will see the Christ. Despite appearances, His mission is proceeding well and many are the changes which His presence has invoked. There are those who doubt His presence in the world. This is natural; only when His face is seen will the doubters believe. Thus has it always been.

Many await Him in the hope of miracles. Many look for His succour and support. Forgoing the miracles of yore, He will address Himself to the problems of the age: hunger and poverty, war and want. When you see Him, you will see a Man Who has given Himself to God. In so doing, He has become a God. So complete is His identification with the Source that naught stands between Him and that Divinity.

Remember, when you see Him, that no law *commands* His presence and return. Responding only to the call to service and sacrifice, He once again shoulders the burden and invests it with joy.

Repeatedly, He has called for your support. Not seldom has He asked you to make known His presence. Were you to fulfil this request, the world would the better be prepared for His appearance. Sad it is that those who long the most act the least.

For the first time in history the whole world will see and know the Teacher. For the first time, together, men will salute the Messenger of God. When they know Him, they will find Him to be a wise counsellor, a true brother and friend. Take heart from this promise, for the day is not far off when men's anguish will be assuaged. Take heart from this promise, for the tide is turning in favour of the Light.

Knowledge of God is essential to man's progress, but God can be known in many different ways. Today, your scientists are presenting facets of God's nature hitherto unknown, and find themselves at variance with the teachings of the churches. The time has come for the churches to re-examine these teachings in the light of the new knowledge now available to man. When they do this, they will find much to discard and much to reinterpret. Only then will the mausoleums of outmoded doctrines and dogmas, which the churches are today, become vibrant conveyors of the truth of God.

In this reassessment, the Master Jesus will play an important part. His is the task to reconstruct the Christian groups along more fruitful lines and to prepare them for their role as centres of teaching and healing. In this He will work closely with the Christ, but Maitreya's mission will embrace all aspects of men's lives. His energy and inspiration will stimulate every field and men will know Him for the World Teacher that He is. Under His guidance, men will refashion the world along more just and spiritual lines and thus begin their ascent to the mountain top of achievement.

June 1985

Maitreya's call

Whenever the forces of Light and Darkness come together to do battle, men may be assured that the victory will be with the Light. However long the struggle, the end is not in doubt. For this reason, there is no need to fear in the present conflict. All outer events notwithstanding, the forces of Light are in the ascendant and steadily inculcate a new and higher rhythm and purpose in men's lives. This being so, naught can disturb the plan for the rehabilitation of the world. The outer signs of turmoil and violence, of hatred and fear, are but the death-throes of a dying civilization under the impact of the new. When the smoke of battle has cleared, humanity will find itself entering into a dispensation unlike aught known before, into, as Maitreya has said, "a simpler life where no man lacks, where no two days are alike, where the Joy of Brotherhood manifests through all men".

To create such a life, much effort will be needed. All must be forged by man himself under the guidance of the Great Ones. All that obstructs the creation of the new civilization must be relinquished, and the stage reset for the construction of more adequate forms. Herein lies the opportunity for humanity to show its true creative genius and capacity for renewal. Man is a potential God and soon that divinity will find expression in the spiritual transformation of the world.

Let it not be assumed that men will re-enter the churches; this is unlikely to be the case. But in every field of endeavour wherein man is engaged, a new, divine livingness will manifest itself and a new radiance issue from the lives and actions of men.

That this will call for sacrifice is obvious, but only for the sacrifice of selfishness and greed. These alone create the divisions which separate the peoples and threaten now the very existence of the race. Such a willing sacrifice will take men to the heights of achievement and confirm them as potential Gods.

Certainly, today, there is a longing for change and a recognition of the need for sacrifice. Wherever thoughtful men and women meet together and talk of the needs of the time this fact is known.

Until now, however, it remains but an ideal; no nation takes the lead and shows the way. Maitreya has come, therefore, to show that only through sacrifice of narrow, selfish interest can the bridges between the factions be built, the tensions resolved, the hungry fed.

Be ready then, to accept the sacrifices which you will be called upon to make: of your privileges and power, your nation's influence and wealth, your unjust share of the world's resources. Be ready to accept that all men are One, that God loves all equally and that each is a reflection of the divine. When you see Him, Maitreya will leave you in no doubt; the course you have to follow will be clear: "Take your brother's need as the measure for your action and solve the problems of the world. There is no other course."

July 1985

The path to the future

Many are the obstacles to progress on the Path but naught hinders more than fear. Fear of failure, fear of ridicule, of suffering, discipline and pain — these are the obstructions which must be surmounted on the Path to Freedom. Sure-footedness is essential on a rocky mountain path; fear contracts the Spirit and renders useless the instinct for danger. There is no obstacle like fear. It obstructs the flow of life itself. It takes away all hope and constitutes the greatest threat to well-being and health. Abjure fear and construct the mechanism of faith. Conquer fear and terminate the torment of doubt. Knowledge banishes fear. Inculcate, therefore, knowledge and trust.

Since 1425, Hierarchy have worked under a new rhythm. Everything pertaining to the Plan has undergone revision and many new projects have been initiated. This has involved a reconstruction of the methods and procedures through which the Plan is implemented, and in many ways denotes a break with the past. While the Masters prepared for Their eventual return, systems ages old have been modified and adapted to meet the needs of evolving men.

In this way have We made ready for Our re-entry to the outer world. When Our faces are seen, you will see also the beginning time of changes which will transform the world. Not all at once will the changes take place, but soon the first firm blows for justice and freedom will be struck, gathering momentum as the months and years flash by. In time, all will be renewed and the peoples of the world will breathe a cleaner and a saner air.

Courage is needed for this monumental task. Many are the challenges which must be met. Not easy is it to change a world entirely, nor to build a new one on the ruins of the past. Have courage, therefore, and rebuild your world. Put fear aside and welcome the future with arms outstretched.

Have patience also, for the foundations of the new must be laid in stone and faith. Treasure the best of the past and restore the old signposts. Otherwise, man would lose his way.

Several times in the past man has had the opportunity to rise but failed to seize the moment. Be prepared to take hold of the future with both hands and fashion a world of beauty. Eschew despair and create with joy and love, knowing that the future stands ready for your embrace.

Steadfastness, too, and hope, are needed for the building of the new. Impress upon yourselves the need to persevere, for many are the obstacles on the road to freedom and love.

We, the Masters, will be among you, and Our experience will save you much travail. Count on Our support and guiding hand to show you the pitfalls on the way. We shall teach you the laws of love and inspire you to live your highest aspiration. We, the Knowers, shall teach you the meaning of Truth, and lead you into the light of your own Divinity.

Allow Us to guide your footsteps towards the future which beckons you onwards. Work with Us in hope and trust and make perfect your way. Leave behind your fears. Take courage from Our example, for We, too, have known the pains and perils of the way.

September 1985

Sharing for peace

When a man shares he grows. Little attention has been given until now to this simple truth. For many, sharing comes naturally, as a matter of course. For others, however, the concept is alien and fraught with suspicion and pain. To these, what is theirs is theirs, almost by divine right, while to share is foreign and absurd. How then can the world move in the direction of sharing and redistribution, prerequisites for world peace?

Wherever men look today they see the results of their inability to share. Across the planet, millions starve and die. Countless others survive in misery and hopeless poverty, condemned to suffer from birth to early grave.

Change will come when men comprehend the reasons for their presence on Earth; when they realize that they are part of a vast evolutionary experiment whose purpose is hidden, to all but a few. When they recognize themselves as souls, parts of the One Oversoul, and grasp the identity of each with the other; when men understand that sharing is the natural order, that selfishness and greed are deviants from the norm, when to share is seen as an opportunity to grow, then will men embrace sharing as an end to their sorrows and their separation.

That time is now upon us. The pressures of inner forces and outer events are making themselves felt on a worldwide scale and are causing a reassessment of man's position and prospects. No longer is it certain that the planet can sustain life indefinitely, subject to its ruthless exploitation by man. Nuclear annihilation is an ever-present threat, while economic competition and financial disarray pose problems which afflict the daily lives of countless millions.

Not for nothing is it now a commonplace for nations to meet to discuss these problems. Such meetings are a sign that man is becoming aware of his responsibilities as steward of the planet, and is ready to take decisions to improve his situation. Foremost among these decisions must be the readiness to share. When the world's goods are shared more equitably, half of man's problems will vanish overnight. Already, there are indications that many realize this, and the call for sharing is rising on every hand. The wise foresee the need for sharing as the only basis of lasting peace, and the heroes of the young lend, too, their popular voice.

This augurs well for the future, for it shows that mankind at last is aware of the choice before it — to share or die — and is ready to act in the spirit of brotherhood and love. No longer are men content to leave their destiny in the hands of others — to governments formed of blind and ageing men — but see the need for direct participation to safeguard their future and their world.

Many still are fearful, but the light of the New Time grows brighter by the hour. Many await the dawn of a New Age with hope and anticipation, aware of the opportunity to serve and grow. They know that they stand not alone but surrounded by others who share their vision and likewise long for brotherhood and peace.

Through sharing alone will that vision be realized. Through sharing alone will that peace be won. That is the message for the present time: share and grow into the reflection of divinity. Share and inaugurate the era of peace and love.

October 1985

Love — the way forward

Each day, man looks anew at his life and fails to discern the causes for his discontent. He blames the weather, his neighbour, his lack of money or opportunity, for his failure to find happiness and inner peace. As a result, he is at odds with himself and his world. He knows no sure faith that life is meaningful or has purpose, and grasps at every ephemeral idea or notion which crosses his path in a vain attempt to satisfy his longing for the surety of knowing 'the Truth'. Time after time, that 'Truth' eludes him, leaving him stranded once more in a sea of doubts. Nowhere can he find the solution to his problems; nowhere can he see the answers to his questions and fears. As time goes on, he lapses into silent lethargy or follows a path of ever more destructive violence. Thus stands man at the crossroads of his life, awaiting a new dawn or a fateful and final slide into catastrophic war.

Into this scene emerge Maitreya and His group of Masters carrying with Them the Banner of Peace and Love. Round Them are gathered Their disciples, ready to do battle in the cause of Justice and Peace. Their war cry is *Unity — Justice* and *Freedom* for all. They know the rules of combat — conquer by Love and Service. They know the needs of the time and are ready for every sacrifice. They know Their tasks and wait, impatient for action. Listen for the sound of Their music — Beauty and Truth. Watch for signs of Their hand — Co-operation, Sharing and Joy.

Make ready to recognize and work with these Warriors of the New Time and fulfil the purpose of your incarnation. Largely unknown, as yet, They are not to be found in the existing groups. They stand in the wings, awaiting the call to service. When that call comes, They will enter into a service for which They are well trained, expressing the needs of all for a world shorn of cynicism and greed; rid for ever of bigotry and narrowness of view; a world in which men will come to know themselves and each other as the Gods they truly are.

Then men will understand that what ails them is their lack of love; their inability to register in their lives their qualities as souls; that daily the soul seeks expression of its purpose, and that being denied, all turns to salt.

Here, then, is the cure for all the ills of men: demonstrate love that every man may share the Earth's abundance. Demonstrate love that wars be seen no more. Demonstrate your soul's love and bring that day forward when man will be united with man and God.

However he may try, man cannot live without love. This fact will soon establish itself in the consciousness of the race, and lead to events unparalleled in history. Shortly will begin a process of transformation unlike aught seen before: gone for ever the sight of millions starving, the daily heartache of the dispossessed, the everlasting travail of the world's poor. Gone, from sight and mind, the threat of self-destruction, the unholy terror which has humanity in thrall. Gone, too, the lack of trust which curbs and limits man's every action and sets him against his neighbour and himself.

All of this shall man achieve by demonstrating Love. Through Love shall man conquer and become a God.

November 1985

The role of man

In time, men will come to understand the true nature of their relationship with the lower kingdoms, and accept gladly the role of steward for their evolution. This will lead to a transformation in all aspects of farming and agriculture, in forestry and fishing. Gone for ever will be the present methods: despoliation of forest and soil; over-cultivation of impoverished land; greedy and reckless pursuit of many species of animal and fish.

A halt must soon be called to this unholy war on nature's bounty. No longer must men allow the poisoning of the earth and waters, which threatens the lives of man and beast alike. No longer is it fitting to engage in farming methods which prohibit the basic rights of movement and access to air and light. The cruel exploitation, for experiment, of countless creatures must give way to saner means of research and knowledge.

Many, today, are concerning themselves with these issues and calling for change. Men's minds are moving in the right direction and naught can halt this momentum. Nevertheless, vast changes are needed forthwith to maintain the ecological balance in the world.

When the Earth is viewed as a living entity, complete in all its parts, each essential to the Whole, a new vision and a new sanity will prevail. Men will come to see themselves as stewards of a natural order, preordained to function in harmony and beauty, each kingdom related, above it and below it, according to the Plan.

Today, vast sums are spent on research into nature's laws. At the same time, enormous resources are wasted and misused. Were these resources directed to stabilizing the natural balance, a new world would emerge. Man would find himself the possessor of secrets long hidden from him. He would enter areas of knowledge until now closed to his enquiring mind. Nature would yield up her mysteries and man would begin a partnership with the creating Logos, taking his rightful place as custodian of the Plan.

Man has the power to make all things new or to destroy his world; never before has such omnipotence been his. To ensure the correct use of this power requires the expression of a wisdom seldom seen today, but one that man must find within himself or die.

Fortunately for the race, man is not alone. From behind the scenes of life is now emerging a group of Knowers; men endowed with all the attributes of God. From Them will flow the wisdom of the ages to guide and shepherd man along the way.

Under Their inspiration, man will retrace his steps and begin anew. Under Their wise tutelage will he begin the ascent into divinity, to demonstrate that divinity, potential, but unexpressed.

Thus will men in time become the Knowers, servants alike of the Purposes of God. From them, then, will flow a stream of universal wisdom to nurture all together in the furtherance of the Plan.

December 1985

Psychism today

In earlier times it was customary to seek the advice of an oracle when faced with some quandary, some difficult decision. The ancient myths are replete with accounts of such events and testify to the deep superstition which prevailed in those far-off days. The oracles became all-powerful and frequently influenced the course of political action. Whole nations were plunged into war and disaster on the word of the oracle.

Today, things are not so very different. Throughout the world, men and women in every sphere of life seek the advice and counsel of 'clairvoyants', 'astrologers' and 'soothsayers' to help them solve their problems and dilemmas. In the vast majority of cases, that advice is spurious and useless, yet people gladly pay substantial sums in the hope of 'higher' guidance. So deeply rooted is the habit of turning to others for help in this way that many people, otherwise intelligent and sophisticated, find it all but impossible to make a decision themselves. At the same time, a considerable industry exists to cater for their demands for guidance. In this situation, all manner of nonsense passes for superior wisdom and trained inner perception.

We are entering a time when the psychic faculties of man are coming under stimulus. Eventually, these faculties will unfold in such a way that the soul's higher knowledge does indeed become available to the seeker. At the present time, however, and in most cases, only the lower psychic mechanism manifests itself and brings through from the astral planes the illusions and distortions of these realms. What use then to seek from the realms of illusion the answer to one's dilemma? Much education and correct training must proceed before the world may properly benefit from the guidance of prepared sensitives.

That such preparation and training will be available is not in doubt. Much thought has gone into the planning of these procedures and the day is soon at hand when the work can begin. In the interim, due caution must be exercised and the sharpest discrimination employed in all approaches to 'psychics'. Better by far it is to make one's own decisions and to learn, if necessary, from one's own mistakes. In this way lies growth and future strength. No man becomes a Master who cannot stand alone and act with purpose and intention. Supine dependence on 'psychics' and 'guides' leads but to inaction and lost opportunity, and serves only those who ply their lucrative trade. Thus do We recommend the sterner course of self-reliance and the discipline of the Spirit, on which anvil the tempered blade of the Master is forged.

The time is coming when no one will sell the gifts of the Spirit. The day is dawning when the joy of sharing these gifts will be its own reward. When insights and knowledge stem truly from the Spirit the thought of payment enters not therein. Soon we will see a cleansing of this field and a proper evaluation of the sensitives in our midst. The presence of Maitreya and His Brothers will bring a new purity of approach, a flood of knowledge and a wiser handling of this entire subject.

January 1986

The Divine science

As we near the beginning of a new era, the thoughts of men turn to the sky and the possibilities which exist for future travel between the planets. Already, instruments probe deep into space, gathering the information which may throw light on the nature of the system in which we live. Men's thoughts turn upwards and outwards for the first time. This concern is new for man. Seldom before has his thought reached further than his own hearth, restricting his vision of the vast scope of cosmos which awaits his exploration. At the same time, new discoveries about the nature of Life Itself are awakening men to the need for an outer expression of the unity which, they now know, underlies our Universe.

Already, vast sums are spent annually to ensure the success of these explorations and much dedication and valour contribute to their achievements. Thus we stand today on the verge of an era of new knowledge, broader concepts, wider horizons and richer experience than aught known before.

At precisely such a time has entered the new Teacher. His will be the task to enlarge even further these horizons for man, to show that all is interconnected, that we live within a family, as brothers, and that each contributes to the well-being of the whole. Thus man will come to sense himself as an integral unit in a vast system which stretches to the stars; as a tiny point of conscious, loving life, without which the Universe would be poorer. Thus man will come to see his greatness, and his function in an endless scheme of interrelated points of light and energy and knowledge.

The first step is to accept that all is One, that underlying the diversity of forms beats the Heart of the One Divine Life. When mankind grasps this Truth there will emerge a civilization based upon that Truth which will carry man to the feet of Divinity

Itself. From that holy place man will see the glories until then hidden from his gaze and come to know himself as the God he is.

A new, divine science will become his. Through its means, man will harness the energies of the Universe for his diverse needs and transform and beautify this Earth. As custodians of this science We, the Masters of Wisdom, will reveal its secrets, stage by stage, as man equips himself correctly for its use.

Then the gateway to the heavens will open and man will find himself on a journey without end. The cosmos, near and far, will be the subject of his research; infinity will beckon him ever onwards and test his valour.

A new stream of thought is entering men's lives which will galvanize them into action. A new, creative potency will manifest itself on all sides and, in gathering momentum, the secrets of Life will be discovered and revealed. Man stands now on the threshold of great things. Marvels await his astonished gaze. The limitations of the past will soon lose their hold and free him to explore the cosmos and himself.

When man sees the Universe and himself as One all things become possible.

March 1986

The emergence of great servers

There comes a time in the history of each nation when its soul quality begins to manifest itself more powerfully and to give rise to the appearance of major figures in the realms of art or science, politics or religion. When this happens, we see the emergence of influential men and women who give colour and coherence to a nation's endeavours. Deeply creative, they inspire those around them with their vision, and help to create the culture of their time. They are the disciples and initiates who articulate for others the genius of their nation.

At the present time, we await the arrival of such powerful figures on the world's stage. Trained by the senior members of the Esoteric Hierarchy, there now exists a group of spiritually oriented men and women equipped to deal effectively with the problems of the time. When the call sounds forth, which soon it will, they will take up the work for which they have been prepared: the reconstruction of our planetary life along entirely new lines.

Working in all fields, this group of dedicated disciples will show the way for humanity to follow. Coming as they do from many nations, they will be able to focus and channel the aspirations of all people for a world of peace and justice. They are, for the most part, unknown at present, but soon their names and work will bring a light to men's eyes, inspiring them with hope and expectation of a better future. They work today unseen but are ready to put their gifts and training at the service of the race. They will be known for their altruistic love and wise judgement; for their sense of duty and dedication to their task. Trained by Masters, they will reflect something of Their detachment and knowledge, bringing a new rhythm and order into our chaotic world.

Shortly, from the blueprint of the future now descending, will precipitate the forms of the new civilization. Each nation has a part to play, bringing to the structure of the Whole its own particular voice. In this, the United Nations will play a vital role, co-ordinating the plans for reconstruction and redistribution. Even now, despite the limitations imposed on it by the major powers, the contribution to world peace made by the United Nations is great. Its agencies educate and bring succour to millions in many lands. As a forum for world debate its position is unique and priceless. Sad would be the day and great would be the loss to humanity were the nations to lose faith in this institution, central as it is to the working out of the Divine Plan.

Many expect Maitreya and the Masters to right all wrongs and to transform the world. That They will show the way, guide and inspire, cannot be gainsaid. That Their light and wisdom will be placed at the service of humanity is equally true. But the work of transformation must be undertaken by humanity itself, cheerfully accepting the changes and sacrifices which must ensue. Only through such willing acceptance can the changes take hold and create the conditions for a new and better life for man. To lead the way, and to build the foundations of the new-age structures, are emerging now the trained architects of the coming civilization. Recognize them by their desire to serve, their wisdom and their manifested love.

April 1986

A call to service

Within the limits set by his present level of consciousness, man has created much. Nowhere is this more apparent than in his scientific achievements, his art, his engineering and architectural skills. Many geniuses have arisen to show the way, men and women dedicated to the task of enriching the culture of our time. Thus, as we stand on the threshold of the Aquarian experience, many new possibilities are opening up for man, calling him onwards to fulfil his potential — a divinity waiting to be revealed.

Viewed from Our standpoint, this is but a beginning, a preparation for the creation of a civilization such as man has never known; a civilization which will not alone rival but far surpass the most brilliant of ancient times. Then, as We do now, the Masters led the way, but openly, known as the bestowers of knowledge and truth. The wheel has turned and We retrace Our steps.

Soon, the world will see the return to the world of the Elders of the race, the Knowers, the Sons of God. Prophecy has foretold Our advent and quickened the expectancy of the disciples, but many such sleep soundly, oblivious to the happenings of the time. There are many who await Our coming with aspiration but envisage it in a far future time. Know they not that Our hand knocks *now* upon the door? Awake, friends! Awake, workers for the good! We need all who would work with Us to transform the world. We need your aspiration, your joy. Your hope and trust We cherish. Make ready to see Us and to welcome Us into your lives.

There is no need to fear Our return. We embody the Centre of Love. That is Our nature and invokes Our service. Know this to be so and fear not. We shall be with you as Elder Brothers, to show you the way. For long have We awaited this opportunity to serve you, counting the years till We can be among you. When you see Us you will know that the time of the end and of the beginning has come: the end of the old separation; the beginning of partnership.

There is now afoot a plan of salvation for the world. This involves the co-operation of all those who long to serve the world. To serve today is not difficult, for the means of service lie to hand and the Earth itself cries out for succour. Choose your field of service and endow it with ardour, knowing that as you do so your soul will equip you for the task. Know, too, that Our hand will strengthen yours and share the burden.

Certain it is that much needs changing; the tempo of that change will depend on you. We rely on your co-operation to carry out the details of the plan. Service calls the vanguard of the new civilization to build the foundations of tomorrow's better world.

Take your places in that roll-call and aid Us in the work of salvage. Pass it not by, when the hour has struck!

May 1986

The need to love

From time to time, there arises in the minds of men the concept of love. The idea of love as a natural instinct which demands expression engages men's thought, and steps are taken, through argument and discourse, to demonstrate that this is so. Thus has it been for millennia. The notion that love is somehow central to man's nature never fails to find adherents. This being so, is it not surprising that so little love finds expression in the day to day activity of men?

Almost without exception, men live in fear. They see the world and life as threatening, and build an armour of defence against these threats. Thus do they limit their capacity to love. Their love atrophies and dies or hides behind aggression and hate. Bereft of love, man sickens. Conscious of his inner worth, unable to call it forth, man projects his fears and hates upon his neighbours and his world.

Where love rules, harmony governs. Without that harmony, naught may proceed with confidence. Failing confidence, little can be achieved. Fear inhibits the expression of love. Love annihilates fear. Seeking to express his love but limited by fear, man loses his way. Lost in the quicksand, his struggles only serve further to entrap him.

Wherein, then, lies the remedy? In order to love, man must trust. Where trust is not, love cannot be. Love arises spontaneously in the trusting heart, for love is the true nature of man. Learn then to trust and demonstrate the love which is ever ready to shine forth. Trust is the acceptance of life in all its pain and beauty. Trust is the sure knowledge that all is working towards the good, that all is under law, and that that law is administered with justice. Learn to trust and banish fear. Banish for ever the mechanism of limitation and open wide the floodgates of love.

When man loves, he draws to himself all possibilities. The magnet of love, through identity of vibration, attracts all requirements. Thus is love the lever of evolution. Consider a world without love; such hideousness appals the imagination. Why should this be so? Instinctively, man recognizes the need for love and soon will understand the need to love. He will come to know that love links him to all others in an endless chain. Tentatively, perhaps, at first, he will begin to trust. Step by step, he will conquer his fear. Then will he enter into that blessed state where fear has no place, where love sits calmly on its throne, bestowing its grace on all who come near.

For man, then, to live is to love. Fear, the usurper, must be eschewed and overcome. Trust engenders love and destroys that fear, revealing the god who dwells for ever within. Trust and faith are one, reflections of the inner divinity. Trust that divinity, allow it to radiate as love, and know the end of fear.

June 1986

The benefactors

Every generation brings into incarnation those souls who are equipped to deal with the problems of the time. This statement is an esoteric truism to which more attention should be paid. In it lies hope for the future and a guarantee of progress. It also gives an insight into the workings of the Plan. Faced as they are with adversity and trial men tend to see the world as hostile and life as haphazard. They fail to see the continuity and beauty of the unfolding evolutionary plan.

In reality, all is working towards the good. Naught there is of trial and pain but leads eventually to greater understanding and peace. Could men but see the intricate workings of that Karmic process, they would marvel at the justice and majesty of the Plan. As it is, they know not that all proceeds under Law. Lost in fear and doubt, they turn their backs upon the evidence of their experience and deny the existence of Law.

Yet a backwards glance through history would reveal the steady onward progress of mankind. Each epoch has seen the unfolding of some facet of man's potential; each century the emergence of men and women of genius whose radiance and resource has enriched the lives of all. Through their discoveries, their arts and sciences, these benefactors of the race have led humanity forward, bearing the fruits of the spirit for all to see.

Thus has it been for untold ages, testifying to the efficacy of the Plan. And thus will it continue till all is perfected and a new day begins upon another star.

Cycle after cycle, bringing their gifts of insight and experience, wave upon wave of souls have met and overcome the challenges of the time. Never, for long, has mankind faltered, however dark the image that history presents. Never, for long, was man left unattended. Brief, indeed, were the terms bereft of guidance, and even then the light was there for those with eyes to see.

Group Law conditions this manifestation while the Law of Service impels the groups to co-operation with the Plan. Myriads of souls await their call to service, drawn to incarnation by the magnet of their ray.

Age after age, the call sounds forth, and time upon time, the groups respond. Hearkening to the need, they enter gladly, ready to do battle with ignorance and fear.

This time of test is no exception. Already in the centres the vanguard wait. Trained and prepared, they know their roles and parts and know, too, that victory will be theirs.

Trust, then, the Plan, and know that naught for long can hinder its fulfilment. Know that the Great Ones, in Their wisdom, foresee all needs. Know, too, that all can enter into service and share the burden of the task.

The present time is one of special opportunity. Seldom, if ever, has such a one been known. Take your places in the forefront of the servers and enter the lists on the side of God.

July 1986

The moment of truth

From time to time, a new situation develops which requires the concentrated attention of Hierarchy to ensure its correct resolution. So many forces, today, are locked in conflict, so great are the tensions, that Hierarchy itself is extended fully to hold the balance. This is only to be expected as the moment of revelation nears. Soon the world will face the choice: to continue in the ways of the past and perish, or to right the ancient wrongs and enter into a new life.

Already, the signs are that humanity is ready for change, is ready for the testing time ahead, but so much now depends upon humanity's right choice that naught can be allowed to distort its judgement. For this reason, all Hierarchy works in unusual tension, conscious of its responsibility to guide men safely through this difficult time.

A unique situation is, now, upon us. Through its representatives, humanity is about to see and know the Christ, to face the challenge and to reap the blessings of His presence. All the world awaits this moment of truth. Soon there will be no gainsaying; men will know for certain that the Avatar has come.

Since He is one of us, a man among men, the Christ will speak for all, make known the needs of a world divided and torn. As He is one of Us, the Master of the Masters, He will lead Us, too, into a new relationship with men, and seek to guide Us on the Higher Way. Thus will His twofold task proceed.

Many, from times long past, will recognize Him and once again follow faithfully behind. Many, new to the fold, will greet Him as their Teacher and confirm, in deeds of spirit, their allegiance to His Cause.

In this way will the past be overcome. Thus will a transformed world come into being, fashioned alike by Masters and by men. When you see Us, you will see your friends and brothers, each a man and each a Son of God. Naught is there strange about Us but Our habit of joy and capacity to love. Let Us share with you the secrets of life and become your Mentors on the Way. Let Us guide your footsteps on the Path and lead you to the Light. Our aim is to serve and to inspire. Our joy is the awakening of your love.

Since each man is a potential God, it behoves each man to manifest his divinity. Our task will be to help you to do this, and by the quickest route. Our experience is long and tested, Our wisdom sure. Our hard-won knowledge will serve you well. This being so, there is naught to fear as you stand on the threshold of the new time.

Each age bestows on mankind a culminating grace. The age now passing has conferred on man the quality of devotion, and on every hand this aspect can be seen. Until now, devotion has been directed to the self, one's country and a far-off God. With Our help and example, men will devote themselves to each other and to the God within all. Thus will it be. Thus will man come to know himself and his brothers as God, and thus will God become manifest through men.

September 1986

The Guardians

Whenever man is at a crossroads, faced with a difficult choice of direction, help, he can be sure, is near at hand. Thus it is today as man stands ready to opt for Justice or death. To aid him in his decision, to outline the possibilities and dangers, to serve him and to guide him, man's Elder Brothers return. For long have They awaited this opportunity. For long have They been ready to emerge. Now that the hour has come, They face Their task with joy, sure in the knowledge of its success. They know that however grave the problems, they will be overcome; however hard the decision, the right course will be taken.

They know, too, that without Their help man would be in danger of self-destruction. They know that there are those who would unleash upon the world the chaos of total war. In such a war there would be neither victory nor future, for all life would perish.

The Elder Brothers stand ready to guard and to guide. They know that men long for peace but feel helpless amidst the forces of disorder and separation, await a sign that their cries for help have been heard, their longing recognized, their prayers for deliverance answered.

The signs are there for men to see, yet, doubting, they turn blind their eyes. Looking beyond, they see not the present. Searching the heavens, they see not the stranger at their door.

Soon, for all to see, the Lord of Love will present Himself to the world. Then will come the challenge for man: to remain helpless in the morass and forfeit all progress for the race, or to conquer greed and pride and manifest the divinity of man. We, the Elder Brothers, watch and wait, ready to respond when men seek Our guidance and experience. That experience is hardly won and constitutes Our right to oversee men's journey of return.

Soon, men will discover that they are not, nor ever have been, alone. That always in times of crisis have the Guardians been near, protecting and guiding from the wings. Within the limits of the Law has Our help ever been forthcoming and on this fact men may rely. They will see Us as Brothers, rather older in experience than themselves, in Whose footsteps they may follow with assurance. As Teachers on the Path of the Infinite Way Who will guide them safely to the feet of God. As co-workers, ready to act together for the transformation of the world and the realization of the Divine Plan.

Thus shall We, the Guardians, be known by men. Thus shall we together build the new world on the foundations of the old, preserving the best of the past while we create the forms of the future.

Naught can stop this manifestation. We, your Elder Brothers, are here. To the ancient retreats the Call has gone forth: Return, return, the hour has come!

In ones and twos We thus retrace Our steps, returning once more to the world of men. Gladly do We do this. Gladly do We accept this opportunity to serve and grow. Our joy is undiminished as We face the work ahead, welcoming the new relationship with men. In partnership shall we create the glorious future which awaits all men.

October 1986

Leisure is the key

Among the many problems with which humanity is faced none looms larger in men's minds than that of unemployment. In the developing world, millions have never known regular work while even the industrialized nations see, each year, the workless total inexorably mount. "Man must work or starve," says the age-old adage. Yet need this necessarily be so?

Without doubt, the main reason for increasing unemployment is the discovery and application of the new technology. More and more, the robot is replacing man in the more complex manufacturing processes. No man can compare, in speed of operation and repetitive accuracy, with the sophisticated machines now in use. This is as it should be. Many may lament the loss of human skills earned through long apprenticeship and training, but man is born for higher and more worthy efforts. Why should men compete with mere machines?

Man is an evolving god and foolish would it be to place a limitation on his creative possibilities. Naught there is which, with time, he may not do. Why, then, lament the passing of a stage in man's long journey to perfection which allows him at last the leisure to expand and grow?

Man stands now on the threshold of a new perception of himself, his purpose and the world in which he lives. This new awareness will evoke undreamt-of skills and talents which yet await expression, and allow men to enter the abode of gods.

When man sees himself truly as he is naught will prevent the manifestation of his divine powers. On all sides this glory will be seen, lighting a path to the farthest stars. Until that blessed time man must learn and train himself in leisure. Without leisure man has little chance to grow. Leisure must be seen as the prerequisite for that creative thought and action which will transform all life for men.

In an age of competition the old adage holds. Work alone confers the right to eat. But man is ready to experience a new relationship; a new and caring co-operation beckons him to be his brother's keeper and to safeguard the right of all to the necessities of life.

More and more, machines will free men to be themselves. Leisure will ensure that each man can reach his full potential, reflective of his stage upon the journey to perfection, adding his gifts for the enrichment of the Whole.

Thus will men see a flowering such as none today can imagine but which one day will show men to each other as the gods they are.

Leisure is the key, and to ensure leisure men must share. Millions starve and countless more grind out their lives in hopeless poverty today. No longer must this sickness be accepted as the norm. No longer can the tensions thus engendered be supported by mankind. Entering a New Age where machines will cater for the needs of all, men must share as brothers and walk together towards the dawn.

November 1986

A question of priorities

Throughout the world today there is a growing sense that great changes are necessary if humanity is to survive. Nowhere is this more obvious than in the political and economic fields. From time to time, and with increasing frequency, world leaders meet to discuss, and hopefully to solve, some of the more pressing problems which beset mankind. This they do under the watching eyes of millions and in response to the growing weight of public opinion. They dare not fail, for they know that the peoples of the world will hold them to account.

The divisions between the nations yawn wide, yet somehow, men know, they must be bridged. The tensions of the present can be supported for little longer. They drain the will and nerve of all but the strongest men.

Into this arena must come the Christ. His will be the task to show the way through the quicksand, to lead men safely to established peace and justice. A formidable task but one for which He is well prepared. He will answer the need of men for leadership and guidance. He will reinstate as normal and right a spiritual connotation to life. He will reaffirm men's worth as potential gods and show them the way to demonstrate that potential. A mighty task but not beyond His strength.

He will lay down certain guidelines, affirm certain priorities. Beyond all others, the task most pressing is the elimination of hunger. Millions starve today while the food that could ensure them life lies rotting mountain high. The world's poor groan daily under the burden of their lot. He will seek to show afresh that men are One, together in life to fulfil the plan of God.

The next priority is the establishment of peace; little hope remains for man if peace is not secured. The way to peace, He will show, the only way, has the signpost: Justice, written large.

Men must learn to share, without which justice is a far-off dream.

The third priority concerns the maintenance of human freedom. Countless numbers now suffer indignities and torture in the prisons of the world, their only crime the crime of independent thought. The Christ will emphasize the need for human liberty without which man is haltered and stunted on his way to God.

Once secured, these three primary tasks will set men firmly on the road to Perfection. Without their achievement man would have little hope to survive. More and more, men begin to see this and seek to find a way to just and lasting peace. Without the acceptance of sharing, they will find, all efforts will be futile, for sharing alone is the key to the future for man. When men share they will know peace. When men share they will enter into their birthright. When men share they will know the meaning and purpose of life.

Thus will Maitreya speak, offering men the choice of glory or death. Confident in their right choice, He will turn their thoughts to the future and show them the dream of God that awaits their astonished eyes and minds. He will help them to envision that future and to turn into reality that dream.

December 1986

Health and healing (part 3)

The problem of AIDS

Without doubt the most important problem facing humanity in the area of health is the newly discovered virus giving rise to loss of immunity in the blood cells, the so-called AIDS. For many, the emergence of the AIDS virus is yet another sign of the wrath of God, and just punishment of evil-doers who ignore His Commandments.

A saner approach would be to see AIDS as a result of man's inability, as yet, to handle the new incoming forces which impinge on all, and which, in a few unfortunate cases, have led through over-stimulation to the creation, for them, of a nightmare, and for humanity as a whole of an urgent major problem. A more tolerant view of this tragedy would be to see its rapid spread as the result of the altogether more open attitudes towards sexual expression which have been adopted in many countries in recent years, and which have brought much benefit, in terms of social acceptance, to sexual minority groups. That this 'permissiveness' has led to such unforeseen results is an indication of the need for balanced and gradual change. It should not be seen, however, as an opportunity to apportion blame or to castigate as evil those engaged in practices other than one's own. Care and common sense are crucial components of a healthier attitude to this new disease.

With cure we are in safer waters, for all would agree on the urgent need to halt its spread. Unhappily, no easy answer presents itself as yet, nor will an answer be forthcoming until the cause is known. Man is far from realizing the effect on his physical body of his growing power of mind and of its ability to cure or kill. Not for nothing, however, is the saying "Mind over Matter" known to all the race. Mankind is entering a period in which his latent powers of mind will be established in all their glory, creating for his delight and use the products of his soul's purpose and joy.

For the present, however, his wayward mind has set a trap for his unruly instincts and wrought of his imbalance a Pandora's Box. The minds of some have been invaded by urgent desire and have turned an impulse of beauty into fear and dread.

Not for long, though, need man await amelioration of his plight. Serums will be found which will halt to some degree AIDS' onward spread. But total cure will not be achieved till man has set his mind and world to right and established a new relation to his brother and himself.

That this will not be easy must be said. Powerful indeed are the forces ranged against this change, and ancient laws, transgressed, exact their due toll. Man's illnesses result from man's imperfect use of the energies of his soul which, inhibited or squandered, find a deviant path for their expression and create dis-ease.

A new and clearer understanding of how man functions is needed and is on its way. This will reveal the intricacies of his energetic network and the inter-relatedness of all the parts. The roles played by man's different bodies, as vehicles of the soul, will become known and understood, and lifestyles will be adapted to ensure their proper use.

This time is not yet but not so far off as some might fear. The advent of Maitreya and His group of Masters will accelerate the speed of change. Their stimulus will bring enlightenment and a readier acceptance of the required adjustments. Gradually, the old rhythms and attitudes will die out and a new and saner outlook and mode of living will bring man into right relationship with himself and others, allowing him at last to find his feet on perfection's path.

January 1987

The case for sharing

There will shortly come a time when humanity must reach a great decision. Troubled as it is on all sides by divisions and cleavage, a new approach must be found to the many problems which beset it. Without such a new approach, there is little doubt, an ominous future would await mankind.

Historically, there is no precedent for the present situation and conditions on Earth. Never before have so many souls coexisted on the planet. Seldom, if ever, have the divisions between the groups been so painful and deep. Never has man controlled such forces of destruction as are now at his command, giving him power to destroy the life in every kingdom. When such destruction threatens, man must take stock and devise new ways to proceed.

Of all the possible ways there yet remains but one untried. Throughout his history one simple answer has eluded man's grasp. The principle of Sharing is the only one which will answer man's needs and solve his many problems, for it is fundamental to the Plan of God Himself. Without sharing, man denies his divinity and stores up for himself all future woes. Without sharing, unholy chaos reigns and withholds from man the Justice which is his by right. Sharing alone provides the opportunity to establish God's Plan of Brotherhood and to remove from the world for ever the sin of separation.

How, lacking sharing, could man continue? How, without sharing, could he hope to survive? So great are the dangers in the present imbalance between the nations that luck alone would not suffice to see him through. A deadly sickness — separation and greed — prevails upon the Earth, and calls for drastic measures to effect a cure.

The simple cure is at hand despite the outer chaos. The long-drawn testing of mankind is all but at an end. Arrayed against the forces which still hold man in thrall, the Hierarchy of Light retrace Their steps and stand together under the banner of Truth.

Maitreya's mission begins with an appeal to men to share. His knowledge of men's hearts leaves Him certain of their choice, and certain of their readiness to make the needed changes. "Man must share or die," has He said, knowing well that men will choose to share and live and to create with Him a better future.

Until now, all efforts to solve man's problems have been directed to maintaining the present structures, however unjust they have proved themselves to be. The cleavages on every hand cry out for resolution and await the application of the Law of Justice.

Fear grips many today as they hear their leaders wrangle; a time is coming when they will leave their leaders far behind. Man is awakening to the call for freedom and needs only true leadership to set the world to rights. Maitreya has come to show the way and to lead men to brotherhood and justice. A new era opens under His wise direction which will demonstrate the true divinity of man, establishing the means of sharing and co-operation and thus fulfilling the Plan of God.

March 1987

The emergence of Maitreya

For several years, many people have awaited, with varying degrees of patience, the emergence of Maitreya into the arena of the world, to present Himself to the people as the World Teacher for Aquarius. Many have found it a tiresome wait indeed, while others have cheerfully worked to acquaint the world of His presence and plans, knowing that eventually their efforts would succeed. The day has dawned when all will see Him. Knowingly or not, all have called Him and He has kept His promise to return.

For years He, too, has awaited the invitation from men to emerge and speak for all. Now that, at last, this has been given, He has taken steps to ensure His recognition and acceptance. Not for nothing has He prepared many groups to acknowledge Him. Highly placed and influential, there are those in varied walks of life who know Him to be here, know His plans and priorities, have listened to His words and believe them to be true. From diverse backgrounds and many countries do these prepared ones come, alike in their desire to serve Maitreya and the world. With their detailed knowledge of His plans they will speak for Him, awakening their colleagues and citizens to the task ahead. In this fashion will He work through them, pointing the way to a better future.

Shortly, His face will be seen by thousands around the world. Television has made it possible for the Avatar to enter the homes of countless people and with simple words to penetrate their hearts. Soon will follow other such appearances until the whole world listens and responds.

In this manner, the world will come to know that the Christ, Maitreya, is in our midst, ready to teach and lead, to serve and guide, to show the way back from the abyss and to inspire the creation of a new era for men.

That not all men, at first, will recognize Him, perhaps, needs to be said. Not all know the true background to His life and advent. But, more and more, they will see the wisdom of His words, feel the blessing of His presence, and know from within their hearts the truth that He utters.

From within their hearts, too, will they respond, acknowledging Him as the Teacher for the Age. From them will He evoke the desire to share, to recreate a balanced and harmonious world. When men realize the urgency of the task, they will unleash upon the iniquities of the present a force for good unlike aught seen before. The transformation of the world will proceed apace and men will work together as brothers for the good of all. Thus will it be. Thus will the New Age be built by man himself under the guidance of Maitreya and His Group. The separation of the past will give place to co-operation and sharing; the selfishness and greed to a new sense of justice. From within man himself will come the urge for betterment, a testimony to the divinity inherent in us all. That divinity will Maitreya show to be the nature of man, and He the Agent of its manifestation.

Already, the signs of His work are apparent to all. The old dogmas die; new brooms are sweeping away the debris of the past. The old men linger but a new force of truth beats on their embattled and crumbling walls. Not for long will they withstand this new force for righteousness and justice.

April 1987

The new simplicity

There will come a time, in the not too distant future, when men will know with certainty that they are Gods. This achieved divinity will demonstrate itself as Brotherhood, and through the creation of a civilization in which humanity will unfold God-given faculties and powers.

Under the stimulus of the Christ and the Masters, men will find themselves the recipients of knowledge and insights which will open before their eyes vistas of new being and meaning. Inevitably, as a result, will flow the creation of new forms, new techniques of living and working, new methods of production and new goals and aims by which to measure man's achievements. An entirely new approach to life will express itself through new relationships and rituals.

At first, the changes will be slow, but, gradually, far-reaching changes will transform the world. Each nation will contribute its special gifts to a new world harmony. Above all, a new spirit of goodwill will motivate men's actions and lead to the creation of truly lasting peace. Thus will it be. Thus will 'The Desire of all Nations' be established in our midst. Thus will the sons of men come to know themselves as Sons of God.

Many today await the manifestation of a great Teacher, an Avatar, a Guide, one Who will take them safely through the labyrinth of present difficulties and dangers and lead them to the 'Promised Land', a land 'flowing with milk and honey', a land of plenty, of abundance. This vision of the Teacher is not entirely false but reflects an outlook of deep materialism. Abundance there will most certainly be, bringing new life to men on all the planes. This 'new life' is the spiritual gift of Cosmos focused through the Christ and presented to all men. But a land of plenty could be every man's today. No need is there to await the Avatar to right the present wrongs. No need for a Saviour is there when man can save himself. "Take your brother's need as the measure for your action and solve the problems of the world." Thus spoke the Christ, outlining the simple steps to justice and plenty for all.

Many await the Avatar to cure their personal ills, forgetting that they themselves have the cure within their hands. "No man is an island", nor was meant to be, and when the needs of all are met the individual will flourish.

Prosperity is a state "where no man lacks", where there is neither very rich nor very poor. Far from this blessed state are men today when luxury and starvation walk hand in hand.

A new simplicity will the Christ present to men, allowing them to share as brothers all. Co-operation will be the keynote of this simple life, the sharing of resources the order of the day. Thus will man's divinity be expressed and thus will the Plan work out through men.

There begins now a great adventure for men which will take them to the highest heights. In simplicity will the new life be known and lived, rich and full in meaning and purpose. From 'The Waters of Life' of Aquarius will flow that spiritual abundance for which all men in their hearts yearn.

In this way a new approach will be made to the problems of money and power, privilege and prestige. The desire to serve will replace the desire for gain, and the longing for justice will supplant divisive greed. Each one has a part to play in the creation of this new freedom. It behoves all who sense the happenings of the time to play well their role.

May 1987

The time ahead

When Maitreya makes His appearance before the world, He will herald the beginning of a New Age for men. In this coming age men will rise to heights undreamt of by those now in incarnation. New teachings will beget new knowledge, new inspiration, new illumination, and all in order and sequence. Hopes will give way to certainties, fears to faith and ignorance to wisdom.

When man grasps the facts of his existence: his threefold nature; his recurring appearance on the physical plane; the great and just Law of Karma by whose action his lives and deaths proceed, he will enter into a state of Being in which all becomes possible. Then will unfold the powers latent in all men which, when revealed, will demonstrate the divine origin of man. Men are Gods, did they but know it. Naught but ignorance blinds them to their glory.

The future time holds for man such promise that, could he see ahead, before his astonished and bewildered gaze would arise sights baffling in their newness. Naught there is in the language of today to describe such creations. Naught can describe the joy known then by men. Nothing can reveal the sense of inward peace and vibrant action. Sanctified by meaning, dedicated in purpose, life will have for men unending creative potential.

Thus far, naught but a fragment of that potential has been expressed by men, so lost in ignorance of their true nature have they been. From now, an upward spiral of creative innovation will grace a new civilization, bringing the light of the Divine Principle into the acts of men.

History reveals that evolution proceeds but slowly; nevertheless, in this coming epoch, man will outstrip, by far, the pace achieved by his most illustrious ancestors. Profound changes in man's social life and organization will release energies hitherto untapped, and unleash upon the world a whirlwind of transformation. Thus will it be. Thus will men meet the measure of their promise and unfold the powers for so long dormant and still.

Creative change will be the keynote of this future time, gathering to itself all possibilities for good. Creative change, men will find, is the basis of life and the origin of cycles. In harmony with the cosmic flow, men will construct a civilization in which time will be no more; "where no two days are alike"; where the arts of life and Being walk together hand in hand.

Preparations for this future time are well advanced. The blueprints of the new civilization impress the minds of men. Already, formulae are being discovered which embody basic truths, and far-sighted thinkers envision a new beauty.

Still, the old struggles to maintain its grip, locked in a forlorn battle with life itself. The end of the old is near, for the sound of the new has found an echo in the hearts of men.

Soon, the Christ will gather together around Him all who can respond to the new note. His Teachings will lead men safely through the maze of illusion and darkness and show them the splendour which awaits them in the time ahead.

June 1987

God's Representative

Whenever man is bereft of hope, seeing no way forward, no way to solve his problems, he sets up an instinctive cry for succour, an appeal to God to help him in his anguish. Thus it was during the war years earlier this century that the travail through which humanity was passing invoked the Christ, called Him forth once more into the world. Never before, through all vicissitudes, has so much depended upon His coming, for never before has man controlled such forces of destruction.

Today, the nations are divided, as ever. Each claims to be the repository of the world's wisdom, offering men the choice between freedom and justice. How absurd it is that men should be proffered such a choice. Freedom and justice are divine and that divinity is indivisible. There can be no freedom without justice, no justice bereft of freedom. Shortly, men will be offered the opportunity to end for ever this travesty of truth and so heal the breach between the nations. It requires but the simple realization that all men are divine and have the same divine right to share in God's gifts and plans. Lacking such realization men would know no peace.

When men see the Christ they will realize that they are not alone, that God's Representative has answered their call and returned to help them. He will remind them of their source in Divinity and of their kinship, brothers all. He will place before them the choices for the future and exercise His right of counsel. He will outline the steps towards a better life for all, a life more in keeping with the spiritual nature of man. He will teach and lead and thus change the world through the actions of men.

At first, progress may be slow as men grow accustomed to the benefits of change but in due course the pace will quicken until all is caught up in a ferment of change. Naught can stop this process, for it finds its origin in the Mind of God. Naught can for long resist the magnet of God's Plan.

Without doubt, the greatest hindrance to the Plan's successful working is the present insecurity of men. They see around them a hostile world, feel threatened on all sides by penury and want. The nuclear threat hangs heavily over all. The counsel of Maitreya will show men that they have nothing to fear but their fear. That a blessed future awaits man if he will but act in his own best interests. That the Intention of God is man's greatest good. He will show that men must act to create the world they want; that He comes not to save but to point the way. He will empower all who take upon themselves the burden and joy of service. He will anoint all who share His burden.

The upholders of the old sense the danger but fight a losing battle. They seek to strengthen the walls of their citadel in vain. Their ramparts weaken as the tide of justice turns. Their buttresses betray them as men strike out for freedom. Into this turmoil Maitreya has come, to put His divine resources at the service of man.

July 1987

The luminous age ahead

It is not for nothing that the world now undergoes a paroxysm of change. Nothing comparable has occurred in historical times; nearly a hundred thousand years have passed since events of such magnitude, of such far-reaching consequence, have taken place. The world is now being prepared for the advent of a new era, unlike aught known before, in which humanity will awaken from its long sleep, shake from its eyes the blindfold of ignorance and fear, enter at long last into the light of Knowledge and Truth, and receive its birthright.

To aid men in this awakening, the Masters of Wisdom have begun Their re-entry into the world, have taken up again Their association with men and stand ready to serve. This They do at the behest of Their Leader, the Lord Maitreya, the Lord of Love Himself. He has alerted Them to Their Destiny and called Them on the Higher Way.

That They welcome this opportunity further to serve brooks no gainsaying. That They know the magnitude of the task let no one doubt. Emerging from Their ancient retreats They enter joyfully into the life of men.

To recreate that life is Their avowed intention, and long experience equips Them for Their task. They know by heart the pitfalls which beset the traveller on evolution's path and seek to guide men safely on their way. Well versed in the methods of ascent, They place Their knowledge at the service of aspiring men.

The world awaits the Declaration of the Christ. This great event, unique in history, will herald the beginning of the new era. It will vouchsafe, too, the end of man's anguish and the beginning of new triumphs for men. When men follow the Christ, which indeed they will, they will come into that birthright which awaits them, and receive from Him the accolade of Joy and Peace.

They will know then the purpose of their lives on Earth and seek to implement that purpose. They will know the intent of their souls and how best that may be accomplished. They will know, too, the ways to establish right relations with both God and their brothers and to give reality to the Brotherhood of man.

All this will men learn from the Christ and establish as the norm. Thus will be fulfilled the prophecies of old and the creation of an era of Peace and Joy, a golden and luminous age of Justice and Truth.

Few, today, can conceive the future which awaits mankind under the guidance of the Christ. Few, indeed, would believe the wonders which He will reveal to men. Few there are who can countenance the changes which will prevail under His leadership to bring men in consciousness to the feet of God.

September 1987

The linking kingdom

The day is fast approaching when humanity will see itself as it really is: a centre of energy in the body of expression of the manifesting Logos. When that day dawns, an entirely new attitude to its meaning and purpose will also awaken in mankind. For the first time in its long history, humanity will become aware of its potential, and strive with conscious effort to realize and express its hitherto untapped resources of wisdom and power.

Humanity is the linking kingdom between the divine and the sub-human and as such carries great responsibility, for it is planned that one day humanity *of itself* will inaugurate and control the evolution of the lower kingdoms. This is not so far distant as many might think for man now stands on the verge of a great expansion of consciousness, which, when achieved, will render into his hands unimaginable power and knowledge.

In achieving this knowledge and power, the first step must be the realization of the Oneness of all life. This is fundamental to all future progress for man. When men know, beyond all gainsaying, that there exists only One Life, manifesting through a myriad of forms, they will begin to see their task as the organizing and distribution of that Life for the greater good of all creation. Thus will men develop the resources of nature in ways as yet unseen, giving new life to old forms and creating new forms for the better expression of the One Life.

In the animal kingdom, through man's energetic stimulus, profound changes will take place. The intelligence factor will grow apace, and, under the impact of man's mind, a new co-operation between the kingdoms will become possible. Many ancient forms will die out, having served their purpose, but, inspired and guided by man, a new sensitivity and response to thought will manifest. This will lead to the establishment of a new relationship between animals and men, one more in keeping with the Plan of God.

A new era opens in which men, as Gods, will demonstrate their divine powers in service to the Plan, reaping therefore the benefits of all true service: greater responsibility and an opportunity better to serve. With these powers being used for the good of all, a new chapter of meaningfulness will open for man, and he will find himself being led from revelation to revelation along the path of discovery of his own divinity. Thus will it be. Thus will men demonstrate their intrinsic spiritual nature, capacity for service and sensitivity to the Plan.

Maitreya and His Group of Masters stand ready to lead the way. They know well the potential of man and, as men, have long since realized that potential to the full. They come to guide, and put Their experience at the service of the race. With Them in the vanguard humanity cannot fail.

October 1987

Continuity of consciousness

Within humanity today a growing number of people are achieving continuity of consciousness and are thus retaining the experiences of the sleep state. This makes for faster evolution as no time is lost in waiting for the filtering down of information to the brain to take place. It also ensures the reception of more accurate information leading to more correct action and results.

This is the way forward for humanity. Until now, the break in consciousness between the waking and sleeping states has proved an obstacle to large scale advance. More than anything else, it has kept humanity in ignorance of the true nature of reality, and, consequently, in superstition and fear.

Nearly a third of life is spent asleep and much information is given and received during that period. Many are the experiences which may be had and known, enriching the life of every individual. Never before, on a large scale, has the opportunity been present for a gradual shift in consciousness to take place. Already, a large group stands ready to achieve this continuity, lacking only the practical techniques for its achievement.

Soon, steps will be taken to make more known and available the information already given on this subject. Much has been imparted which awaits study and application; few, today, realize the treasure-chest of instruction which has been recorded and published.

Mental polarization is the key to this achievement. Correct alignment of the astral and physical bodies provides the basis on which mental polarization can gradually be built. This achieved, continuity of consciousness naturally unfolds. There are, of course, degrees of this achievement and the process covers a considerable period of time.

Much has been written about the need for spiritual detachment. This quality most readily provides the field for the correct interpretation of phenomena and information carried over from the sleep state. Otherwise, despite continuous consciousness, much distortion can ensue.

Spiritual detachment results from decentralization. Through service and correct meditation, the orientation of the disciple shifts from his limited self to the not-self. This begets a state of divine indifference in which desire subsides and the true, inner man can appear.

With his appearance, the way is open for continuity of consciousness to begin. Safely, the out-of-body experience can be correctly registered and known, and a new chapter opened in the life of the disciple. The Halls of Learning or of Wisdom become his conscious fields of knowledge, depending on his level on the Path.

So far, we have discussed only the continuity of consciousness between the sleep and waking states. A further expansion of awareness awaits the disciple who can bridge the gap between the two great areas of experience to which we give the names of life and death.

Life alone exists. Death is but the name for another level of experience of life, continuous and unbroken except in man's limited consciousness. The time is coming in which the experience we call death, the intervening period, and the return to outer manifestation will be recalled in full consciousness by man. Then will man lose the fear of death and reap the harvest of the inner planes of knowledge and bliss in total awareness of his true identity as a Son of God.

November 1987

Fear of change

Without doubt, the greatest hindrance to change is the present state of mass consciousness. The masses of humanity are deeply fearful of changes the outcome of which they cannot foresee.

Thus it is today among the community in which the Christ has made His abode. Notwithstanding His presence and inspiring exhortation, relatively small are the numbers who *act* upon His words and seek to implement change. Others listen gravely and nod assent, curious only to know who thus so wisely counsels and entreats.

Perhaps the fear of deportation, inducing caution, conditions their response. Perhaps they are not typical of the world at large. But seldom it is that one will arise and ask how to proceed to change the consciousness of men.

Fear of change is endemic in the human psyche. From earliest times man has learned to resist, and has set up barriers against, inevitable change. Childlike, man has clung to the familiar and the safe, whatever the pain involved and however short the term that safety might prevail.

Nowhere is this more obvious than in the political field. Millions today live in conditions of abject misery and abuse, exploited by tyrants masquerading as their leaders. Yet the people, for the most part, suffer in silence, fearful that resistance will make the unbearable even worse.

Can humanity be persuaded to look on change with a bolder eye; to accept that the ills of the world must be cured or man will perish? For how long and how deeply must men suffer before taking action on their own behalf?

Maitreya's task will be to show men that their suffering is unnecessary; that the remedy is in their hands even now; that together they are invincible. He will show that the only barrier to

123

freedom from fear is fear itself; that a new world awaits its creation, based on justice and trust.

When men see this they will support His cause, and set in motion the changes which will renew the world. Gathered together in common Brotherhood men will demand the freedom and justice which is theirs by right. Thus will it be. Thus will the institutions of the past give way to the new forms, whose nature will allow the expression of the true divinity of men.

That not all at first will welcome these changes is true. For many they herald a bitter taste indeed. But gradually men will find that the changes are for the best, and a new buoyancy of spirit will enter their lives.

Renewed and refreshed by the lifting of the burden of fear, man will tackle anew the problems of our time, and set in motion a steady stream of changes which when completed will bedeck this planet in a raiment of light.

December 1987

The new education

In seeking insights into the direction which education in the New Age might take it will prove useful to establish the basic purpose which education serves and so throw light on the inadequacies of present educational approaches.

Firstly, it must be understood for whom education exists and the process by which it carries out its function. This may be less obvious than at first sight may seem to be the case, for man has long been ignorant of his true nature and constitution, taking the part for the whole, and ignoring, to a large extent, his essential being.

Man, as a soul in incarnation, is an emerging God, and, through the Law of Rebirth, is advancing slowly to the demonstration, in full splendour, of that divinity. Education, in its true sense, is the means by which an individual, through a gradual expansion of conscious awareness, is fitted and fits himself for that goal. All that aids this process is education, however formal or informal the method might be.

In today's sense, education is a feeble thing indeed, ensuring only the minimum requirements for an understanding and control of man's environment. Few there are who learn more than the rudiments of life's meaning and purpose, caught up, as most people are, in the daily struggle for existence.

Whole nations, today, are all but illiterate still. Elsewhere, facts-full minds stand idle for lack of meaningful work. Education for jobs has replaced education for life while, more and more, the stresses and strains of such imbalance erupt in violence of all kinds.

Education should be understood as the means by which the indwelling God is contacted, known and given expression. Traditionally, religion has been seen to serve this purpose and religious education remains a bulwark in many countries today.

However, religion is but one of many paths to God, and ways must be found which will allow all men to know and to express their experience of divinity.

To this end the new education should address itself. The fact of the soul, the Divine Intermediary, must gain general acceptance, and techniques of contact with this higher principle attain common usage.

When the ray structure, evolutionary development and purposes of the soul are known and documented, a more scientific approach can be made to the education of both children and adults, and a new meaning given to the process by which men learn to become Gods.

All of this awaits the earnest endeavours of those working in the educational field. Fitment for such tasks should be the aim of all aspiring to teach the young. Never has a better opportunity for service presented itself to those ready for the challenges of education for life in the New Age which now opens before us all. A new vista of possibilities will soon appear as men grapple with the problems of separation and division. This will release the forces and inspire the techniques of training and teaching which will bring men in due course to the feet of God.

January 1988

The new revelation

Whenever man stands at a crossroads, as he does today, he becomes the recipient of close attention and aid from that group of Elder Brothers, the Spiritual Hierarchy, Who, from ancient times, has stood guard over his welfare and progress.

Thus is it now as we await the formulations of the New Age structures. To assist and guide man in his deliberations, the Masters are taking up Their posts in the cities of the world. Unknown, as yet, to all but a few, They represent the highest man can achieve on this planet: a perfect expression of the Love nature of God, consciousness and control on all planes and a knowledge, tested and tried by long experience, of the Plan of Evolution and the process of its implementation.

Never before in man's long history have the possibilities for rapid advance been so great. Never before, in such numbers, have the Masters dwelt among men. This alone is remarkable; it presupposes great changes, already occurring and still to come.

Chief among these changes is the readiness of men for new revelation. The thirst for knowledge has brought man to the door of knowledge unlimited. Beyond that door, man senses, lies a treasure trove of mysteries to be solved, worlds of meaning to be conquered, vistas of beauty to be experienced and known. Man begins to question the purpose of his existence and to search for means whereby that purpose can be fulfilled.

Thus it is at the dawn of the New Age. As always at such a time, man approaches life with a deeper reverence, sensing its spiritual basis, and raises his eyes and heart to those realms from which all revelation comes, thus invoking the revelation for which he longs.

"God works," the adage goes, "in mysterious ways." Yet always is that mystery open to interpretation and understanding. Age after age, the mysteries have been revealed; new insights have opened the door to greater knowledge and a new light has entered the minds of men.

Today, a great new light is awakening humanity to its purpose and destiny. That shining brilliance will reveal to men the Purpose underlying the Will of God, and will galvanize mankind into the creation of those relationships and forms which will serve to demonstrate that Purpose in all its beauty and power.

Such a time as this has seldom been. Man is on the threshold of a new understanding of himself and of those forces which lie behind all appearances. Soon he will know, beyond all gainsaying, that God is, and that man is God.

March 1988

At the door of initiation

When people near the gate of initiation, at whatever level, a profound change takes place in their life patterns and associations. All that was familiar and comforting loses its flavour and becomes stale. All that tended to support and comfort falls away. A new openness and vulnerability takes the place of assured habits of thought, and an unfamiliar humility descends upon the seeker. The old certainties disappear, the world changes shape and nothing is as it was.

When this happens, the individual experiences a profound sense of unease, of impending loss, often of despair. All seems black and bereft of hope. The old loses its appeal, the future beckons menacingly.

Thus it is for the individual disciple. Thus, too, is it for humanity as a whole. As it stands, now, at the very door of initiation into a new state of consciousness, humanity steels itself for the experience of the new, the infinite tasks ahead, the creation of a new world. Bereft of guidance, it would founder quickly and suffer painfully. Without higher help, its progress would be slow and fitful, its future uncertain and bleak.

Help, however, as always, is at hand. Never, in man's long history, has that help been unforthcoming. Now, in time of greatest need, many are the hands held out in succour, many the forms this aid has taken.

Chief among these is the reappearance of the Christ. In answer to mankind's call and need, Maitreya has shouldered, once again, the burden of appearance. Today He awaits an invitation to come before the world as the World Teacher, the hope and saviour of men.

He comes Himself and this time not alone. With Him today are many of His Brothers, Who, like Him, have mastered the lessons of this Earth. They come to aid and teach, to point the way, to release to men the blueprint of the future in all its beauty.

Other hands, as yet unseen, lend, too, Their gracious succour to the world. From distant worlds this help descends and protects, saving man much anguish and woe.

No need is there for men to fear. The aid is adequate, the succour is in time. Man must now accept responsibility for his own salvation and set in motion the changes for which he longs. Maitreya and His Group of Masters will lead the way, outline the path, but man must take the first steps to rehabilitate his world.

When these first steps have been taken, then will the Masters add Their strength and knowledge to the task of transformation. Then will the world respond to a new note, a clearer call. Then will men awaken to a fairer day, and restore the ancient allegiance of man and God.

Thus will the Plan of God begin to be fulfilled in all its beauty and colour. Thus will men know the truth of their divinity and the certainty of progress into that divinity.

April 1988

The hour approaches

More than ever before, man is ready to receive new teaching. Perplexed and afraid, man nevertheless senses a new Revelation and new revelations of his purpose and nature.

Without doubt, man now realizes that he stands at a crossroads. Whither to go is his problem; which path to take. One, he knows, spells oblivion for his species, perhaps for all the world. How then to skirt the dangers which lie waiting on that path; how to avoid the pitfalls which he sees clearly ahead? Bit by bit, he inches slowly forward, with careful reconnoitre and many a false step. Lacking trust, he doubts the value of conciliation; seeing the dangers, he knows he must not fail to find the right path. Thus he stands today, seeking and searching, and ready for guidance.

With that sure guidance the Christ will enter the arena of the world. Awaiting, patiently, His opportunity to reveal Himself openly, He will meantime address the problems of the hour, present their solution and seek to inspire mankind to action.

At last, He believes, man is ready to act on his own behalf. Already, the signs of reconciliation are plainly to be seen, and a new level of hope uplifts mankind.

That hope is now based on a sure foundation. Never before, with such serious intent, have the nations sought the road to peace. Never before, with such apparent ease, has compromise been possible. Never, not in his boldest dreams, has man thought likely the steps being enacted on the world stage today. Dark and dangerous corners though yet there are, much is changing for the better in the outer life of man. This is but the echo of the inner transformation which proceeds, everywhere, apace.

From His centre, Maitreya uplifts and upholds the world. His energies, directed with consummate skill, heal the cleavages, destroy the ancient dogmas, and purify the ways of men.

Those who seek to impose their selfish will and hold to the forms of the past will soon relinquish their power. Bereft of support, they will fade into the darkness of yesterday. In their places a new generation of leaders will arise, men and women of goodwill, filled with the urge to serve mankind.

Into their hands will be given the reigns of power. By common consent, their altruism and wisdom will fit them for the tasks of reconstruction which lie ahead. Aided by the Masters and the Christ, they will set in place the foundations of the new era and herald a future based on tolerance and love. Thus will it be.

Thus will the Christ work through all who seek to serve their fellow men, and thus, gradually, with minimum cleavage, will men remake this world.

May 1988

The Great Lord emerges

Passports will become a thing of the past. In the coming time, people will be free to enter and to leave any country at will. So great will be the trust engendered by Maitreya's presence that all doors will be open, and a great and enriching interchange of peoples will take place. Thus, men will learn to know and to love their brothers, seeing them as little different from themselves. Thus will it be.

Within weeks, Maitreya's open mission will begin, drawing to Him those who care and wish to serve the world with full heart. Those around and close to Him will prepare the ground, outlining His precepts and teaching. When a certain saturation has been achieved He Himself will enter the world's stage.

Already the policies of nations are being reshaped by His influence. Already, many in high positions know of His presence and await His Announcement. Thus does He work quietly, affecting, under karmic law, the future of the race.

That future holds for man unbelievable promise. From the Day of Declaration will begin a process which will transform this world, and take men to the highest levels of achievement.

On that day, men and women everywhere will experience the love nature of God and know it as their own. Through their hearts will flow Maitreya's Ray, evoking from them an understanding altogether new. Sharing and Justice will be His call, and, thus guided and inspired, men will respond in full measure, remaking the world under His wise counsel.

Not for nothing has He waited till now to make His appearance. Only now are men taking steps to put their house in order. Thus only now can He come forward and lead.

On the Day of Declaration, He will outline the future for man, showing the alternatives which face the race today. Man's choice, He will show, can only be for sharing, for none other can sustain the planet longer.

Many are the tasks which lie ahead. Great is the inertia which grips still this world. But already a start has been made and the future beckons brightly.

Men should know that all are needed to overcome the evils of the past. Division and separation have ancient roots and will not easily relinquish their hold. Each one, therefore, should see it as their task to aid the Christ in His work of transformation, giving of their best to reconstruct the world.

Soon the world will know of the Splendour in its midst. Soon will men weep for joy at His appearance.

Soon, too, will they take upon themselves the task of succour, re-establishing the true unity of men. Thus will it be. Thus will men know, at last, that Brotherhood which they long have cherished but till now were unable to find.

June 1988

The Great Approach

In every century a group of disciples is given a special task: the discovery or announcement of certain ideas and truths; the revealing of hitherto unknown facts about the nature of man or the universe; the enrichment of man's spiritual life through art or religion; all of these avenues of approach have been used by the hidden Hierarchy to awaken man to the Reality in which he lives. Age after age, this process has continued, lending continuity to the teaching methods by which the Masters work. As the world stands poised on the threshold of the Aquarian dispensation all is in flux, all undergoing the ferment of change.

So, too, is it in Hierarchical circles. Without exception, the Masters Themselves are experiencing a reorientation of procedures and methods unlike aught known before. During the last five centuries, They have gradually inaugurated changes in approach in preparation for the Great Approach, the externalization of Their work in the world.

Not for nothing have They tested and looked afresh at every long-tried line of action, adapting where necessary to the new and growing sensitivity of men.

Now, waiting in the wings for the Day of Declaration which will signal Their Approach, the Guides of the race stand ready to serve advancing mankind. From the ranks of men the Masters have come; to Their ranks They beckon and welcome men.

That Their task will not be easy They know well. Long centuries have conditioned Them to work unseen and unannounced. Now, in the full light of day must They guide the destinies of men, leading them consciously to the mountain top. Averting Their gaze from the higher to the lower centre, They must together demonstrate Their readiness for the Higher Way.

Although long-trained and prepared, much remains to Them unknown. Men, from their divine free will, dictate the rate of progress and response. Only thus can the sons of men become the Sons of God.

Men await the coming of the Christ yet know not that He is here. So blind are they to the reality of life that they see not the Promise in their midst. Not alone the Christ but the vanguard of His group are now among you, awaiting the call to enter the affairs of men. Soon will They take up Their willing task and shepherd men into the fields of Knowledge and Love, Sacrifice and Service, Justice and Brotherhood.

Thus will men avail themselves of the higher knowledge of their Elder Brothers, and create with Them a civilization worthy of the name. Thus will men come to know that they are not alone, have never been so, nor will ever be. Always are the Masters at hand when help is needed; on that may men depend. Now in full measure will that help be forthcoming, given openly for all the world to see.

Thus will the centres come together and the Lord's Will be done. Thus will it be.

July 1988

The Waters of Aquarius

Each age brings into incarnation those groups of souls whose energies can find a consonance with the prevailing energies of the age. In this way, the necessary forms through which the specific intentions of an era can be expressed are certain of formation. Thus it is today as we stand at the threshold of the Aquarian Age.

More and more, adolescents and young adults will be found to be singularly well equipped to respond to the incoming energies of Aquarius which tend to synthesis and fusion. Likewise, they will be able to take advantage of the opportunities which, uniquely, will be presented to them, and will find and create the structures on which the civilization of the coming age must be built.

Maitreya, as may be expected, has His plans well laid. These involve the setting up of centres and institutions in which the required teaching will be given, experiences met and lessons learned.

In this way, groups of young and mobile pioneers will chart the new ways of living and relating, seeking ever to infuse their lives with the loving, blending energies of Aquarius. Wise experiment will lead them step by step to the creation of viable and trustworthy forms which, gradually, will be adopted by all.

Thus the new era will emerge from the chaos of the old. Thus the restrictions of the present will give way to a freedom altogether new, in tune, at last, to the life-giving waters of Aquarius.

What these forms will be no one yet can tell, but they will evidence a new livingness and creativity, and a new responsiveness to the needs of all. In time, the Masters Themselves will enter more directly into the arena of men's lives, and, interacting and advising, will add Their long experience to that of men. Much will then be learned which for the present must remain unknown. Vast vistas of knowledge, which if revealed too soon would hinder their onward stride, await men's questioning minds. When responsible hands are ready to receive and wisely dispense, bounteous blessings of knowledge and wisdom will be theirs.

The world awaits Maitreya as the Water Carrier. Unknown to most, the Waters of Aquarius flow daily from Him to all the world, blending and fusing, awakening men to the Glory in their midst. Soon they will see and know Him. Soon will they recognize and follow Him. The day is not far off when the bells of celebration will joyfully ring.

September 1988

The Avatar

Breath held, humanity awaits the appearance of the Avatar. Knowingly or not, millions now stand ready to receive the Teacher, the Revealer of new Truths and the guarantee of men's future and divinity.

All now conspires to bring about this blessed event. Cosmic and planetary, the Forces of Regeneration reap now the harvest of Their sowing and bring into being the condition which allows Maitreya to appear. Forced by force of law to withhold, for a time, His open mission, He knows that the law is being fulfilled, the debts are being paid, the opportunities taken; and that now in full splendour may He appear, and receive the love and service which, many will avow, they are ready to bestow on Him.

His Grace already does embrace the world. His Love enfolds the nations, East and West, North and South. None escape the arrow of His Love.

Daily, His Ray awakens men to their true destiny, and conjures anew their hope and trust.

From far and wide the representatives of the people gather at His side, and He endows them with a wisdom altogether new. Soon, this enlightened group of men and women will present their story and experience, and prove past all gainsaying that the Christ is in our midst. Millions then will hearken to this promise and demand to see the Representative of God. Under many names will He then come forward and thus fulfil the hopes of every faith.

His call for Justice, Peace, and Brotherhood will then be heard among the nations, avowing God's concern for the well-being of men everywhere. His voice will remind the peoples of their origin and destiny, and bring them, in trust, to the feet of God.

That His task is well prepared you may be sure. His disciples, inwardly trained, have long engaged themselves in this work of preparation and know well their various roles. Called into action, they will carry the work of reconstruction to every corner of the world and replace misery with joy, separation with unity, hatred and malice with altruistic love. Thus will it be. Thus will the New Time enter its course of splendour, and thus will mankind realize the promise which His presence brings.

That not all will testify to His Glory is certain; for some, the Mantle of God has too brilliant a light. But most will see in Him the fulfilment of their hopes and dreams for justice and love, for sanity and freedom. And to Him will they turn their eyes and hearts, seeking guidance and comfort, inspiration and purpose, enlightenment and love. These in abundance will He bestow upon the world. A vast River of Truth is He, nurturing all who from these waters deeply drink. A Fountain of Love is He, enclosing all within His heart. An Avatar like none before is He, come to lead men into the realization that they, too, are Gods.

October 1988

A new era has begun

At this point of planetary crisis, few, indeed, realize the enormity of the tasks facing both Hierarchy and humanity, and even fewer the magnitude of the work of transformation for which this world calls. Nevertheless, great forces of reconstruction are at work, and, ere long, the evidence will be there for all to see. Already, many are the changes which none can deny.

More and more, the peoples of the world are realizing that their destiny lies together, that none can escape the imperatives of the time. Soon, the majority of peoples will subscribe to a new formula, a new enunciation of their common heritage and future, and embody this in constitutional form. Thus will begin a new era in the long evolution of men.

In the meantime, much can be observed and learned by those attuned to the true happenings of the time.

As we watch the Law (of Cause and Effect) in action, producing pain and suffering as well as correction and transformation, we can see the inevitable process of this great Law. All comes under its command. None, not even the Christ, is beyond its call.

Recently, there has been a growing realization that the Christ is in our midst. This is due, in equal part, to an inner response, however oblique, to His energies now flooding the world, and also to the work of those now serving to make known His presence among us. That the majority should find this information unlikely is not to be wondered at; it tends to undermine the established norms so long held sacrosanct.

Yet those in His community who know Him are not in doubt. They know that the Teacher for all men is here, and await His emergence into more public life.

They know, too, that this must take place gradually, step by careful step, so that the free will of men is not infringed.

When men see Him, they will find Him corresponding to their hopes and aspirations, their thoughtform of perfection. Some will reject Him totally, insulated by fear from the experience of the real. But the majority, by far, will see in Him the fulfilment of their dreams of justice and peace, harmony and grace, and welcome Him to their hearts.

Thus shall we see the implementation of a long-laid plan to bring humanity into the experience of itself as God.

This process is now under way, and soon the first signs will be apparent. Men will take upon themselves responsibilities long since relinquished, and achieve the hopes and dreams for so long cherished. Then shall we know, in truth, that the new era has begun.

November 1988

The coming harmony

As we come closer to the Day of Declaration, we find a growing presentiment that soon all will be changed, all known landmarks obliterated or pulled down. Already, the signs are there for the knowing eye to see that the end of the epoch is at hand. Already, many fear the gathering storm of the century's end, and search for safety in mountain and desert retreat. They fear the destruction of the familiar pattern of their lives and await the cataclysms conjured by their fears.

That the world is experiencing rapid change is true. Each day brings its quota of events. None can deny the hectic rhythm of transformation now sweeping over the world, nor the new climate of hope which this engenders.

The work of the watching Hierarchy therefore is no easy one. Theirs is the task to guide events in such a way that minimum cleavage results. Given full rein, the forces of reconstruction and change would sweep away all opposition to their plans and sow the seeds of future discord and strife; held too strongly back, the forces of reaction would deepen and prolong their weakening hold over the destinies of men. In this transitional phase between the ages, steady but ordered change is the prime requirement, and the Masters bend every effort to achieve this goal.

To effect this balanced forward movement, the energy of the Spirit of Equilibrium, overshadowing the Christ, has been released and now saturates the world. More and more, it will bring all factions to the moderate central point, and consensus will replace opposition as the order of the day. In equal measure to the present tension and conflict, this divine force will restore harmony and peace. Thus will it be. Thus does the Great Lord work to make this world safe for men.

When all is ready and prepared, when world events have signalled their warning to men, Maitreya will step forward and claim His rightful place as Teacher. From that point onwards, a new spirit of co-operation will make its appearance and lead to the rapid transformation of all our structures. Men will accept the guiding wisdom which His spiritual status confers, and stage by stage, in mounting momentum, will remake their lives in relation to the spiritual blueprint with which He will endow the world.

His present work is to restore and maintain balance, thus saving humanity much needless pain and suffering. Already the evidence is there that this is being achieved, and a new spirit of conciliation engages the minds of those who lead the peoples. Soon the world will see the Teacher in their midst. Many have experienced Him in one way or another and await His public appearance with joy. There is not long to further await the Avatar, the Christ, the Teacher for all men.

December 1988

The reordering of priorities

Such is the pressure under which humanity lives today that only the few can perceive the transformations which, daily, are occurring on a global scale. A momentum of change has been established which naught can halt or deviate. Thus it is that the world is undergoing regeneration, purification and pain, preparatory to the creation of an entirely new civilization.

The new civilization will be built upon the foundations of the past, but, necessarily, much of the old must be swept away, corrupt and useless as it is. For those with eyes to see, the new indications are already evident. Wherever men turn their eyes today, a new landscape presents itself, new ideas engage the mind, new structures take tentative shape. A world in flux is transforming itself, the growing pains of change are felt by all.

Into this situation has come the Christ, eager to assist men in their hour of need. That He can help there is no doubt, but men must want the changes He will advocate and implement them of their own free will. Naught will be forced and naught imposed, for otherwise the Law would be infringed.

The speed of change will be conditioned by men's capacity to absorb the measures for which an ailing world cries out: sharing and justice, co-operation and acceptance of the rule of law. Only thus will men find the peace for which the peoples yearn.

To aid men in their task, the Christ has formulated certain priorities which, when implemented, will establish balance and order, and so create the harmony on which well-being and peace depend.These priorities are simple and self-evident, yet nowhere do they exist to any great extent. Enumerated, they cover the essential needs of every man, woman and child: the first priority is an adequate supply of the right food. Secondly, adequate housing and shelter for all. Thirdly, healthcare and education as a universal right.

These are the minimum requirements for a stabilized world and will become the main responsibilities of governments everywhere to ensure. Simple as they are, their inauguration will have far-reaching effects, and will usher in a new era for this Earth.

The creation of weapons of war looms large in the priorities of many nations today. From this time forward, these new priorities must take precedence, and engage the resources now given over to 'defence'.

When this is done, a great creative wave of joy will sweep across the planet and men in every nation will respond. Co-operation and sharing will become the order of the day, and peoples everywhere will find a new purpose and meaning in their lives. Maitreya will be present to advise and guide, and under His wise direction the world will be made anew. This time is now at hand.

January 1989

The need for trust

There will come a time when men will look back on this period of travail as one of rediscovery of meaning and purpose amid a chaos of false values. For untold ages, men have set their sights on the acquisition of wealth and power, prestige and acclaim. The subtler arts of spiritual knowledge and wisdom have attracted but the few, and perforce men have walked the stormy way of warring faction, ignorance and fear.

Today, at last, a new light is bringing men to the realization of their future glory as co-workers and co-creators with God. Many are the trials which await men on the path to such a destiny, but never before have they been so ready and prepared to meet this challenge. Against all the odds, and in spite of all appearances to the contrary, mankind is about to emerge from its chrysalis of darkness, its impotence and fear. With growing boldness and assurance, the steps of men are set in the direction of unity and justice, co-operation and sharing, simplicity and trust.

That such a trust is necessary brooks no gainsaying. Naught can be achieved until the bonds of trust are set. Hitherto, the absence of trust has hampered the highest aspirations of men, cleaving the nations and placing in jeopardy the future of the race.

Trust, the reflection of love, arises spontaneously when fear subsides. Trust alone can create miracles of co-operation and lead to actions otherwise impossible.

Thus it is in the world today. Under the impress and inspiration of the Christ, the leaders of the nations are beginning to trust.

Much remains to be done but already the signs are there for all to see. A new chapter is opening in the long story of man which will set the seal on his future glory.

The growing sense of interdependence is the proof that man has not totally lost his way, that he has stepped back from the brink and is entering a new era of co-operation and realism.

In the individual sphere, the need for trust is paramount. Naught so corrupts relationships as the absence of this precious jewel. It matters not that trust is broken or betrayed; trust begets trust and allows the sweet flow of love to take its course.

Few today can envision a world in which trust truly reigns. Few there are who can visualize the calm, experience the beauty, of such a time.

Let your imagination conjure a world free from fear and crime, competition and greed. Open your mind to the concept of universal justice and peace, manifested joy.

Do this and glimpse a world in which the trust of the uncorrupted child blossoms again in the man free from fear. In that world all becomes possible. Man stands now on the threshold of its discovery.

March 1989

The Plan

Step by step and stage by stage, humanity is achieving a degree of Oneness. Each day that passes brings some new insight or event which underlines this process and shows conclusively that the Plan is working out.

The Plan of which I speak embodies the Purposes of the One we call God and focuses His intention for all the kingdoms of Creation. No one can know, in its entirety, the manifold aspects of this Blueprint of Evolution, but the broad outlines, at least, have long been the concern and privileged service of the Spiritual Hierarchy under the leadership of the Christ. With the many aspects of this Plan They daily work, seeking to inspire, through humanity, its gradual fulfilment.

The time has come for humanity to enter more deeply into a knowledge of the Plan and thus, in full consciousness, to evolve according to the Will of God. Where man's will and God's Will coincide, all proceeds normally and well. Where this congruence is absent man is afflicted by all manner of ills, each of his own engendering. Thus it truly can be said that man creates his own destiny; his halters and fears are his own, his suffering self-made.

Today, the Plan unfolds at an unprecedented rate. Miracles of change are occurring on a global scale, confounding the hopes of those who would for ever enthral the peoples, and keep them submissive to a nefarious foe. New energies saturate the world, awakening man to new possibilities and relationships. New teachings and teachers present themselves to men, each in his own way illuminating a strand of the complex pattern of the Plan.

Thus does the Plan proceed through mutation and change, bringing all gradually to the envisioned goal. Wherever men turn their eyes today they can witness this happening; a paroxysm of change engulfs the world.

The task of the watching Brotherhood is to oversee these changes and contain them lawfully within the confines of the Plan. Thus do the Masters work, relating the Plan to the possibilities presented by men.

Each step towards synthesis taken by men gives opportunity for further unfoldment under law. Thus do men, themselves, control the progress of the Plan.

Entering our life today are forces altogether new, heralding a civilization based on Brotherhood and Love. These forces likewise herald the re-entry of the Christ into the midst of men, accepting the challenge as Teacher for the new time. Working in full knowledge of the Plan, His task is to take humanity in the direction of its ordained destiny: the fulfilment of the Will of God for the perfection of all men.

Thus today does the Christ work to accomplish His task as the Great Mediator, the Representative and Knower of God.

April 1989

Awakening to responsibility

In former times, changes took place slowly, and for long centuries society remained relatively static in its structure and activity. Furthermore, large areas of the world were unknown to each other. Communication, even between near neighbours, was spasmodic and confined to traders and soldiers for the most part.

Today, all of this is transformed. In almost every corner of the world communications flourish, and bring the events of each day to the attention of all. Nowhere is it possible to be unaware of the swift and often savage happenings which assault the eyes and ears of billions daily. In a very real sense the world has shrunk to village size and, as in village life, the actions of one affect the lives and interests of all. No longer can any nation stand aside and claim immunity from the results of its misdeeds. Power alone no longer confers this privilege. More and more, the nations are awakening to their mutual dependence and responsibility, and this fact augurs well for the world.

At long last, under pressure from their peoples, governments are accepting the need to cherish and nourish the environment on which all future life depends. Without such wise husbandry, the future for mankind would be bleak indeed. Gradually, it is being realized by those who make decisions that time is not on the side of those who despoil and poison the planet, that resources are not unlimited, and that nature recoils from exploitation and assault. There is a growing awareness that careful and concerted action, on a global scale, alone can remedy the many transgressions of the natural order which man's ignorance and greed has brought about. A start is being made, but many years of dedicated action will be required even to halt the menace of pollution and depredation which threatens man now.

Fortunately, not all in the future sounds so dark a note. Man, as ever, is not alone, and steps have been taken to release to him the knowledge of new and cleaner and safer modes of generating power. Technologies altogether new will transform daily living and leave man time and impulse to explore his own Being and purpose.

Thus equipped, man will learn to work and live in harmony with nature, coaxing from her richness a brimming cornucopia sustaining all he could desire or need.

When men see the Christ the issues will be clearly placed before them: men now face the challenge to work together for the well-being of all, and to remake their ways of living with sufficiency the key, or to sound the death knell of a planet already sorely stressed, and so place their future in greatest jeopardy.

Maitreya, Himself, has no doubt that men will hear and answer His call.

May 1989

New light, new understanding

Each age brings to humanity a new challenge and opportunity. The dawning Age of Aquarius will present men with challenges and opportunities in such abundance that, before its end, giant strides along the evolutionary path will have been taken by all. We are now at a turning-point, not only of the present world situation, but also in the destiny of the ancient race of men. Humanity stands poised now to enter consciously into a new dimension of life.

For five long centuries, the Masters have awaited this time, ready to add Their gifts and wisdom to the efforts of men. Knowingly or not, men have outstripped themselves and, against all expectations, men have become ready for a new revelation, ready to receive new light and knowledge, to see new meaning and purpose in their lives and to demonstrate this growing awareness in technologies, sciences and relationships altogether new.

Not for nothing has it been said: "When the pupil is ready the Master comes." This is as true on a mass as on an individual scale. Today, humanity as pupil, as world disciple, tested and tried, is ready to enter into new life, the life of service to the race.

The shift in consciousness now taking place will reveal to men that their sense of separation is illusion, that naught exists in all creation unconnected to the Whole. This dawning awareness and readiness for change of men has invoked the Teacher and the Teachers, for such We are.

Under Our wise counsel, men will find themselves galvanized into action in every department of life. Soon, the changes will be there for all to see. Soon, the Representative of God will establish Himself firmly in the hearts of all mankind.

Responding to His stimulus, humanity will seek ways to implement the new directions which His presence will reveal, and order their lives according to a new and higher rhythm.

When Maitreya reveals Himself before the world, statesmen of every nation will gather for advice, and a new realism will reflect itself in their decisions. His call to action will resound throughout the Earth, evoking response from young and old, rich and poor, firm and halt. Never before in Earth's history has such a time been known, the planet galvanized to act together for the good of all.

Many who know Him now already hearken to His call; inspired by their experience of His presence they dedicate their lives to service and ready themselves to follow His lead.

Thus will it be when all shall know Him, when He presents Himself as Teacher for all nations, and takes upon Himself the task for which He has returned: the salvation of the peoples, the revealer of new light, new understanding, to men.

June 1989

The pairs of opposites

Since man first emerged on Earth, his history has been one of conflict and strife, aggression and war. Seldom has there been a time when these tendencies have not been uppermost, until it would seem that they represent the essential nature of man. Yet, despite all evidence to the contrary, this is emphatically not the case. Why, then, does man present such a distorted image of himself? From whence comes this capacity for chaotic action and destructive violence?

Man is essentially a soul, a perfect reflection of God. Through countless incarnations over untold ages, man's soul seeks to express its divine nature in time and space. Creating for itself a physical counterpart, the soul endows that with the means of evolution to its own perfection. Thus does the Plan of God work out.

The key to this development is aspiration. Indwelling in all men is the desire for perfection and the urge to express the good, the beautiful and the true — the attributes of the soul. No one, however faltering in action, is bereft of this desire for betterment, however expressed. In no one does this longing not exist.

How then to account for man's aberrations, his violence and hate?

The answer lies in man's unique position, the meeting ground of spirit and matter, and the tensions which their concurrence evokes. Man is an immortal soul, plunged in matter, subject, therefore, to the limitations which that matter imposes. His struggle for perfection involves the bringing into total union and resolution of these twin poles of his nature.

Through repeated incarnations, the evolutionary process gradually achieves this aim, until the quality and radiation of the matter coincides with that of spirit. The Plan is fulfilled and another Son of God has returned home.

For long ages, the dominance of matter precludes a major expression of the soul; evolution proceeds but slowly. When, at long last, the opposing poles of his nature are resolved, man realizes that the dichotomy is but seeming, the oppositions unreal. Then he sees that all is One, spirit and matter but two aspects of one divine Whole, the limitations of the past naught but illusion.

Without the struggle of opposites and the friction which ensues, man's progress would be slow indeed. Friction is the fire which impels him on his way, aspiration the light which calls him ever upwards. Thus does man discard, in time, the limitations of matter, endowing it with the radiance of his spiritual truth. Man's task is to spiritualize matter and to bring the substance of the planet, in every kingdom, into a perfect reflection of the Heavenly Man Whose body it is. Conflict and war, violence and hate, are but the passing manifestation of man's inability, as yet, to demonstrate his true nature. The time is fast coming when his truth will prevail, his beauty radiate and his good demonstrate for all to see.

July 1989

The Age of Light

In each century, a few men emerge who tower over their contemporaries. Their gifts are manifest, their genius shines forth for all to see and acclaim. We know them as the great discoverers, the painters, writers, musicians and scientists whose work has led humanity forward in a growing awareness of itself and its potential.

In recent times, their emphasis has been on science and the expansion of human knowledge. This has prepared the way for an extraordinary awakening of men's minds on a scale until now beyond hope of achievement. Man stands today on the threshold of a new enlightenment, of discoveries which will cast into the shade all previous accomplishments.

This coming time will be known as the Age of Light, and Light in all its meanings and manifestations will become the provenance of man. Already, the signs are there for the discerning that man is knocking on the door that leads to the Chamber of Light. Ancient darkness and ignorance are being banished as men grapple with the implications of new insights and technology. Soon, the Science of Light, the Divine Science, will be revealed to man's astonished gaze, and a major landmark on man's journey of evolution will have been reached.

Until now, only the specialist few have access to this Science of Light, but, already, steps are being taken to make its benefits available for all. The needs of all for power and light will be met safely and simply, the sun itself being harnessed in this cause.

United in love under the Banner of Maitreya, men will forge new pathways to the stars. As man explores her mysteries, nature will yield up her secrets, and reveal the ordered beauty underlying all.

Thus will begin a new and simpler life under the guidance of Maitreya and His Disciples. Cheerfully, men will relinquish the divisions of the past and enter into a new harmony with all that lives.

For long, men have searched in vain for the key to this yearned-for harmony. Always, their highest aspirations and efforts have been to no avail. Now, for the first time, the dawning realization of oneness is impressing men to share, and to regulate their living along more just and safer lines.

The new Era, the Era of Light, is upon us, and in this coming time men will find the inspiration and guidance which their forefathers lacked, or ignored. Now, at last, men and the Masters will work and move forward together, united in the common bond of Brotherhood and Trust. Our example will inspire men to superhuman efforts and achievements, and bring the Light into the hearts and minds of all. Thus will it be. Thus will the great secrets of creation be revealed. And thus will man become the creator and regulator of his own destiny, a God-like Being, worthy of the name of Man.

September 1989

The Era of Righteousness

In time, men will come to know the importance and value of the present period of transition when sweeping changes are taking place across the planet. They will know, moreover, that the traumas attendant on these changes are inevitable, temporary and healing.

They herald an era in which a new balance will be struck between the need of individuals for freedom and self-expression and that of society — groups and nations — for discipline and order. The competition of the past has led to deeply stressful conditions in that relationship, giving rise, again and again, to outbreaks of violent protest and revolution, with their inevitable, and often savage, repression.

Throughout the world, today, individuals are demanding, often for the first time, a say in how their country will be governed, in how their destinies will be fashioned. The old practices are being questioned, and a growing intolerance of ancient corruption is being seen on all sides.

Naturally, this healthy response of the masses finds little favour in the centres of power in any country, threatening, as it does, their monopolies of privilege and prestige. However, a new world is being wrought from the injustices of the past, and naught for long can withstand the high tide of change. The energies released by Maitreya and His helpers are awakening men to a new awareness of themselves and their potential, and a growing confidence in their ability to manifest the future they envision for their kindred.

They lack, as yet, the worldwide leadership and inspiration to voice and channel their demands along logical and constructive lines, thus enacting change with minimal cleavage and pain. Maitreya has come to take His rightful place at the head of this vast army, to speak for and support the dispossessed around the world. His call will echo their cry for help and justice. His counsel will embrace their needs.

At last, the thought is dawning on the race that the future is not the bleak doom they had supposed and feared. A new light, Maitreya's light, has brought new hope to mankind, enabling old divisions to be seen afresh, and to be broached in a spirit of co-operation and mutual trust.

This new spirit is fast gaining ground, and, despite the efforts of the Earth's destructive forces to seize each opportunity to create disorder, a major change has taken place, a new high point has been won.

It will not be long till the yearning of men is answered, their needs addressed, their aspiration given voice. Soon, for themselves, the people of the world will recognize that their Elder Brothers are among them, that Their leader, too, is present, that Their light cannot be extinguished, and that, for all the signs to the contrary, the new Era of Righteousness is being fashioned now.

October 1989

Infinity the goal

It has always been the policy of the Spiritual Hierarchy to keep humanity informed of, and in touch with, all aspects of esoteric knowledge that can safely be made open and exoteric.

For long centuries this has been possible to but a limited degree. Over the past century, however, more information has been given, and more knowledge released, than at any time in the history of the race. That this is so reflects the growing comprehension by man of the subtle inner laws governing the outer appearances of things and events and, at the same time, his sensed need to play a fully conscious part in his own evolution and development.

Standing as we do at the threshold of the new era, we may look with confidence to an unprecedented release of hitherto guarded teaching which, when absorbed and understood, will throw yet greater light on the mysteries of the universe and the nature of man's Being. We, the Protectors of the race, look forward to the time when all can be revealed, when man and the Masters work together openly and in full trust, knowing that no harm can come from such co-operation.

That time is not yet, but already steps are being taken to ensure a closer collaboration than ever before. Among the first group of Masters to take Their places in the world are Those Whose task it is to stimulate such closer working together, and to gather around Themselves groups of trusted disciples who can be relied upon to impart the teachings to others without distortion.

Several modes are being researched and experiments conducted, and in this way We receive the necessary information on which to proceed without loss of time or energy. Flexible as We are to all changing circumstance, naught of importance is undertaken by Us without proper preparation and planning. Thus has it always been.

Few today can realize the enormity of the task which confronts the Masters Who first emerge and work alongside men in such close partnership. Throughout past ages, Their attention has been turned to the higher planes of life, the realms of consciousness Their primary concern. In growing numbers, They must now focus Their gaze on the life of everyday, accepting a role they have long since outgrown. Nevertheless, naught daunts Them or cools Their ardour for this work; of Their willing service all men may be assured. Theirs is the task to lead men to the mountain top on the sure path that They Themselves have trodden, thus setting the seal on Their achievement.

Soon, the first group of Masters will be known, Their names familiar to the disciples of the world. With growing confidence and trust, humanity will turn to Them for guidance and advice. Thus will They effect great changes through men themselves. They will inspire the creation of a New Dispensation in which the knowledge and understanding of men will reach to the stars and beyond, seeing infinity, only, as their goal. Thus will it be.

November 1989

His name is Love

It is becoming more and more obvious that the changes taking place in the world, apparent to all, are connected and interrelated, leading to the correct assumption that they share one common cause.

Every day brings news of some event, political or environmental, social or scientific, which underlines the transformation now occurring on a global scale. Never before in our history has change proceeded at such a hectic pace. Never, until today, has man begun to comprehend the implications and possibilities inherent in such global change.

All proceeds to plan, and gradually men begin to understand that there is a Plan, that naught takes place by chance, that control and guidance and intention play their parts in the unfoldment of that Plan. So great, so widespread, so sudden and unexpected are the changes under way, that few today can doubt that some unseen hand initiates and guides the outer transformations.

That such a hand is that of the Christ many find difficult to accept. This is but to be expected, conditioned as men are by the narrow viewpoint of traditional belief. Nevertheless, it is indeed the Christ Himself Who orchestrates these changes, appearing before men in one or another guise. Many today work under His inspiration and guidance, creating the new forms through which to manifest new life. Others, unknowingly, hear His call and respond, seeking but to serve their brothers. A vast army now exists to follow His lead; in every land they arise, calling for justice and freedom.

A new climate of hope exists in the world, created by the energies of the Christ. Tirelessly, He works to produce this change, and so foster new faith in the hearts of men.

When men see the Christ in person, they will quickly assume a new attitude to life and its problems. They will understand that the problems are man-made, exist in man himself, and are not the fault of an uncaring God or the result of mindless chance.

A new sense of responsibility will endow men with the impulse to act for the betterment of all. Co-operation, caring and trust will soon replace the present self-concern, and a new phase will open in the evolution of man.

The new awareness grows apace. Already, the signs are there for the discerning that humanity is growing up, taking stock of its situation and preparing to change.

Naught can hold back this tide of change when, under the inspiration of Maitreya, men begin to see themselves as One. The sense of separation will gradually recede as men face together the tasks of reconstruction and succour which call out to be done.The day draws near when all shall see the Christ. By what name they know Him matters not; His name as Love is etched deeply in the hearts of all true men.

December 1989

Day of destiny

There is growing evidence, in the changes now taking place at an accelerating pace, that some force (or forces) guides the destiny of the world. Few can believe that the historic transformations, the upsurge of aspiration for freedom and participation now witnessed on a massive scale, result from mere coincidence and have no inner cause. Few would deny that the speed alone of these momentous changes suggests otherwise, points to the growing awareness by millions that their day of destiny has come, and that power, from now, rests with the people, and must be wielded for their good.

A new sensitivity to energies is manifesting today, and it is to new and powerful energies, scientifically blended and directed, that we must look for the origin of the outer events; energetic stimulus precedes change, always and everywhere.

From whence do these energies come, and who directs them? Students of the Wisdom Teaching will know that behind all outer events stands the Spiritual Hierarchy of Masters under the leadership of the Christ.

It is They, in Their Wisdom, Who guide the destinies of the world and wield the energies and forces which bring about all change. Theirs is the task to oversee the present climactic world situation and to ensure that out of chaos harmony and equilibrium prevail.

Much has been written about the Masters and Their work; much more, as yet, awaits elucidation. Not all that is written and taught has the hallmark of Truth, but, nevertheless, vast numbers today know of Their existence, acknowledge Their divinity, and look to Them for guidance and succour. They seek Their inspiration and value Their counsel.

The time is fast approaching when the Masters Themselves will make Their appearance, and, scattering the clouds of superstition and doubt, will reveal Themselves as normal and human, albeit divine and perfect, men.

The world awaits the appearance of the Christ, and, soon, the expectations of countless individuals will be fulfilled. His mission has already begun; the changes which proceed apace bear witness to His presence. The signs are there for all to see, not only for the discerning, but for those who must hear a thunderclap to sense a storm.

Soon, the final preparations for His emergence will be in place, awaiting the outer events which must precede His declaration. Dignitaries around the world await His Call, ready to reveal their experience of His blessing. Many who already know Him stand poised to speak. From all nations and peoples will come the representatives of each, eager to add their voice to the hosannas of esteem.

Maitreya's task has but begun yet already the nations shake off the stranglehold of the past. What then can be imagined when in full vision He stands before the world, His teaching and counsel uplifting the hearts and minds of all?

January 1990

The threshold of rebirth

More and more, it is becoming clear that humanity has begun to change direction. Until but recently, men seemed set on a suicidal course, a fatal leap into the abyss which would have ended for ever man's sojourn on this planet.

That danger is now passed. No longer need the nations scan the skies for enemy 'warheads'. No longer need the oceans hide the stalking submarine. Gone for ever, did men but know it, is the threat of mass destruction, the annihilation of the race. Great and difficult problems remain to be solved, men live still with the habit of fear, but a new and growing optimism and trust begins to make its appearance, heralding a new era in human affairs.

For many, however, little has changed. Locked into poverty and disease, hunger, oppression and squalor, the dramatic events of a transforming world pass them silently by. Too great are the problems even to subsist for them to show much global concern. Each day brings its quota of suffering and fatigue, its share of illness and death. Millions, therefore, pass their days in ignorance of the changes which now grip large areas of the world.

But not for long will this be so. Soon, the new energies will penetrate the hearts and minds of all those hitherto immune to their galvanizing impact, and from their midst will rise a cry for action to alleviate their lot. Thus will it be. And thus will the poor and dispossessed make known their demands for justice, for dignity and freedom. For too long has their voice been silent. For too long have the rich nations looked the other way. Now, at last, will their cries for help be heard, their needs accepted and met.

Soon, for themselves, will men see and understand the reasons for the changes now occurring daily. They will know that naught happens by chance, that great and natural laws condition the lives of men, that the thoughts and actions of men, not God, are responsible for the quality of their experience, and that, more and more, into their own hands can they take the reins of government. No one, no class, is 'born to rule'. Only when the needs and rights of all are justly met will harmony prevail.

Much, much, remains to be done but already men begin to sense that this is so. The new energy lights new hope and courage in countless hearts and guarantees the formation of structures and constitutions embodying the noblest ideals of men.

In the wings, awaiting His entrance into the arena of the world, stands the Christ. His energies go before Him, doing their transforming work, creating the equilibrium longed for by all men. Many now sense His presence, whether by name or not. They sense the release of new life and hope when they had all but given up. They feel, too, their growing power and ability to shape their future. When they see and hear Him speak, naught will halt the crescendo of change which will then ensue as He gives voice to their deepest longings and needs.

The world stands, expectant, on the threshold of rebirth.

March 1990

They will not be denied

With every day that passes, more and more people are becoming aware that something new, quite unusual, is happening to them and the world. They sense that events are under way which will reshape the future and carry them they know not where. This expectancy simultaneously frightens and thrills. They feel a growing confidence that mankind is not doomed, but, against all odds, has, they know not why, come through the fire that threatened its existence.

They feel, too, a gathering power within themselves with which to effect changes in their lives, and so control their destiny. Thus disappearing for ever is the time when governments rule against the peoples' will and force their unwelcome doctrines on the passive populace. The days of the autocrats are numbered and, one by one, they leave the stage of their inglorious reign. The new times are with the people and from their ranks will the new spokesmen come.

Waiting, behind the scenes, stands the Christ. In patient silence and unhurried, ceaseless toil, He fashions the means of His emergence before the eyes of men. All, now, is prepared. The final touches, only, await His hand. Soon, the world will know that the Teacher is here; that the Son of Man has returned; that the Representative of the Most High has placed Himself at the service of humanity once again.

His call, resounding through the world, will draw the best from all who find in Him an echo of their heart's desire for justice, freedom and love, and, in ever-gathering force, the cry for their enactment will rise from every nation. Thus will it be. And thus will He focus the will, and become the outspoken voice, of a myriad aspiring souls.

His voice is not the only one that men will hear. Throughout the world, in every country, groups await the opportunity to speak. Prepared and trained they stand now in the wings, ready to serve when called. They know the needs of the time and the answers to the problems which beset mankind today. Little by little, these problems will be conquered and a new chapter opened in the evolution of the race. Before too long, these wise ones will come forward and place themselves at the disposal of the world. Their altruism will recommend them to the peoples and their judgement will win the trust of all.

Take heart, therefore, from all of this, and know that new and better times are on the way. Take heart and know that naught can stop the momentum of change that now grips this world.

Formerly, people awaited events in passive acceptance of fate. Today, a new consciousness informs the minds and hearts of men and awakens them to their inborn need for justice and freedom. They will not be denied.

April 1990

The hour has struck

With each month that passes, the world is awakened anew to the irrefutable fact that something quite extraordinary is happening on planet Earth, something for which no precedent exists. Today's world is on a 'roller-coaster' of change. Events crowd one upon another so quickly that there is neither time nor opportunity for even the most experienced observer to take stock. Astonishment, bewilderment and wonder are the usual and natural reactions to the current transformations.

Whenever accelerated change occurs, man's normal response is one of fear. Little is it to be expected, therefore, that many today can avoid the experience of fear as they witness the dissolution of the old familiar landmarks, however limiting they may have become. That which is familiar, however cumbersome, is oft preferred to the untried new.

Nevertheless, many experience today a secret inner joy, a sense of some impending delight, a renewed and vivid hope that all will be well, that the future holds promise of a new and better life for one and all.

That that hope will be fulfilled there is no doubt. Despite the present chaos, the pain and suffering of millions, the trend of world affairs is towards a sensed interdependence, an accepted responsibility for the well-being of each other, and a new determination to take all steps necessary to achieve that aim.

From behind the scenes, We of the Inner Government watch with growing satisfaction the evolving process by which man, little by little, edges closer to right action and right alignment with the Plan of God. We know there is much to be done. We also know that there exists in the world a band of dedicated workers whose task it will be to lead the way into the new dispensation. Equipped with the skills and insights for which the new situation calls, in total altruism and glad desire to serve, these forerunners will map the new territory and guide the footsteps of the pioneers.

Rome, we are told, was not built in a day; nor will the New Jerusalem be fashioned overnight. Nevertheless, the first steps have been taken, the new direction becomes ever clearer, and a vast body of men and women stand ready for the task of reconstruction.

Shortly, Maitreya Himself will open the door to the New Time. Appearing for all to see, He will claim His rightful place as the Teacher for the age, and demonstrate to the world His right to point the way.

That He, Himself, knows the awesome task which lies ahead for Him there is no doubt. Never before has the Teacher embraced the problems of humanity worldwide. But He alone is equipped to undertake His Mission, and none better equipped has ever graced this Earth.

He comes, moreover, not alone. His group of Masters, too, are on Their way. Many now reside in the midst of men, unknown as yet but ready to emerge.

Soon the world will know and salute Them, and invoke Their Wisdom and Love in the remaking of this world. The hour has struck.

May 1990

Magic, black and white

Several years ago, I suggested in these articles that before long we would see the advent of new and wonderful technologies which would enhance the life experience of all. Included in these advances, I wrote, would be many new approaches to healing and the eradication of disease. Now, as the century's end draws near, we are beginning to see the manifestation of the new technology which, in its many different applications, will revolutionize conditions on Earth.

A beginning is being made in what has been termed genetic engineering, and, some think, with dire results. Many of the experiments now being conducted are along right lines and augur well for the future. Many, already, contribute to human well-being and happiness and enrich men's lives. However, not all that is being done can be seen as harmless or for the ultimate benefit of mankind. Many are the experiments, carried out behind closed and secret doors, which add not a whit to man's understanding of nature or the laws which govern life. Great care must accompany the exploration of the process by which life finds form. Too great a focus on the material form itself, and the means by which it can be manipulated, can lead to disaster. Much that is being done today comes, for this reason, under the heading of black magic.

In the popular mind, black magic consists of rituals and ceremonies devoted to the devil and his nefarious ways. While many such rituals do, indeed, take place, and are more common and more widespread than many might suppose, from the viewpoint of the Masters true black magic is magic misapplied, restricted exclusively to the manipulation of matter. It is here that the White Lodge parts company with the denizens of Form.

For the Master, magic consists of the organization of all necessary aspects for the enhancement of consciousness, and thus of evolution. For them, the Form is but a means whereby Life finds expression, and not, of itself, a Principle, or of major importance. For this reason, They watch with concern the application of a purely materialistic view of life in the experiments now being conducted in hospitals and laboratories around the world.

Human individuality is sacred and all perfectionment proceeds through the Laws of Evolution and Karma. No two human beings are, or ever can be, alike, yet soon, evidence will be forthcoming that the 'perfect' human being is now achievable by genetic engineering techniques.

Here, indeed, is a misuse of man's divine powers. To see man as a plant or a strain of corn open to manipulative techniques of perfectionment is to ignore man's innate divinity and the spiritual basis of life. Sadly, even as it dawns, the new and life-enhancing knowledge is being corruptly applied, not necessarily for monetary gain, but out of a mistaken concept of the meaning and purpose of life.

Soon, steps must be taken to slow the progress of this materialistic science, to better oversee the directions in which ambitious minds are moving, and to safeguard for future generations a science based on Life and not alone on Form.

June 1990

A time to serve

For many years, Maitreya has sought to influence world leaders into taking the decisions which will make future world conflict not only impossible, but unthinkable. Slowly, but ever more surely, the powers have edged their way to solutions, based on compromise, which augur well for the future of mankind. Much is happening behind the scenes, far from the public gaze, which, when completed, will guarantee future world peace and satisfy at last the Desire of all nations.

Men can now, with confidence restored, set about the tasks of transformation, political, economic and social, which will engage their best minds and efforts for many years. For too long have they laboured under the threat of war. For too long has that threat misdirected the energies and wealth of nations great and small. Now, at last, can the peoples look to the future with hope and assurance that all will be well, that never again will their bright flowers of youth be sacrificed in vain.

Maitreya has said that each one is important, none too young or too weak to serve. Knowing this, there is but one path to take — the path which, through service, leads to God. In this coming time, many will find this the shortest route to the Source and the purpose of their incarnation.

Maitreya awaits the engagement of all who would transform the world, for "Nothing happens by itself; Man must act and implement his will". Relieved of the threat and the burden of war, those who wish to serve the world should enter now the arena and do battle with injustice, poverty and pain.

Seen in retrospect, history presents a picture of ordered, sequential change. All seems inevitable, gradual, guided by some unseen hand. In reality, the changes have been often swift and sudden, calling into question the adaptability of men. At this momentous time in the long history of the race, men are witnesses to changes both sudden and radical, galvanizing in their import, and radiant in their promise. Now is the time, as never before, for each one to grasp the opportunity to serve in some way, to influence the direction of change, and ensure the creation of a just and stable world.

Maitreya beckons and points the way, but men themselves must envision the future and build the foundations on which, in all its beauty, it may rise. We, the Elder Brothers, stand ready to assist in the preparation of that base; to ensure that the needs of all are acknowledged and accepted, that the Law of Brotherhood underlies all plans.

When We enter, openly, the life of men, Our task will be twofold: to inspire the willing acceptance of those changes which will guarantee the further expression of the Will of God, and to guide humanity in the implementation of the practical steps by which God's Plan can manifest. We are here to serve, and, if you are willing, we shall together transform this world.

July 1990

Life abundant

From time to time, it becomes apparent to many that a crisis point is being reached in the history of the race. Today is such a time. Seldom, in man's long experience, has this been so abundantly clear. On all sides, the portents of major change are appearing, creating an atmosphere of expectation almost tangible in its potency. Everywhere, new ideas are emerging, new patterns are being created, new and healthier approaches to living are being advocated. All of this points to man's readiness for a great step forward, itself the response to an expansion of conscious awareness. Man is growing in stature every day.

Despite all appearances, notwithstanding the ugliness and cruelties which abound, man's inner divinity is gradually shining through, and gives joy to the hearts of Those of Us Who work on the inner side of life.

Soon, men will see that a new time is arriving, a new epoch beginning, a new and substantial shift in human consciousness taking place.

Many are the signs which point in that direction, many the manifestations which guarantee that man stands now at the threshold of a great adventure, one that will bring him to the feet of God Himself. When men realize the significance of this time they will thank God for the opportunity thus presented and for the beneficent Grace now afforded. Thus will it be. And thus will men come to know their part in the Great Plan held, till now, in the Mind of the overseeing Logos.

They will realize, too, their responsibility in the working out of that Plan, and bend their wills to its implementation. They will know themselves for what they are, immortal Beings, and seek to create a civilization which will demonstrate that divinity.

The time is at hand for the emergence of the Masters, the Elder Brothers of the race. For long have We lived in isolated seclusion, awaiting the day of Our return. Soon the world will know that We exist, that Our beneficent supervision guarantees the survival and evolution of the race of men. Before long, men will acknowledge Our counsel and reap the benefit of Our experience. Much do We have to give and gladly shall We share Our knowledge and guidance. We shall show men the way to God, a path well known to Us, and guide their footsteps thereon. We shall inspire the creation of a new culture which will bring to men the gifts of God. Thus shall we together work in the formation of the new civilization. Thus shall we together serve the Plan of the Creator.

Men await a new manifestation of Divinity. That Divinity awaits an invitation from men to appear among them. Thus do men stand, poised, at a new beginning, a new awakening, ready to receive the gift of Life Abundant from the Source of Life Itself.

September 1990

The wane of fundamentalism

Whenever men sense the onslaught of change, the tendency is to 'dig-in', to return to origins, to re-establish and strengthen the links with the past. Thus it is today as men, in all areas, religious, political and economic, feel the impact of the energies which challenge their assumptions and prejudices and threaten the continuance of their much-loved way of life. Fundamentalism has reached the acme of its power in all three of these fields and faces, from now, a sure decline in influence.

This is already to be seen in the weakening power of communist ideology, especially in Eastern Europe and the USSR; in the gradual erosion of classical capitalist theory and practice, worldwide; and, in the religious field, in the diminishing authority and prestige of both the Roman Catholic and non-conformist branches of Christianity. Only the more evangelical groupings in the West, and, in the East, the various branches of Islam, have still, for the masses, their magnetic appeal.

For the world as a whole, this is a development much to be welcomed, a sure sign that the dogmatic attitudes of the past are being superseded and that the time for the emergence of new forms is at hand.

For a time, militant fundamentalism will continue to influence the decisions of governments, especially in the Middle East. But, gradually, a more pragmatic approach to problems will prevail, and the influence of the Mullahs will wane.

The people themselves will demand reforms which, inevitably, will undermine the authority of the religious canon and weaken the power of the priests. The time for this is not yet but it cannot long be delayed.

Then we shall see the resurgence of a new spirit of common sense, practicality and proportion in the affairs of those nations hitherto enshackled by the snares of a dogmatic ideology, unrelated, for the most part, to the real world. A new spirit of compromise, enterprise and goodwill will overcome the isolationism of the past, and a new chapter will be written in the annals of these ancient peoples and cultures.

At the present time, it would seem that whole nations are caught up in the glamour of a 'holy war', and many are the factions which promote and encourage this call, but the wiser heads are not without support, and the realities of a modern, interrelated world will bring reason to bear, and lead, in the end, to an established peace, peace with dignity for all the peoples concerned.

October 1990

The need for action

Many times before have I spoken of the need for action to realize men's plans and dreams of a better life for all. As Maitreya has said: "Nothing happens by itself; Man must act and implement his will."* With this in mind, let us look to the problems which most demand attention, and seek to throw some light on their solution.

The major problem awaiting resolution is that of achieving just and lasting peace. Without peace, today, there would be no future for the race. The nations, even now, are edging slowly towards this goal, but certain basic requirements must be met before real peace can be assured.

Firstly, true peace depends on trust which arises only when the Law of Justice is fulfilled. The great and widening gap between the lifestyles of the rich and poor, nationally and between the nations, is, today, the greatest block to the achievement of peace. Divergent ideologies play their divisive part but this factor is diminishing in potency. More important, by far, is the ingrained complacency and greed of the developed world.

Peace results from balance, whose absence guarantees conflict and war. The achievement of balance requires the recognition that all are interdependent, peoples and nations, and that the needs of all can be met by just sharing. Until that realization dawns *and is followed by action* we shall know an unstable world. While half the world goes hungry and millions yearly starve true peace remains a dream.

The present crisis in the Middle East has brought home to the industrial giants the folly of selling arms to emerging nations. Iraq is but one of many countries whose ambitions have been fostered by this cynical trade. The factories of the West cannot be allowed to prosper in maintaining the regimes of tyrants and reactionaries around the world.

Events in the Persian Gulf have at last focused the need for an integrated solution to the problems of that region. No resolution of the present situation is possible without an Arab-Israeli accord, and an end to the bitter enmity which has festered there since the founding of the State of Israel. The Palestinian people must, and will, have their homeland. Nothing less will satisfy the legitimate aspirations of that long-suffering group, and nothing less will bring an end to the recurrent crises which have maintained tension, and thus threatened world peace, for so long.

Events are moving fast. If the leaders grasp this present opportunity and, with wisdom, take the longer view and withhold their military hand, the world could see emerging the end of hostility and war, a just redistribution of resources, and a new and saner relationship between the nations.

For this Maitreya has worked long and hard, counselling the main protagonists in the various crises as they have arisen, seeking to endow them with His insight and breadth of view. Their gradual response to His endeavours allows Him the sooner to come openly before the world.

November 1990

Message from Maitreya No. 31

The dream of brotherhood

Before long it will become apparent to all but those who will not see that a profound change has taken place in the affairs of men. From every corner of the planet the signs are showing of an extraordinary transformation which has gradually established itself in the minds and actions of men and nations. Each week demonstrates a new situation, each day adds its quota of change. Can all of this be *par hasard*, can chance alone be held responsible?

The more perceptive will see in the changes taking place a pattern, a logical movement in unison towards some envisioned goal, a gradual replacement of divisions and confrontations by measured analysis and wise compromise.

The quickening pace of change reveals itself most clearly in the political field where an altogether new relationship now pertains. Gone are the days when men looked fearfully to an inevitable holocaust, ending for ever man's inglorious reign. New horizons beckon, new hopes and reconciliations are in the air, and, despite present crises and temporary impediments, man's forward march seems now assured. Willingly, men are beginning to see the need to act together and the advantages to be gained thereby. Cautiously, step by careful step, they are testing the waters of co-operation and finding them to their liking.

Thus are men appoaching the time when with one voice they can demonstrate their grasp of the Plan which brings them into incarnation and provides them with the opportunity to serve, in time and space, the vision of their Maker.

For long ages men have dreamed of brotherhood. That deep, persisting aspiration underlies countless aberrations and atrocities of the past. Never have men abandoned that ideal but, despite all setbacks and discouragements, have kept aloft their hopes of its eventual consummation. Now, at last, the first dim outlines of the necessary forms are beginning to be discerned as men move towards the next phase of their involvement in the adventure of life.

Under the inspiration and guidance of Maitreya and His group of Masters, men will find an increasing ability to make the right decisions, to act correctly in relation to the Plan. This will lead inevitably to a growing sense of brotherhood, to an understanding that only as men move together can they forward move at all.

Naught hinders but the political will. The peoples everywhere are ready for the adjustments in their ways of living which will herald the age of brotherhood, and await only the leadership and counsel of Maitreya. Then will the people establish for themselves right relationship, accepting the role of participators in the management of the world.

In the not distant future, a renewed hope will arise in the hearts of men that the dream of brotherhood is no chimera, no fruitless longing, but a reality to be established here and now.

December 1990

The dark before the dawn

Recent events in the Middle East and other areas have shown, once again, how precariously poised is peace, how tender and vulnerable a flower it is as yet. Nowhere, it would seem, have its roots gone deep; nowhere, it would appear, have men tended carefully its early growth. The bright promise of the year now ended seems clouded and fraught with danger and mayhem. How to account for such dramatic change?

Men tend, in the midst of such change, to see each event as separate unrelated acts which, multiplying out of their control, threaten their very existence. The reality is somewhat different.

All change results from response to energy, and today, as never before, man finds himself bombarded by powerful forces, new and unfamiliar, with which he must cope. That he is coping reasonably well is not in doubt. Despite all appearances, man is better equipped to use these forces than hitherto but, as yet, these unaccustomed stimuli galvanize him into actions, precipitate or clumsy, the results of which he cannot always foresee. So powerful and omnipresent are these new energies that a period of slow adjustment is inevitable.

We are witnessing simultaneously the rebirth of hope and freedom on a mass scale and the last efforts of the old order to re-establish itself against the tide of evolution. The New Age is on its way and naught can halt its progress, but man himself determines the speed and ease or otherwise of that forward movement.

New forces are gathering to avert calamitous war. Wise men from many countries are making their voices heard and are calling for discussions to avoid such folly. Through them does Maitreya thus guide the actions of men from behind the scenes; His inspiration will lead the nations back from the abyss. Thus will it be. And thus will men come to understand the sanctity of peace, the necessity of justice, the beauty of the rule of law.

Each day that passes brings nearer the Day of Declaration when Maitreya will appear openly to all the world. On that glad day the shared joy of men and women everywhere will transform the present clouded picture of anxiety and fear.

The current turmoil and threat are but the prelude to a new era of peaceful co-operative effort to right the wrongs of the past; to create justice among the nations; to resolve ancient disputes and to uphold the international law.

When men look back on this time they will see it as the dark night which precedes the brightest dawn and will be glad to have lived at this eventful period.

The world awaits the Teacher. The Teacher awaits His opportunity to emerge and, in full view, teach and serve.

January 1991

The people's voice is heard

Almost without exception, the nations of the world are caught up in a new experience: the emergence of the articulate masses. Long gone are the days of silent submission to autocratic rule. Instead, the peoples everywhere are on the march, demonstrating their will and demanding their democratic rights.

With some, the heady excitement and exultation leads them to excess and premature expectations which are doomed to failure, but a movement is afoot across the world which promises to transform it. Steadily, the signs are appearing that the people are awakening from their ancient slumber and are taking the future into their hands.

While We watch silently from behind the scenes, the nations, groaning in their travail, are giving birth to a new concept: the one humanity. For long have We worked for this prize; for long have We sought to inspire this noble realization. At last, men everywhere are grasping the meaning of their existence and sensing the need for justice and participation. Few there are who would gainsay this need; men differ only on the means of implementation.

When Maitreya appears openly before the world, this process of self-discovery and expression will receive major stimulus. Under His direction, many millions, hitherto disfranchised, will regain their self respect, enter fully into the organization of their lives and societies, and, in so doing, fulfil their destiny. A new, socially conscious humanity will gradually find its voice and role, and, inspired and energized by Maitreya and His Group of Masters, will build together the structures of the New Age.

Gone for ever will be the divisions of the past; gone for all time the mistrust and competition which today tear the world apart.

Awaiting His advent, many, meanwhile, prepare themselves for action. They know that a major task lies ahead, for the present divisions run deep and have their roots in the distant past.

Nowhere are those divisions more evident today than in the Middle East. The present crisis focuses dramatically the plight of mankind: when many nations spill their blood and their treasure in unnecessary war. The leaders have betrayed the people and led them to follow a chimera. When the bestiality subsides the people will not forget.

A woeful legacy awaits both sides in this useless and bloody battle. When men count the cost and weigh the achievement, the true folly will dawn. When men's pride and ambition outdistance wisdom the time for change has come.

The task of reconstruction will not be easy; many sources of tension remain to be addressed. Above all, Israel and the Palestinians must find the just solution to their problems without which no lasting peace is possible. This cannot much longer be delayed.

March 1991

The teaching of Maitreya

Within a relatively short time, many people will have convincing proof of Maitreya's presence in the world. Steps are now under way which will make this possible. This is not to be seen as the Day of Declaration, on which glad day the entire world will hear His Call, but a step towards that consummation. Many, even now, are aware, in one way or another, of His imminent Advent, and interpret this according to their background and tradition: as a warning of judgement and travail, or as a manifestation of God's love much to be desired and welcomed.

For the student of the esoteric tradition and teaching, the emergence of Maitreya is the natural outcome of His own fixed intention to return, at the earliest opportunity, in response to cyclic law. Having taken His place within humanity, He awaits an invitation to fulfil His Plan of succour and instruction. Men will find in Him neither Judge nor Saviour but a Friend and Teacher on Whom they can rely.

To be sure, His Teaching will bring men to salvation, thus fulfilling their destiny on Earth, but salvation, they will find, marks the end of their own inner journey to perfection, and cannot be conferred on them by any saviour, however great.

His Teaching will evoke in them an awareness of the Self and lead them step by step to a total realization of their oneness with that Source. Thus will men come to know themselves as the Divine Beings they are, and thus will this achievement glorify both God and man.

His Instruction, already begun, will illuminate the workings of the Laws which govern all life and elucidate for men the purpose of their presence here on Earth. He will show how action begets reaction and thus how men create, themselves, the circumstances of their lives. In this way will men come to understand the need for harmlessness in every situation and relationship.

His Teaching will remove, for men, the fear of death; His very presence will be the guarantee of immortality. His words will conquer, too, the fear which stalks through most men's lives, crippling their spontaneity and joy.

His experience will guide men through the labyrinth of the evolutionary journey, ensuring safe and sure passage for those who can follow His footsteps. As Friend and Guide, Teacher and Mentor, this Eldest Brother of humanity will fulfil His task.

Through His presence and example, men will come to understand the nature of God, and be inspired to emulate that Divinity. Thus, gradually, men will come to show the beauty of that Divine nature and create around them its reflection. Thus will grow a civilization blessed and radiant with the love and wisdom which are His hallmark. He will look upon His and their achievement and be satisfied. Thus will it be.

April 1991

The Middle East

Recent events in the Middle East have focused world attention on that troubled area in a new way. Gone are the assumptions that, if left alone, the many problems there will sort themselves out or go away; that conflict and division are endemic and, if contained, of no great account, and that nothing can be done for this historically and strategically important part of the world.

The nature and technical advances of modern warfare have changed such thinking and are leading to a reappraisal of the role that the United Nations might play in that theatre. For the first time, the possibility of a nuclear-free zone for the Middle East is receiving serious attention. Also, for the first time, a final and fair solution to the Israeli/Palestinian conflict is seen in many quarters to be of paramount importance, while a new urgency can be heard in the voices of those demanding democratic reforms.

Herein lies the challenge and the opportunity for the community of nations to address these many problems with energy and wisdom. Gone are the days when *laissez-faire* will suffice to keep under control the many warring factions and interests which struggle for supremacy. The international community must accept responsibility for maintaining peace and prosperity in the region, must use its new-found authority to bring to the negotiating table the representatives of the various peoples, and must guarantee the implementation of the compromise agreements which would follow serious negotiations.

Only thus will fair and lasting solutions be found and true peace restored. The time is ripe for such action. The time has come to lift for ever the dark clouds which, for many years, have menaced world peace and which, today, literally darken the sun.

To reach such agreements and implement such action will not be easy; no simple solutions stand ready to hand. Much will depend on the readiness of the various contenders to look with realism at the future prospects of the region *without* far-reaching changes of approach. A stark and bitter future, indeed, would follow their refusal to address the problems with wisdom and goodwill.

The time is not far off when wiser minds than those now grappling with the situation may offer Their advice. The long-withheld hand of Hierarchy may soon be extended openly in aid. With this in mind, we may look more hopefully to the future of this long-suffering portion of the world and see a new light scatter the dark clouds of hatred and war.

In recent weeks, the Master Jesus has appeared in vision to the soldiers of both warring sides, each claiming His appearance as a blessing on their cause. Soon, Maitreya Himself will appear to many and proffer His assistance. His guidance, if followed, will lead the world back to sanity and safety, and open the way for the demonstration, in the Middle East, of the rightful brotherhood of those now divided and estranged.

May 1991

The coming of the Great Lord

For some, the coming into our lives of Maitreya augurs naught but fear, disaster and other portents of doom. They see Him as the arch fiend, the Antichrist, and tremble at His name. So distorted is their understanding of their scriptures that they see the manifestation of God's Representative as the embodiment of evil. Thus it was in Palestine long ago when Jesus taught His simple law of Love. Among His adversaries then were many who now await with dread Maitreya's appearance. They recognize, again, the intonation of love but, conditioned by fear and misunderstanding, prepare to reject it as false.

When Maitreya makes known His presence and role, they will find, to their astonishment, that He means them no harm. On the contrary, they will discover, His love for those who fear and oppose Him equals that for the multitudes who will welcome Him with open hearts. They will find, too, that gradually their fear and dread will soften into a growing recognition of His divinity. Step by step, their doubts and fears will change into admiration and eventual trust, and His counsel and advice will they eagerly seek. So will it be. Pockets of opposition may persist for long but, in time, all but the most bigoted will accept Him as Teacher and Friend.

When they do, they will find in Him a Counsellor and Guide Who will take them into the understanding of their own divine origin and nature. He will free them from the fear which blinds them now, and enable them to savour the reality of Being untrammelled by doctrine and dogma. Many there are who fear the coming of the Lord of Love; their own experience of that love will set them free.

Within weeks, many for themselves will hear and see the Great Lord. They will know and recognize Him and establish

Him in their hearts. News of their experience will travel far and wide and awaken humanity to the miracle in their midst. In their own tongue, He will outline His proposals and views and seek their co-operation and help. In this way, a new climate of expectancy will be created by Maitreya Himself. This will lead directly to the Day of Declaration and the beginning of His open mission.

He will seek to allay the fear of those who see in Him the advocate of evil, Satan's henchman. He will succour and heal them and bring them, too, to His fold. He will present to them the Master Jesus and other Masters and thus remove the doubt borne of their confusion. Thus will it be and thus will the Lord of Love complete His task, bringing, eventually, all the Sons of God under His divine tutelage.

June 1991

Maitreya's light

The day is fast approaching when many will know for certain that Maitreya exists, is tangible and knowable, and awaits recognition. Fulfilment of the laws governing His emergence proceeds apace and allows Him more open contact with humanity. For little longer must He hide His light, appearing only to the selected few.

Soon, many will experience Him directly in full vision and physical presence; they will hear His call to them for co-operation and help. In this way, the day is being prepared for His appearance before the world.

When that blessed day arrives, the world of men will know that God has sent His Representative, that the Teacher is among us, that the age of ignorance is at an end.

From that time forth, if men hearken to His words, a new spirit of hope will galvanize all nations and lead to an era of peace and well-being such as few, today, can conceive.

Gone for ever will be the old hatreds which have poisoned planetary life from ancient times. Gentile and Jew, Muslim and Hindu, will find a common ground in their shared humanity and the age-old antagonisms will melt away in the warmth of His light.

Little time remains for men to wait before they see the Teacher, and when they do they will come to understand the reasons for their existence, the purpose of their lives.

They will renew their faith in life and create around themselves the fabric of a new and better civilization whose keynotes will be justice and sharing, harmony and love.

They will look to the future with hope rather than despair. They will plot the heavens as maps for coming journeys, and welcome infinity as a concept of beauty and promise. They will love life and all who live, and enter again within God's Plan.

Thus will it be, and thus will the Great Lord fulfil His mission: the salvage of humanity and the restoration of God's Will.

Naturally, not all of this great progress will happen overnight. Many chains still enshackle man's consciousness, and deep chasms of ignorance and superstition bedevil men's thought. Nevertheless, a start will soon be made to shine the light of knowledge and understanding upon the many problems which beset the world and, with tolerance and good faith, much will quickly be achieved.

Maitreya comes not alone, but at the head of His Group of Masters. They, too, with Their Initiates, will take humanity in hand, and, fulfilling Their mission of service, will lead men into the New Age.

Their experience will guide men and quicken their evolution; together they will create the new forms and institutions through which men will demonstrate their experience of the divine. Thus will it be, and thus will the ancient vision of man's perfectioning see its beginning realization.

July 1991

The call to service

When the call to service sounds, it behoves each earnest disciple to grasp the opportunity presented with both hands. Seldom is the call repeated, for the Masters have little time to waste. "Many are called but few are chosen" should read: "Many are called but few respond."

Thus it is in the Great Service; only the elect realize the blessing conferred by the opportunity to serve the Plan. Service is the sacred duty which allows the disciple to shorten by many lives his sojourn on this Earth. Many know this but balk at the lightest task. Many forget the pledge they made long ago and shrug off the inner unease. Not for nothing do the Masters sadly shake Their heads and search once more among the waiting lights.

Not all who serve realize they do so. So instinctive is their response to the soul's or Master's call that they plunge in boldly without a second thought. So decentralized are they that the world's need is their only concern. They serve as they breathe, but in relation to the needs of the time they are few indeed. We on the inner side look for those who know, somewhat, the Plan, and whose priorities are sound. We search for those whose ardour is strong and whose hearts are aflame with love and sacrifice. We welcome such brave ones into Our midst and gladly present a field of service. Then We stand aside and watch. Over and again, their first glad steps slow and falter. Too often, their bright expectations turn to boredom and doubt, their lofty aspiration shrivels and dies.

The failure of faith looms large in these sad happenings. Without faith nothing lasting may be done, and for lack of this one quality many promising disciples have failed. Not for nothing, down the ages, have the teachings emphasized the need for faith, seeing it as the very heart of service.

Faith, to be sure, does not mean blind acceptance and belief. On the contrary, true faith rises only when the intuition, the voice of the soul, prompts an inner knowing, and, past all gainsaying, the heart tells you: this is true. When that moment comes, clasp firmly to you this new-found truth and "stay there".

When the voices of envy and doubt assail you, keep serenely to your task. Remember that your mind belongs to you and no one has the right to tell you what to think.

Cultivate a wise rhythm which will allow your service to expand naturally. Eschew a service done in fits and starts for in this way is all momentum lost. Remember that you are here to serve the Plan. That, if you did but know it, is your soul's wish. As you make contact with the soul, the objectivization of experience begins to take place. The soul has no preference, no desire; it relates only to that which is consonant with its purpose, which is to serve the Plan of evolution to the greatest degree possible.

The time will come when the influence of the Masters will provide a field of study and experience by which those now standing on the threshold will enter into the realm of light and knowledge and know themselves for what they are. There are many awaiting the creation of a New Age whose manifestation will profoundly affect the structures of their time. Serve and grow, serve and grow should be the keynote of your lives.

September 1991

True and false Christs

From time to time, a Master may take upon Himself the task of inspiring large numbers of people who, strictly speaking, do not constitute His immediate group. This is frequently done when an opportunity arises whereby His thoughts and plans can gain wider recognition and response.

Today, several Masters are involved in an attempt to influence constructively many not fully prepared for this stimulus. The hazards are obvious: over-stimulation, negative reaction, glamorous misunderstanding, all are possible. Nevertheless, much can be achieved with a carefully selected group whose aspiration is high and whose priorities are sound.

At the present moment, for example, there are many well-meaning individuals who consider themselves to be the Christ, the Lord Maitreya, or the Messiah, and who await a call from humanity to come forth. Their presence indicates that humanity is prepared to see the Christ, that the message of His coming has gained acceptance, and that the time for His return is nigh. Responding to the unusual stimulus, their hearts react ahead of their minds, and they feel called and destined to fulfil the Saviour's task.

That they could not possibly do so is not important. Only the few believe them, in any case. Nevertheless, they act as a signal to many that the time is ripe for the appearance of the Teacher, and so help to establish the climate of expectation and hope. Well-known or not, they keep before the public the idea of the Christ's return and strengthen the hand of those who work with Him.

Needless to say, media representatives enjoy this manifestation more than most. With impunity, without commitment, they can safely publicize these "Messengers of

God", sure in the knowledge that no one takes them seriously, no one is offended, or shocked, none feel threatened or betrayed.

In the face, however, of the presence of Maitreya Himself, these same media workers know not what to think or do. More and more, and against their better professional judgement, they are coming to realize the truth that the Christ is in the world, working behind the scenes to bring about the changes which, daily, dazzle all beholders. They resent His apparent inaccessibility and understand not at all the Laws which govern His emergence into the world of men. They fail to comprehend *their* role in that Emergence and stand, baffled, awaiting events to which they can react.

Soon, these events will galvanize the networks to action. Soon, the world's reporters will flock to certain cities where many will have seen the Christ. There they will find the "proof" they seek, and, following their "story", will make known His presence to all men.

October 1991

The pressure mounts

It is the experience of many that the world is 'speeding up'. Events crowd in at such a pace that few can relate or understand them. What is missing in the average person is the ability to take an overall view, to grasp the significance of certain pivotal events and relate these to the world as a whole. Moreover, many lack a sense of the inevitability of such events and find themselves shocked and stunned by their apparent random occurrence. They look helplessly on, while the drama of world change overwhelms them and fills them with fear.

Not for nothing has this period been called 'the end times'; it represents for many the end of all they hold most dear. It also represents the time of change, the end of all that hinders the further progress of the race.

Maitreya has said: "My Coming portends change. Likewise, grief at the loss of the old structures. But, My friends, the old bottles must be broken — the new wine deserves better."* We are witnessing the destruction of all that blocks the way forward for man, that limits his understanding and prevents the expression of his innate divinity. We are watching the formation of new patterns of thought and feeling, of new awarenesses, and from these will flow the new forms, the relevant structures, with which better to express the hopes and aspirations of men. These are now in the making. The pressure mounts. Hence the hectic pace.

Behind the scenes, We work. With love, We send the forces which destroy the old, outworn forms. With love, We watch the collapse of totalitarian greed. Lovingly, We turn the lever which controls the pressure which could destroy the world.

Again and yet again, We increase the tension, watching how men respond to the higher pulse. As opportunity allows, We release the forces which beneficently act on the hearts and minds of those who serve, and potentize their work. In this way, a new world is being built, one better suited to the evolving needs of men.

The next few years are crucial ones in the development of this world. Much depends on the correct response of humanity to the inspiration and guidance of the Christ. If man wills, the transformation of existing structures can proceed quickly and with minimal stress; a glad acceptance of the need for change would ensure that this were so. However, not all men see the world in the same light, and for some the needed changes will appear as backward steps strongly to be opposed. Who, then, decides?

Man, himself, must decide the speed and scope of change. In this way, free will is not infringed. Gradually, men will come to understand that radical change is inevitable and the sooner undertaken the sooner enjoyed.

November 1991

Message No. 82

The problems of change

It is not uncommon for events to proceed at a pace so fast, so relentless, that the people most involved can bear no more; they undergo a reaction and withdraw their interest and involvement. Thus it is today in many parts of Eastern Europe where, only a few months ago, the call for change was at its height. Over-exposed to emotional debate, many grow listless and tired, disillusion and apathy replacing the high enthusiasm and expectations of so little time ago.

For them, 'politics' is no longer the answer; the daily need for food and work more pressing priorities. A deep and dangerous ennui fast replaces the thrilling hopes for a new start, and men turn to demagogues and adventurers for leadership and guidance. That precious right, the right to vote, is being willingly forsaken, old patterns re-emerge, and a climate of despair grips many hearts.

Not all, however, is gloom and despair. A new and growing sense of the spiritual basis of life is manifesting more and more, and, inevitably, men turn to religion as a surer source of inspiration and tutelage. Throughout Eastern Europe, the churches gain authority and power; the people shift allegiance and look again to the old signposts.

Not all they find within the churches answers truly to their spiritual needs; daily, however, there is a growing awareness that Deity manifests in all, and needs expression in the lives of all, here and now.

That this requires the establishment of new and better institutions, political and economic, has dawned on but the few, but the time is coming when this logic, too, will be grasped.

Then the groups, political and religious, will join forces in a common aim: the reconstruction of their countries along truly spiritual lines.

Already, the signs are that the present disillusion and discontent will be relatively short lived; that soon the people will reassert their aspirations for a happier and more just world, and this time on a broader front, addressing the total needs of men, inwardly and on the physical plane.

Then we shall see the fulfilment in Eastern Europe of an ancient longing for a society based on spiritual truths: the Brotherhood of men, justice and freedom, right relation of man to God. The deep religious feeling of the region, long suppressed and now reawakening, will flower in a renewal of hope and an understanding of the task ahead for humanity. In that task the people of Eastern Europe will play their full and unique part.

December 1991

End of a dark chapter

World events are moving to a climax. Soon, the peoples of all nations will realize that they are living at a crucial turning-point in the evolution of the planet and, together, are making history. For some, the passing away of the old is fraught with pain and fear. This is inevitable as the outworn forms disintegrate in violent chaos. Much blood is being spilled now in the gestation of the new.

Nevertheless, for those who have the eyes to see, the most remarkable transformations are taking place across the globe which augurs well for the future of the race. Unheralded as many of them are, these changes for the better have crept up on humanity unawares, and, quietly and unsung, perform their benevolent work of salvage. Thus are the people themselves creating the new structures, painfully and haltingly at present but soon to accelerate to a momentum past all imagining.

When the changes are at their height, Maitreya Himself will step forward for all to see and add His counsel to the deliberations of the people. Thus will the future direction be safe guarded and much painful experiment be avoided.

Paramount among His concerns is the welfare of the poor and dispossessed. Half the world's population enter this category and present an enormous challenge to the goodwill of men. Maitreya's intention will be to inspire and galvanize that goodwill and so end for ever this injustice. That it will not be easy He already knows; deep-seated and tenacious are the greed and selfishness of men. But, gradually, people will come to see that it is in their own best interests to share the resources of the world, that naught else can save them from disaster. When men gladly and willingly accept the need, the blueprints of sharing will be unrolled and presented to the nations. Thus will end for ever a dark chapter in the history of this planet and men can start again on the upward path.

Whenever the cry of despair finds utterance on a mass scale, the Forces of Light, the Elder Brethren of humanity, by law, respond. Today, from all corners of the planet, that cry of anguish issues from a thousand million hearts, bringing to their aid the Masters and Their Master, Maitreya, the Lord of Love.

Behind the outer events, the transformations, lies Their unseen hand. Their energies engender vision and courage, and, in due course, an all-inclusive synthesis. The present discord and disarray will give place to a new harmony among the nations — reflecting the growing harmony arising in people everywhere in response to Maitreya's presence. Soon, for themselves, men will know that the future is bright if they heed His call, that He is here to stay, and to lead them, if they are willing, along the path which leads directly to the Source of all.

January 1992

A new world in the making

Many will remember how, only a few short years ago, the world braced itself for nuclear destruction. Few there were who expected humanity to survive the war of words, the 'cold war'. Rather, most awaited the fateful 'count-down' and resigned themselves to eventual oblivion.

Recent events have changed such fatalism and brought new hope to despairing humanity. The bridges between the nations are being erected one by one and the barriers diminish daily. Soon, a new dawn will shed a brighter light on man's problems and show the way to their solution.

Above all, the nuclear threat has receded, mankind breathes gratefully anew, and in the atmosphere of trust thus engendered, the stockpiled horror loses its terror for the race.

However, many nations, large and small, have placed their faith in nuclear weapons, hoping to outface their enemies or rivals for influence and power. This presents many problems, for few acknowledge possession of the bomb and most are reluctant to relinquish its potency in use. Nevertheless, significant strides towards disengagement and disarmament are being taken by the major powers and this bodes well for a reduction of arms around the world.

Until now, the confrontation between the United States and the Soviet Union has, of necessity, dominated world thought and action, and this in every sphere, politically, economically, and militarily alike. The new relationship now being forged between these erstwhile enemies marks a turning-point in world affairs.

At last, the problems which demand attention can be addressed wholeheartedly, without being weighed in the context of the 'cold war'.

At last, the emerging nations can grow without the necessity of subservience to one ideology or another for their aid. The sharp demarcations, ideologically drawn, are losing their definition, and a new freedom and flexibility is beginning to be felt.

Much now depends on the ability of the leaders to sustain the momentum and to create the conditions in which a lasting peace can be assured. As yet, the sharing of resources, on a world scale, has not been given attention, but this remains the major issue to be resolved. Until that is achieved the world cannot know true peace.

Nevertheless, a new spirit of co-operation and mutual trust is beginning to be established, and that alone is a major hurdle overcome.

Much there is of confusion and potential danger in the world, but now, for the first time in half a century, the peoples can look forward with growing confidence to a new world in the making.

March 1992

The bringers of treasure

It will not be long before the Masters make known Their appearance in the world. With Their leader, the Lord Maitreya, They, too, have awaited the opportunity to emerge and to take Their places openly among men. For long have They known that this day would come; for long have They prepared Themselves for Their arduous task. Notwithstanding the completeness of Their evolution and understanding, it is no easy duty that They are called upon to perform. Not for nothing have They trained Themselves to work on the inner and the outer planes, for that simultaneous action is crucial to the externalization of Their service.

We know that Our appearance will change the lot of men. We know that Our experience and wisdom will serve men well. We know and comprehend the enormity of the problems which await solution. We are not daunted but approach the new day with joy. Nevertheless, We recognize the necessity of men's co-operation and trust. We know We cannot, under law, act alone. A new and closer relationship between men and Us will become the order of the day, and thus shall We forge a ladder of ascent by which means many, becoming ready, in due course will enter Our ranks. Thus shall it be.

Not everyone who knows of Our existence expects Our imminent appearance. Caution and doubt prevail in the hearts of the learned and blind them to the truth. Soon, however, like all the world, they, too, will rejoice that the Masters have returned, that the Mentors are among men, that the Elder Brothers walk once more on the Earth. Together, We shall create the new forms and institutions to enable a better expression of that divinity which rests potential in all men. Together, We shall bring order from the present chaos and control the destruction which inspires the present anguish. Together, too, We shall enter deeply into the meaning of life, unfolding new capacities and insights. A new science, inspired by Us, will adorn the new civilization and lend men the appearance of Gods. Thus shall men enter into their birthright and understand the ways of God.

When you see Us, remember that We once were men like you. Remember that We are a mirror reflecting your future and can show you the way to that future. We come to teach and to inspire and to lead men out of darkness into light. We have seen a measure of that light and know well its radiance. We offer to share with you, humanity, Our treasure.

April 1992

The promise of the future

Every so often, in response to human need, the door is opened which separates Hierarchy from mankind and, to a greater or lesser degree, certain teachings and information are released for the benefit of those who can make use of them. Now is such a time. For those with "eyes to see and ears to hear" these articles constitute one of the ways in which new information can be given at this time, the ancient truths remembered and a new light focused on the perennial values which underlie human evolution.

It has been My endeavour, over the years, to present to the readers of this magazine a picture of the life ahead, to inspire a happy and positive approach to that future and to equip them with the tools of knowledge to deal correctly with the problems which daily arise upon the way. From My vantage point of experience and insight, I have sought to act as "look-out" and guard, to warn of approaching danger, and to enable you, the reader, to act with courage and conviction in service to the Plan.

For many, this has not been a task performed in vain; many have found in My words both inspiration and guidance. Many await, avidly, their monthly libation of truth. Others read calmly, with a distant eye and even more distant mind and heart, while others again are baffled and know not what to think.

In recent articles I have concentrated on the emergence of Maitreya and of Ourselves, His Disciples. This is the central happening of this time, without precedent in untold millennia. The climax of this process is now being reached. Frequently, now, Maitreya appears before many hundreds to inform them of His Presence and to invoke their aid. Soon, these appearances will reach the ears of media and investigation will begin. That investigation will reveal the presence of an extraordinary man, endowed with unusual powers and offering unusual answers to men's problems and needs.

We stand on the threshold of a new era. Most people today can feel the winds of change which sweep across the world, pointers to the new time. Amid the chaos and the breakdown of old certainties and forms can be felt a new world waiting to be born. A better world. A safer, saner and a fairer world.

My task has been to keep these hopes and plans before you, to inspire your co-operation and active service, to guide your footsteps when they might have faltered, and to awaken in you the realization that you are not bereft and alone.

I am happy to be of this service; I welcome the opportunity to lighten your burden and to hold before you the golden promise of the future.

May 1992

The Fiery Light

Whenever a new Light enters the world the effects are far-reaching, if not always immediately perceptible. Subtly, through the planes, that Light engenders new relationships, affecting the very nature of substance itself.

Today, profound changes are taking place in the natural, as in the human, world in response to the fiery forces now saturating this Earth's space and Being.

Never before, at such a tempo, has this planet been so subjected to stimulus. Never before, in so short a time, has so much been achieved. Men would stand amazed did they know the extent of the changes, now and yet to come, which the Fiery Light has wrought within their world.

That the changes are and will be for the better, men must at this stage trust. Only a heightened Consciousness can as yet assess their value to the world. But openly, for all to see, many of these beneficent changes are already apparent to men in all walks and stations of life. Each new day brings further evidence of the transformation proceeding steadily and swiftly across the globe.

Many have asked: from whence do these changes come? What is afoot that so much is made anew? In which direction are we heading, so suddenly and so headlong? Unable to see the total picture, however, many are afraid; the fragmented details alone are registered and disorientation results. Were humanity able to see the situation as a whole, they would see a world in the throes of a new birth with its bittersweet mixture of pleasure and pain.

They would stand, patient, expectant and full of hope, for the new forms to be created which will adorn the New Age civilization. Above all, they would themselves act in the creation of these structures by means of which their aspiration can be given voice and shape.

Those who know that Maitreya is among us can enjoy a secret happiness. In the midst of every upheaval, every apparently backward step, their awareness of His potent presence and eventual Emergence provides an inner glow of faith and trust, a sure expectation that, amidst the turmoil, all is well.

Many, as yet, are unwilling to accept that other than the most strictly material causes lie behind the present transformations, while admitting that their scope and speed are without precedent. Soon, for themselves, they will see that a new Light and a new Light-Bringer radiates our world, that nothing of note which happens does so by chance or the "law of political/economic dynamics".

Soon, the whole world will awaken to the presence of the Avatar, the Messenger of Divine Will and Love, the Advocate of Peace and Justice, "the Teacher alike of Angels and of men".

June 1992

The people's voice

Very soon, another sign of Maitreya's presence will be presented to an expectant world. From far and near, the news of an astonishing manifestation will travel, awakening the slumbering sceptics to the miracle in their midst. In time, even biased and cynical media will find it difficult to gainsay the experience of thousands that the "age of miracles" has no end. Naught can halt this process, for the seeds are already set.

Without doubt, we are entering a new phase in the reappearance of the Christ, one that will convince many that the time is not far off when He can openly walk among His brothers and sisters once more.

Meanwhile, those whose intuition leads them to believe in His return will find their faith strengthened and assured, their hope uplifted, their aspiration quickened.

Many are the ways to serve but one among all today has priority: the Christ needs your willing help. Tell the world of His presence and His imminent emergence and aid Him more than you could know. Build together the thoughtform of this event and create a climate of hope. More than anything, this will ensure His smooth re-entry into a troubled and chaotic world.

Wherever men gather today their thoughts turn to the future. Dark or bright, according to their natures, men sense that the future is suddenly upon them, that it cannot be a continuance of the past and present they have known but will be altogether different, for better or worse.

The powerful events — now daily happenings — throughout the world are awakening men's realization that they are witnessing the death-throes of a dying culture, and, by implication, the creation of a new.

The form that the new culture might take remains, for the most part, vague and unsubstantial, but one factor has already

215

registered itself in the minds of public and media alike: the growing strength of the people's voice and the growing determination to make that voice be heard. *This is the most important political event of our time.* Throughout the world, the peoples of the nations are taking control of their destiny and demanding their rights. The inner call for freedom, intrinsic to their divinity, unites people of all races and creeds, and, in growing crescendo, will echo and re-echo until the last bastions of tyranny crumble and men can inherit their birthright. That is the future awaited by all men.

July 1992

Growth of consciousness

Throughout the world, there is a growing understanding that humanity is undergoing a profound change in consciousness. This reflects itself in many ways, not least in the efforts being made to explore the nature of consciousness itself, to investigate the connection between consciousness, mind and brain, and to study the effect that these three, singly or in unison, may have on matter and the natural world.

The old, mechanistic views of nature and of the forces at work within her are fast disappearing and a new awareness is dawning of the unity underlying all manifestation. More and more, the concept that all is energy, that energy and matter are different states of one reality and can be affected by thought, is being accepted on a wide scale and is changing men's view of life. Enlightenment is growing apace and soon the methods and technology will be found to demonstrate this fact. This is of profound significance for the future evolution of the race.

As we enter the New Age, a new urgency is being felt to explore the outer and the subjective worlds and to understand the relation between these two aspects of creation. Many scientists around the world are bending their enquiries in that direction, prompted by the need to demonstrate and prove their intuitive belief that all is interconnected. The acceptance of a super-personal self or soul is gradually gaining ground and is leading to a new synthesis in men's view of reality.

Eventually, the common ground of all such investigations will exist in the awareness that consciousness is the attribute of the soul, that the mind and brain are conduits, vehicles for its manifestation, and that there is no break or separation in the connecting links between them.

Until now, the nervous system has been seen as the pathway for signals, electrical in nature, from the brain; brain, the command post, through that intricate system, initiates the actions and reflexes, mental, emotional and physical, by which we recognize and demonstrate our livingness. To a limited degree, this, of course, is true. The complex computer of the physical brain does indeed co-ordinate and organize the multifarious information and stimuli streaming, moment to moment, through that sensitive apparatus. However, as understanding grows of the nature and source of consciousness, a truer picture will emerge of the status and function of the brain as the focal point for the infinite variety of impulses reaching it from higher principles.

For many, too, the mind is the man. They see themselves, through identification, as mental beings, capable of thought and action, completely autonomous and separate, whose very existence stems from the ability to think and measure. This, likewise, is but a shadow of the true relationship existing between man and mind.

Man's mind is an instrument, a body, more or less sensitive, depending on the person, by which the mental planes can be contacted and known. The plane of mind, the mind-belt, is infinite in extent and serves as the conduit for all mental experience.

When men realize this, they will understand how telepathy is the natural result of this relationship, and a new era of mutual communication and understanding will begin.

The nervous system will be understood as the connecting link between the soul and its vehicles, the means by which the soul, in incarnation, grips and demonstrates itself through its reflection.

In this way, consciousness, the nature of the soul, expands and grows, shedding its light through all the planes, awakening man to his destiny as a Son of God.

September 1992

The Plan works out

It is with the greatest interest that Hierarchy watches the events now unfolding in the world. So many and so diverse are these happenings that only the practised eye and understanding mind can make the connections and see, therefore, their underlying logic and inevitability. Without such broader vision, humanity is, at best, bewildered, at worst, fearful and dismayed. When all seemed set fair for prosperity and peace the prospect now looks bleak: economic hardship and growing ethnic strife add their daily quota of pain to perennial starvation and injustice. What has gone wrong, many ask, faith and courage shaken by events. When will the new time start, as promised?

This, a time of transition, is inevitably one of difficulty. All that we are witnessing results from the impact of great energies and forces which, playing upon humanity, call forth their various responses. These, unfortunately, are not uniform and homogeneous but are conditioned by separate interests, ambitions and desires, individual and national. Hence the plethora of nationalistic movements and ethnic demands now coming to the fore.

Looked at from Our viewpoint, these demands are the legitimate but distorted reaction to the energies engendering the desire for freedom which now saturate the world — applauded when acted upon to overthrow an oppressive political regime; condemned, and rightly so, as the instigator of fratricide, atrocity and war.

There exists the notion that, as the "inner government" of the planet, Hierarchy is in control of all events, large and small. This certainly is not the case. Nor could it ever be, without the infringement of men's free will. The task of Hierarchy is to implement the Plan of God through "The Centre which we call the Race of Men". This must be done while respecting, at all times, man's divine free will. *Thus, look not for perfection in the working out of the Plan from day to day or year to year. The long-term aim is assured, of that there is no doubt. Man alone dictates the vagaries of the path by which it proceeds.*

Soon you will see a lessening of the tensions which today grip the world. Events are nearing a crisis which will resolve these disparate forces and allow saner viewpoints to be heard. Economic necessity is forcing even the richest nations to think more globally and more in line with group need. Soon, the straits caused by greed will force a rethinking of economic theory and practice and lead the way to a fairer world. This day is not "just around the corner" but not too far off. Fear not, the Plan has not gone wrong. The Plan, indeed, works out.

October 1992

Waiting for the new

The world is waiting. Not with bated breath but with a growing sense that events are moving towards a crisis, the outcome of which is unclear. No one knows how things will turn. The professionals, politicians and economists alike, flounder helplessly in the cross-currents, unable to plan in the conflicting directions they are forced to take. Daily, new problems arise to test the goodwill of the most enlightened, while, behind the scenes, the ruthless greed of speculation brings nations to their knees.

Whenever such a situation arises, men grow fearful, and when in fear they strike out in anger. Thus it is today in many parts of the world. A growing intolerance, of refugees, of foreigners, discolours the democratic process, as living standards fall and security is threatened. Political extremists, waiting in the wings, seize their opportunity, and emerge to lead unthinking youth in imitation of the past.

Nothing can halt this slide towards chaos, as market forces crush the life of men in their unholy grip. Nothing can save this civilization, based as it is on competition and greed. The old order is dying; nay, it is already dead. Commercialization, another name for mammon, has usurped the law and become the state religion around the world.

Were men alone in this maelstrom, pitiful would be their plight, sad indeed would be their fate. Nowhere could they turn for succour, no one could they ask for aid. Forces quite beyond their control would drive them remorselessly to war and FINIS would be written large over man's life on Earth.

However, man is not alone nor ever has been, but, buttressed by his Elder Brothers, he makes his journey under supervision and guidance; not alone, but in the safe company of those who have gone before and know well the way.

Into the centre of the storm this group of Elder Brothers is returning. One by one, They take Their places in your midst, ready when called upon to offer Their advice and help. For centuries have They awaited this opportunity to work directly in the world of men. Now They come, bearing gifts of wisdom and love. Under Their leader, the Lord Maitreya, They will turn men away from the brink of self-destruction and open a new chapter in the history of the race. From the ruins of the old, a new civilization will be built by human hands under the inspiration of Maitreya and His Group. Fear not, for the end is already known. Humanity will overcome this time of crisis and enter into a new and better relationship with itself, its planet and its Source. Maitreya has come to make all things new. Knowingly or not, the world is waiting for the new.

November 1992

We await the Call

We watch, and wait. Despite all evidence to the contrary, We know that Our Plan works out. The time draws near for Our open manifestation, fulfilling the hopes and dreams of men everywhere for guidance and succour. Long have We awaited this hour. Long have We worked to train Ourselves for the tasks ahead, when men will know Us for what We are — your Elder Brothers. It is Our aim that *together* we will build the new civilization, and in that endeavour make two Centres one. It is with hopes high that We re-enter your world, seeking to serve men in their hour of need. Allow Us to teach you the way to fulfil your destiny and join the ranks of the Perfected Ones. Make haste to greet Us and to welcome Us into your lives, for We need your willing co-operation to serve you well. Behind the scenes, as yet, We work, awaiting the day of Our emergence.

Meanwhile, a new world is being fashioned, step by step. The birth-pangs of that new world are there for all to see but only the practised eye can discern the pattern which, slowly, gains coherence and form.

What we are witnessing is the destruction of all that prevents the manifestation of men's divinity. Freedom and justice are divine; hence the new-found impulse, demonstrating throughout the world, to liberate millions from the thralldom of the past. Painful are these first, urgent steps, but men know in their hearts that the time for change is nigh. For too long have men exploited men. For too long have the rich increased their riches at the expense of those bereft of all. A new realism slowly permeates the thoughts of men as they contemplate the excesses and failures of the past decade.

Witness to all of this, We assemble Our forces and prepare to do battle with poverty and greed. Our Banner spells Freedom,

Justice and Love. On these three Principles We stake the future of this Earth.

When you see Us, you will know that your regeneration is at hand, for We bring Our experience and wisdom and lay them at your feet. These are yours to take and make your own. We shall aid you in their absorption and use.

Many wonder at this time how conflict can so erupt and halt the smooth progress to change that they would wish. Many are the factors involved, but new, liberating energies force men to action, not always at a time of Our choosing. Action leads to action and builds a momentum oft-times naught can hinder. Our task is so to balance these energies and forces that minimal damage results.

When the Call goes forth for Our emergence, men will seek Our advice and regulate the changes in the light of a higher wisdom. We await Our task with joy.

December 1992

The One who knocks

There comes a time in the life of every nation when a period of soul-searching must take place; when the ideals enshrined in its constitution, written or not, must be looked at again in the light of actual achievement, and a reassessment of that achievement made. When this is done with honesty and candour, a new and sobering realism will replace the present self-congratulation in which the leaders of many nations indulge, hoping thereby to maintain their faltering grip on the lives of their peoples. Their time is all but over.

Events shortly to occur will redistribute the power of governments and emancipate the people. The sham democracy of today will give way to true participation, and open a new chapter in man's long quest for justice and freedom.

Even as these words are being written a plan is being set in motion which will speed this process and bring joy to the pain-wracked hearts of millions. Patiently they wait, the unexpectant poor: herded like cattle in the parched and pitiless desert; homeless and workless in the proud cities of the world; farming barren rock in the high plateaux. They await deliverance which now knocks upon the door.

Soon they will see their deliverer; many have already done so and live but to see His face again. In the battlefields which disgrace this time, He appears with equal Grace to all. Soon, the many miracles He has wrought will endear Him to the hearts of men and women everywhere. The healing waters will be discovered, one by one, and a great cleansing of men's temples will begin.

History teaches that nothing happens twice in the exact same way. Time and evolution ensure renewal of events. Those who await a saviour in the manner of the past will wait in vain. New times demand new methods and new problems new solutions.

Thus it is that Maitreya addresses Himself to the present situation, to the problems which beset all men: hunger and strife; planetary equilibrium; sharing and justice; the ways of peace and war. That He comes to aid men is not in doubt, but He comes, primarily, to teach. Heed, then, His teachings, for they contain the essence of life, and by their guidance and inspiration can you reach the stars.

When you are asked, "What will the future bring?" tell them this: a bright star has forsaken its rightful place in the firmament and has chosen to walk among men, bringing gifts as yet unseen on Earth. By name Maitreya, this Blessed One will teach men the ways of what they can become. He will show them the secret entrance to the heart of God and lead them therein. He will walk with men and angels and relate these two. By example and teaching He will show the way to self-salvation. He will regenerate and rejuvenate the world. Listen for His knock.

January 1993

The end of hunger

Much attention is given today to the question of hunger. Many agencies and groups around the world focus exclusively on this issue. Why, it may be asked, is this so? Why should one, albeit important, factor in men's lives command so much attention, engage so much concern, arouse such controversy and inspire such dedicated service and self-sacrifice?

Men know by direct experience that hunger, as a continuing state, is unnatural and does violence to our humanity. They know that from the inception of life on planet Earth all living creatures must eat to assuage their hunger and so maintain their physical manifestation.

Over the ages, as a result of climatic change, large sections of humanity have battled, with the animals, for survival. They have known hunger on a scale unmatched today. Technology, science and fast communications have eliminated, for the majority in our time, the suffering of mass hunger and starvation.

The question arises: why, in a world so well endowed, does hunger exist to such degree? Why, with food enough and more for all, do millions still sadly starve and bring disgrace on man's divinity?

By what law do men assume the right to mark those who shall live and those who must die? From what complacent depths are such judgements made?

By what initiative, what new-found grace, can men stem the tide of this iniquity?

Soon, events will force men to re-think the purpose of their lives and recognize their common heritage. Soon, a new levelling will teach both rich and poor their natural brotherhood. Presently, the Teacher Himself will demonstrate His solidarity with all groups and kinds of men, and, in emulation of Him, will today's cleavages be healed.

Mark well these times; they are the beginning of the end of the old, the birthday of the new.

Today, the leaders of nations wrestle with events beyond control. Forces they know naught of drive them to unplanned and oft hysterical response. They flee from chaos into chaos, led by their own dogma.

Meanwhile, We patiently wait. We know the outcome of man's present dilemma, and aid to the full extent of karmic law. We know, too, that man, *of his own free will,* must choose the path to future glory: the path of brotherhood and love, justice and sharing.

We rally to man's need. We strive to teach and serve. Man himself must act, and test his divinity in the crucible of experience.

The signs are there for all to see: the signs of the new time, when hunger will be no more.

March 1993

The Teachers are ready

Without doubt, events are moving to a point of climax. Daily, the news communicators report the growing incidence of crime: violence, murder, torture and rape. Fear grips the elderly and discourages the young; hope fails in the cities as the drug kings rule. Across the countries of the West, a deep malaise asserts itself and corruption, great and small, becomes the order of the day.

Driven by market forces, governments vie with one another in fierce competition, sacrificing thereby the livelihood and well-being of their peoples. In the name of business efficiency, healthcare and education, once hallmarks of civilized life, fall foul of the predator's claws. Rootless and hopeless, millions face the future with despair.

Blinded by "the logic of the market", the ideologues enact their unholy ritual on the long-suffering poor. Nor do they see the inevitable result of their folly: the collapse of the structures they seek to control. Whatever they do, whichever way they turn, they find the working of the Law against them; cause, and its effect, may not be denied.

Soon, the remnants of this civilization will be seen for what they are — the frail and final fragments of injustice and greed. Soon, the people themselves will usurp this faltering power and claim their rights as citizens of the world and children of God.

The sickness at the heart of the present dispensation is selfishness, complacency and fear. Where these three reign, separation and exploitation, handmaidens to ruthless greed, inevitably flourish.

Only a rethinking of the meaning and purpose of life will suffice to steer men from the edge of disaster. Only a new sense of realism will provide the key to unlock these mysteries. When man's erstwhile temples, the stockmarkets of the world, crumble and crash, that key will turn and reveal a new beauty waiting to be born.

Then men will know themselves as brothers, searching in the dark for the same guiding star. They will come to see that the only way forward is together, in co-operation for the general good. They will realize anew the reason for their presence on Earth and seek to implement, in every possible way, their understanding of the Plan. Thus will it be.

Thus will men accept the counsel of their Elder Brothers, and know that through all vicissitudes they have never been alone. Always, behind the scenes, have stood these wiser and more experienced Way-showers, ready, when called upon, to shine Their light on man's problems, and to illumine his way. Now, as never before, does that light shine brightly, and no longer from afar. From the midst of men's anguish does that light now serve as beacon, gathering all who are ready to ease humanity's pain. The call to service has sounded, the Teachers are ready. Awake, awake!

April 1993

The future of freedom and justice

Seldom before has the world seemed so beset with problems. Across the globe, in almost every country, forces are afoot which disturb all balance and security. Chaos and mayhem wreak their terror on an ever-increasing scale. Millions suffer the most degrading hardship and want while whole nations convulse in the throes of change.

Into this cauldron has come the Christ. Recognized or not, His hand can be seen behind the outer turmoil, guiding and cementing the forces for good, ensuring their final triumph. Little as it may seem, a new order is being created from these warring forces, a new livingness from the ashes of the dying forms.

As commercialization spreads its cancer around the world, poisoning the life-blood of human relations, commerce and government, more and more are awakening to the danger, and are searching for new modes of intercourse and trade.

While ruthless and ambitious men spread havoc in their homelands, igniting the fires of hatred long slumbering in the hearts of their peoples, a new willingness to aid the victims and to counter the aggression asserts itself in the forum of the nations.

The hand of the Christ strays never from the helm. Only the fulfilment of the Law limits His range of action. Always, His forces are alert and ready to intervene when too heavy a weight would crush humanity's cause.

Take heart, then, from the knowledge that these days of fire and fear will end; man's long suffering and pain will soon be over. Take courage from the knowledge that man is not alone, that his Elder Brothers know and watch each painful, passing phase.

Prepare, now, to see and build the future. Envision it enfolded in your highest aspiration. Learn to be detached amid the present chaos and add not your quota of fears to the encroaching dark. Nearer than you may think is the day of rejoicing; hatred, too, in time, runs its course.

Awaken, soon, to the new day. Polish, anew, each bright aspiration. A new light, the Light of the World, is now, once more, among you. Reveal the growing light which now enters each sentient being, and redress the imbalances of old.

We watch and wait and are with you. Each day brings Our presence closer to your ken. When you see Us you will know that the time to work together for the safeguarding of the race has arrived: no longer must "market-forces" blight man's ascending path. No longer must cruel ambition hold sway over the lives of the people. Never again must millions starve in the midst of plenty. No more must the future of the young be sold above their heads. The future of freedom and justice beckons. Accept it, accept it.

May 1993

The mantle of power

There are many today who fear that an escalation of the fighting in former Yugoslavia will lead, inevitably, to a third and catastrophic world conflict. The Balkans has replaced the Middle East as the key to Armageddon in the thinking of those who, interpreting wrongly their scriptures, hold such expectations before the world. Did they but realize how inadequate is their understanding of the forces now at work throughout the planet they would save themselves and those who heed them much heartache and worry.

Fear of such an eventuality is behind the present inaction, however rationalized, of many nations, particularly the United States. Such fear paralyses decision-making and leads to confusion and doubt.

Needed now is leadership, firm and clear. The Assembly of Nations, hesitant and divided, should voice aloud the concern of all peoples for the victims of fratricide and authorize the economic and military measures which will bring it to an end. Nothing is to be gained by further delay. Sanctions, alone, will not be sufficient to force the issue and halt the momentum of carnage; military forces, commensurate with the task, should be made available and ready for use. Only thus will the power-hungry leaders call a halt to the slaughter. Only thus will their counterparts around the world, riding on the aspirations of their peoples, take pause for thought.

Soon, the nations will come to realize the necessity for corporate action in solving the many problems which beset the world from day to day. Little as it may have seemed likely in the recent past, it is these shared problems and anxieties which are drawing the nations together in mutual preservation. So dangerous, now, are the forces available to errant groups and individuals that only concerted action by the nations can hold them in check.

Gradually, slowly, step by hesitant step, the United Nations is coming into its own, donning bravely the responsible mantle of power. It represents the rallying point for the highest aspirations of men for justice and peace and must be prepared to act to ensure their preservation. Nothing less will guarantee a future free from the threat of fratricidal war. War, today, must be made illegal and the instigators answerable to Law. The nations must be prepared to enforce the law and to accept the price of action. Until true and lasting peace is assured such policing of the world remains the sole recourse.

Meanwhile, much of good pertains among the mayhem. Far-reaching changes are making their presence felt in all areas, and a new realism is gradually dawning in the minds of governments and peoples. The old glamours, though strong, are gradually losing their grip, and a healthier sense of purpose colours the new approach to the pressing problems of the time. That these problems will be solved is not in doubt.

June 1993

At the crossroads

Daily, men are becoming aware that the present systems — political, economic and social — are no longer sustainable and must be replaced. The question arises: in which direction to go? How best to modify or transform existing structures without falling completely into chaos? Fearful of the future, unable to see clearly, men stand at the crossroads waiting for guidance.

That guidance, they may be assured, is not far to seek. For long ages, the Guides have been ever-present, ready when called upon to offer the fruits of Their experience and wisdom. Today, in the very midst of men do the Guides now stand, prepared to teach men the ways of the new time. A new dispensation awaits the Sons of Men.

Certain it is that the old structures must go; they have long outlived their usefulness and block the further progress of the race. Within these outworn institutions, too, lie many dangers, hazards which men ignore at their peril. When men realize this, they will grasp the opportunity to remake their world along saner and more compassionate lines. In time, they will come to understand that the world of men is one, that nature provides its nourishment for all, that sharing is the only means to ensure justice and peace. With these truths in mind, humanity will bend its efforts and resources to creating the new structures and forms which will allow men to live more fulfilling lives. Thus will it be.

To this end, We, the Guides of the race, will make known Our presence, and aid to the full extent of the Law. Thus will Our hard-won experience be put at the service of the race. In this way, a new era of close co-operation will begin between the Teachers and the world of men. In this way, too, an acceleration of men's evolution will take place, and more and more will find themselves within Our Ranks.

Our preparations are complete, Our plans well laid. We await only recognition and an invitation to enter, openly, men's lives.

The tasks before the race are great indeed. They will require the full co-operation of all. Our help and advice will lighten the burden and guide men's footsteps along sure and proven paths. Many await Our emergence with hope; that hope will not go unfulfilled. Service and love condition Our actions. In emulation of Us, men will reveal the love which lies dormant in each heart, and, serving gladly the needs of all, will reflect the divinity which underlies all things. Thus will it be. Thus will men prosper and know the ways of God.

July 1993

The New Life

Not for the first time, the world is rocking to the sound of exploding bombs. As old, corrupt regimes stumble and fall, the chaos-mongers set to work, sowing their anarchic terror in a vain attempt to halt the process of change.

In growing numbers, countries long steeped in the mire of corruption and misrule are undergoing the purifying fire of the new energies now saturating the world. Naught can escape this process of transformation and renewal. Nothing can resist the fire of the New Life which bursts forth in every sphere.

Preparatory to change must come a gathering inner tension. Such a tension is building throughout the planet as the old energies and forces give way to the new. Recent events are but a prelude to a worldwide process whereby the true needs of the people will gain ascendancy over the despots and corruption of the past. Car bombs and terror will not prevail. The people have scented liberty and justice and nothing can thwart their will.

These selfsame energies exercise their magic in the religious as in other fields. The mounting power and influence — in all religious groups — of extremism and bigotry heralds the advent of a new tolerance and breadth of view. The old order, in Church and Temple as in State, cracks and crumbles, and soon will be replaced. The appearance before the world of Maitreya and His group will speed this process and usher out the ancient, dividing dogmas. The energies of renewal seek new and finer forms; the New Life burgeons forth in all directions.

Without doubt, the forces of chaos are reaching the acme of their power. This ascendancy will be short-lived as the forces of reconstruction wield their beneficent sway. New energies inspire new ideas and ideals and it is these which alter the framework of men's lives. Watch for the signs of the new dispensation: Tolerance and Goodwill; Democracy, Justice and Sharing; Co-operation and Interdependence. These are the signs of the New Time when men will walk proudly and free.

Shortly, the truth of these words will become apparent as events move closer to their inevitable climax. Even the Angels hush and whisper in expectation of that time. When the Great Lord shows His face men will know that the time for change has come: the time to make amends, to heal old wounds, to rectify the past, to light the lamp of the future, to close the door on evil, to cleanse and purify the structures, to welcome bravely the new, to walk unfamiliar paths. They will know that there is no turning back from the future, a future which will reveal to them the meaning of their existence and the nature and purpose of God. They will know that the time has come to remake the world.

September 1993

A new realism

Many people are awakening to the fact that life, from now on, must and will be different from that hitherto known. They sense a culmination in human affairs, a new direction beckoning, a weariness with the past, a readiness to try new paths. The outer events confirm the reality of this experience: daily, the communicators flash their news around the world, telling of the latest invention and medical insight, the unexpected compromise, the meeting of minds long since estranged. A new hope is gathering momentum despite the many areas of anxiety and doubt. People know that nothing lasts for ever — the crippling want and fear or the horn of plenty.

The recent breakthrough in the Middle East talks, deadlocked for years in an arid confrontation of suspicion and hate, betokens a new realism now entering international affairs. Freed from confining dogma and ideology, men can reach agreements once thought to be impossible. The very word is fast losing its meaning as events prove the opposite.

Nothing of this happens by chance. Much work and long-laid plans lie behind each manifestation. Men delude themselves if they see humanity as the sole instigator of change. For untold centuries men have followed a path laid down for them and overseen by others — We, the Custodians of the Way, present it to men to tread, and seek to guide them safely through its many hazards.

One such awaits humanity as events unfold: the stock markets of the world, gambling parlours for greedy minds and idle hands, stand poised to fall and lose their power. No country truly is in charge of its destiny today; unseen calls to 'buy' or 'sell' dictate the strength or weakness of proud and powerful nations. Each is threatened in this casino game.

Faced with such departures from the norm, how can men deal with the problems thus presented; how cope with the manifold changes which must ensue?

Men need not fear the lack of guidance. We, the Elder Brothers of the race, have foreseen each eventuality and know well the answers to men's plight. Be assured that Our help will be forthcoming, that Our advice will be yours for the asking. We know the true needs of the race but men themselves must choose with free will and glad acceptance.

If men choose rightly, for a just partition of resources, Our hands are freed to help them even more. Our experience and knowledge will be freely given, Our wisdom and love put at the service of all. We await with confidence the appeal of men. Then will We enter openly into your lives as trusted Brothers and Friends. Our teacher and yours, Maitreya, the Great Lord, stands ready in the wings to begin His Mission. The call from you will bring Us forth.

October 1993

The new and blessed time

Each generation faces problems commensurate with its ability to solve and overcome them. The Law of Rebirth ensures that each new incarnating group meets the requirements of the time. In incarnation now are those well equipped to solve the many problems with which men grapple today.

No need is there for despair. Immense, indeed, are the tasks ahead — nothing less than the transformation, total and complete, of every aspect of life on planet Earth; but step by step, in growing momentum, rest assured, these tasks will engage the minds and hearts of those with insight, energy and will enough to fulfil them.

Thus does the Plan unfold, thus do men grow in the realization of their part in the intention of our Logos. Thus has it always been and thus will it continue till the completion of the Plan.

From now, however, men will face these tasks not, if only seemingly, alone, but in the company of Those Who, already, have achieved: men's Elder Brothers, Teachers and friends. We stand ready for the tasks ahead, knowing the outcome, and that it will be good.

We know, too, that in the maelstrom which now rages around mankind there is a growing sense of an order which, if sought, can be created; a growing comprehension that, if men have the courage of their inner understanding, the way forward will be revealed, the safe harbour reached. Men, everywhere, sense this but look to their leaders for guidance and the signal to advance.

Today, it must be said, such leadership is wanting. With few exceptions, the people's representatives fight ancient battles for lost causes, and struggle, impotent and in despair, against the tide of history, the forces of the New Time.

Men await a signal from a higher source. Consciously or not, they know that these are not the usual times but times of major import, maximum tension and unlimited possibilities. They turn to the old Truths, the time-worn scriptures and rituals of the past, but, dimly unsatisfied, sense, and wait for, the revelation of the New.

That New Revelation, too, awaits man's searching heart; the simple realization of brotherhood will fill the outheld Chalice. Men, in millions, stand ready for this blessed consummation and turn their heads upwards in expectation and renewed hope.

Not in vain do men wait. Not purposeless is their hope. Maitreya has come to fulfil the pledges, to reunite man with man and men with God. He has come "to make all things new," to fill man's Chalice with the nectar of Love, and to lead men safely into the New and Blessed Time.

November 1993

The destined hour

As the destined hour approaches, mankind awaits the Messenger. Already, the signals flash around the world that the Expected One is indeed among us. The longed for, impossible dream becomes a fact. Suddenly, a new wave of expectation grips the hearts of many and turns their minds to the central event of our time.

Across the world the signs have done their work. More and more, men recognize their import and grasp gratefully anew at the comfort that they bring. A fresh joy rises in the hearts of those who know the truth: that the Messenger stands ready to emerge into the full light of day, awaiting only the call to begin His mission. Soon, that call will sound forth and a new era will begin.

So far, only those of special sensitivity have sensed aright His presence, but before long millions will acknowledge their experience that the Son of Man has returned, that the Lord of Love is here. Men will flock to their temples to give thanks to God. Thus will it be and thus will be fulfilled the first stage of the Plan.

News travels fast — or so it should when it cheers the hearts of men. Yet for long have many rejected that which would renew their hope. From spiritual blindness or fear of disappointment men have ignored the evidence of their eyes — that the world is being transformed, that the impossible has turned to fact, that the fear of annihilation has been lifted from their minds.

Now, many hearken to the marvels in our midst and turn their minds to ways of helping fellow men. A flood of further miracles awaits men's astonished gaze, ensuring their acceptance that the Great Lord is with us. The fearful will learn and understand that the "end time" is not the end of all time but a point in the cosmic history of the Earth. A new openness and tolerance will make itself felt and a brighter chapter will open for men.

Be ready for the new. Reject not the unfamiliar. Great wonders will shower their blessings on men. The obdurate and the narrow of mind will fear for a time, but hate will eventually melt in the glow of Maitreya's love.

Be not afraid for the future of Earth. A new and better husbandry will replace the present ignorance and more stable conditions will prevail. Simpler and truer joys will take hold of men's hearts and usher out the present unease. Men will come to know themselves as brothers all, and, sharing justly, transform the lives of men. Thus will it be, and thus will men know the secrets of the universe and, reaching upwards to the stars, claim their birthright as Sons of God.

December 1993

The path to Divinity

Very soon now, the world will know that the long wait is over, that the Son of Man has kept His promise, and that a new era has begun. When men see Him they will understand the reasons for His appearance and the need for their co-operation, for He will outline the major needs of the time and invite their help in reconstructing the planet. Much there is to do, for a whole world awaits its transformation. Many hands are needed, for the changes involve all men. When Maitreya enters, openly, the stage of modern life, He will beckon to His side an army of willing helpers. Through them He will administer and oversee the planet's restoration.

Time, now, is short indeed before Maitreya's face will be seen, His presence known, His counsel listened to with care. His advice will cover the gamut of present ills and point the way to their amelioration and cure.

His voice will speak for those who suffer most: the halt, the lame, the outcast and the poor — for all who suffer silently and needlessly. He will galvanize those who long to help their brothers and set in motion the new crusade of service. Thus will it be. Thus will Maitreya inspire the formation of groups of planetary pioneers, whose task it will be to bring succour to the long-suffering needy of the world. A sustained programme of aid, far outdistancing anything so far seen, will quickly restore the lives of those in greatest need.

On all fronts the obstacles to progress will be tackled one by one: the greed and selfishness so prevalent today will give place to a broader view of community; the basic needs of all will take priority; the new concern for nature and environment will be embodied in legislation, universally accepted, and will lead to a wise husbandry of nature's gifts; international travel on a massive scale will reduce the isolation and prejudice which narrows the vision and keeps in ignorance so many millions today; the hold on men's minds of the old ideologies will gradually weaken and give way to a new tolerance and trust. Thus will emerge a new atmosphere in which the most ambitious changes can take place in a spirit of goodwill. The General Good will replace self interest as a measure of men's actions, and in growing harmony the peoples of the Earth will move forward into the New Age. Thus will it be, and thus, under the guidance of Maitreya and His Group, will men find themselves once more on the right path — the path to divinity.

January 1994

The dormant fire

Before long, the world will awaken to the realization that the New Age has begun. From all sides, the evidence is growing that an entirely new form of living is beginning to take root in the consciousness of humanity. More and more, the sensitive members of the race are intuiting the understanding of what it means to be human and how best to manifest that practically in everyday life.

Daily, new concepts enter the mind-belt and make their impact on the sensitive minds of men everywhere. Moment to moment, new awareness grows of the underlying needs of the human race as it stands at the threshold of the new cosmic cycle.

Above all, mankind is realizing its oneness, its interrelationship, its need for one another, and, step by painful step, is moving towards that manifestation. Much there is of discord, disharmony and strife, but the new awareness blossoms of the identity of each with each. Never has the world been so ready for change; never has the imprint of the Plan been so fruitfully received.

Be prepared, therefore, to see a new sense of urgency grip those whose task it is to formulate the new ideas, give form to the new concepts, and articulate for all the challenges and rewards of the new time.

Maitreya awaits the cosmic opportunity to present Himself to the world. He seeks the cycle most propitious for His plans, and gathers to Him an army of helpers. Thus does the Great Lord summon His forces to do battle with the tyranny of the past. From all corners of the world these stalwarts gather, ready to place their love and strength at His command. Never before has such an army graced with its ardour and resource planet Earth. Never have such multitudes answered the call to service and succour. Never, till now, has the need for their service, nor the prize of victory, been so great.

Many await, with expectation, the sight of Maitreya's face, the sound of His voice, the tenor of His teachings. Many thousands around the world, knowingly or not, have already seen Him, heard His call, felt the warmth of His love. Daily, that love pours forth upon the Earth, kindling the selfsame love that is the true nature of men, and bringing into grace all who can respond and act.

Thus does the Great Lord work. Thus does He ignite the fire which lies dormant in the hearts of all.

March 1994

A world in change

Whenever change looms large on the horizon, humanity undergoes two reactions: fear and expectant exaltation. Dependent on many factors — age, education, social status and personal disposition — man's response to change lies broadly in these two directions. Change, even for its own sake, for some is the nectar of life; others it fills with fearful dread.

Today, both of these responses to a world in change are everywhere to be seen. Many millions sense and fear the end of all that they hold dear. Millions more await with hope the possibility of a new life, eagerly anticipating new freedoms in a more just world. Change, the harbinger of the new, knocks heavily on the doors of all, calling them to prepare themselves to construct and know a new world, a better dispensation than that which now disgraces man. Each answers the call in his own way: in fear, reluctant to lose status, possessions and pride; and hopefully, welcoming an end to the old limitations and division.

Maitreya stands ready to emerge. His emergence alone will precipitate an avalanche of change which, gathering momentum, will transform the landscape of modern life. Gone for ever will be the iniquities of the past: millions adrift, penniless and starving in a world of plenty; men, educated and proud, begging for coppers in the major cities of the world; multitudes tortured and crippled, left dying on streets once shared by friend and foe alike.

Many struggle for freedom but deny it to others, forgetting that freedom itself, like justice, is indivisible. Many search for solutions to their own sensed need, forgetting that only through interdependence can the needs of all be met. Maitreya's call will resound in men's ears: share and save the world. Co-operate and know true freedom. "Take your brother's hand and know him as yourself." Thus will it be. Thus will the Great Lord inspire the changes so needed in the world, a world groaning in agony between the old and the new.

When men understand the necessity of change then will they gladly accept that which frightens them today; understanding and courage go hand in hand. A newfound tolerance will sweep away the old mistrust, old scores will be forgiven and the dawning light of wisdom will enter the minds and actions of men. When men realize their oneness, and act on that awareness, all becomes possible. Then will the thoughts and actions of men add lustre to the Plan of the Creator.

April 1994

Reflections of the Divine

There will soon appear before the world a man of unique stature and achievement, one whose qualities of love and wisdom are apparent to all who meet Him. Waiting for the hour of greatest opportunity, Maitreya counts the days when, within the Law, He can most readily acquaint mankind with His presence and mission. Soon, around the globe, the news will travel that the Son of Man has returned, that the Way-shower is here, that the eldest of men's brothers has indeed kept His promise and emerges forthwith. That blessed day approaches fast and naught can halt its progress.

When, as all will, men hear the inward message of the Christ, theirs will be the task to realize that from that day forth naught will be the same. Never again can the old injustices hold sway. Never, with impunity, can nation set itself on nation. Never more can the old fears govern and rob man of his birthright of peace.

Many will find themselves opposed to that for which Maitreya calls: justice, sharing and freedom for all. Many will see in such radical reform an end to their privilege and power. So, indeed, will it be, but the iniquities of the past must perish with the past — the future holds for all men greater joy in right relationship.

May it be that when you hear the call for a new start you will find yourself in the vanguard of those who stand for change, happy to lower your demands on life that others, too, might live. Only thus can the world be redeemed and turned again in the direction of the Plan.

None should fear a total disruption of life in the immediate time ahead: minimum, indeed, will that disruption be as the needed changes transform the existing order step by careful step. Never has the need for change been so urgent and so apparent.

Never, before, has man sensed the danger of inaction, and stood, as now, ready to open his heart to the plight of his brothers and the future of his planet.

Maitreya, too, stands ready to lead the way into the future. He knows well the enormous tasks which lie ahead but, undaunted, trusts in man to fulfil his role. He knows that His leadership and guidance will release the best that humanity has to give, and, nurturing that aspiration, will awaken the divine nature which is the birthright of all men. Thus will it be. Thus will the Great Lord, the Teacher and Redeemer of men, begin His mission. Thus, too, will humanity know peace and justice, freedom and love and come to see themselves as reflections of the Divine.

May 1994

The era of light

Down the ages, man has ever sought the light which he senses to substand his ignorance and fear. When threatened by some dark and awesome catastrophe, real or imagined, he instinctively turns inwards, invokes the light of his soul, and seeks guidance therefrom. Such action is but natural, for deep within the consciousness of every man, woman and child lies the awareness of being a soul. As progress upon the evolutionary path is made, that certainty deepens, the conscious link between the soul and its reflection strengthens, and the light of the soul the more readily is contacted and known. Thus the light of understanding grows.

Humanity stands now on the threshold of an era in which that light of consciousness will manifest on an increasing scale, expressing itself in every field of human endeavour as a growing awareness of the meaning and purpose of life on planet Earth. Many, now, are aware of a higher and higher stimulus, edging them ever nearer to an understanding of themselves and their environment.

Many are awakening to a new-found freedom on the super-mundane realms and, in faith, experiment in areas hitherto unknown. Dangers there are in such untrained endeavour, but, slowly and surely, the nature of Reality is being revealed to the enquiring public, the new discoveries are being absorbed, and a steady advance is under way on a wide scale.

We Who watch from the inner side of life are heartened by this evidence of response to Our work. Ours has been the task to guide men safely through this most difficult time of transition, to help them clear the hurdles which each succeeding stage presents, and so prepare them to become co-workers with Us.

Despite all appearances: despite the many travesties of justice, the iniquities and savage cruelties which pertain, man has made real progress on his onward path. With Our Advent, the momentum of this progress will multiply a thousandfold, and, in growing wonder, man will learn to create in the full light of his soul. Thus will it be. Thus will men achieve that which has been ordained: partnership with the Divine, and thus, too, will men satisfy their longing for light, for the direct expression of their nature as souls.

Whatever hinders the full expression of that nature will gradually fall away and be surpassed. The key to such progress lies in right relationship, and, little by little, that is beginning to dawn on the enquiring minds of men. Many now see clearly the only forward path. These, the vanguard, will show the way for the others, and so herald the establishment of the era of light.

June 1994

The voice of Maitreya

With each day that passes, the appearance before the world of the Great Lord grows ever closer. Very soon, now, humanity will know that there lives among them a man of most unusual attributes: a capacity for service conditioned only by the Karmic Law; a knowledge of that law unique even among His peers; a wisdom fashioned from the experience of millennia; from the depth of that experience, a vision of the Purpose embodied in the Plan of God; an ability to speak, simply, to the hearts of men; an awareness of the needs of men and of how these needs can be assured; a concern and a love for all, boundless, fathomless, beyond all possibility of man's imagining. A Hero, a Titan, is in men's midst, and soon will they awaken to His presence.

Soon, very soon, now, Maitreya plans to address a large section of mankind and to acquaint them with His hopes and plans, to share with them His vision of a better world for all. From that time forth, the process of His emergence will continue apace, and, gathering momentum, will bring Him openly before the world. Thus will the Son of Man fulfil His promise to return, and thus will men know that the time of their deliverance is at hand.

While awaiting an invitation to emerge and speak directly to men, Maitreya has not, you may be sure, stood idly by. Powerful and deep are the transformations which His presence has already wrought, and, even as these words are written and read, further profound changes can be expected to appear.

A new voice is being heard in the affairs of men, articulated by a few sensitive minds among the leaders of the nations. More and more, this voice will give expression to the foremost needs of our time: peace, tolerance, forgiveness of past wrongs, co-operation and sharing for the benefit of all. That voice will issue from the hearts and minds of all who love their fellow-men, creating an invincible demand for world reconstruction and renewal. That voice is the voice of the new era. It is the voice of Maitreya.

Add your voice to that gathering clamour for peace and justice and become aware of your place in history. A new world is in the making and requires the involvement of all: all have a part to play in this great undertaking; none should feel too young or too old to voice aloud their aspirations.

Soon, Maitreya, Himself, will focus this demand for a new way of living, adding His insight and experience to the cry from men for justice and peace. Soon, the inadequacies and contradictions of the present dispensation will force upon the nations a new realism. In that clearer light the new era will come to birth: the tensions and suffering of so many today will give way to renewed hope and vigorous involvement in the reconstruction of the world.

July 1994

To serve anew

Since the time is short indeed till mankind sees the Christ, it would be wise to consider, somewhat, the likely repercussions of that momentous event. Firstly, men will awaken to a new situation, one altogether unfamiliar and strange: nothing similar will have been the experience of anyone alive; no one, anywhere, will have heard before the thoughts broadcast on that day of days. Never, before, will men have heard the call to their divinity, the challenge to their presence here on Earth. Each, singly, and solemnly alone, will know for that time the purpose and meaning of their lives, will experience anew the grace of childhood, the purity of aspiration cleansed of self. For these precious minutes, men will know afresh the joy of full participation in the realities of Life, will feel connected one to another, like the memory of a distant past.

Suddenly, men will realize that their life till now was a shallow thing, lacking, for the majority, all that makes life dear: brotherhood and justice, creativeness and love. Many will know for the first time that they count, that they matter in the scheme of things. An unfamiliar sense of self-esteem will replace their present hopelessness; drugs of all kinds will cease their hold on men. Quietly, men's tears will flow in humble gratitude and longing for the good.

From that time forwards, a new spirit of sanctity will prevail upon the Earth; men will walk on tip-toe for a time. Soon, however, men will realize that the changes needed in the world are vast, manifold, requiring patience and dedication, imagination and trust. Before long, men everywhere will engage themselves in the work of reconstruction, the rehabilitation of the world. Succour for the poor and hungry will take pride of place, and so will end for ever a blasphemy in men's midst: millions will know for the first time the quiet happiness of satisfied need — no more will the dying forms of the starving disgrace the screens of the affluent; no longer will men watch their brothers dying before their eyes. So will end a dark chapter in the history of the race.

Changes, unequalled in extent, will engage men's minds and hearts; naught but the finest of the past will prevail against the onslaught of the new. Daily, the transformations will be recorded for men to compare and admire; a new world will be constructed in the blazing light of day. All will, in their way, participate, each will add his vision and contribute to the whole.

For many, the very presence of the Christ will constitute a problem — their long-held beliefs will be shaken to their core. For them, a period of heart searching will be inevitable as they seek to understand the meaning of the new dispensation; ancient beliefs die hard and hurt bitterly in the process. Nevertheless, millions will respond with a glad heart, happy to accept the Teacher in their midst. Few, in time, will stand against the common acknowledgment that the Christ, in the person of Maitreya, walks once more upon the Earth.

Those relatively few who have led the way in preparation for this time will find themselves offered another field of service: an educational endeavour vast in scope. From all sides will come the queries; a long-felt hunger for knowledge will, like a dammed-up river, overflow and burst its banks. Many will seek to know the background and history of this event; for others, the immediate future will be the chief concern. Still others will feel the need to analyse and to question every explanation, unsatisfied in the end with aught but their own beliefs. Persuasion and tact, therefore, must be the order of the day, so to avoid the charge of bigotry and pride.

Societies, worldwide, will play their part, assuring the broad dissemination of the needed teachings. Much remains to be given, but, already, much remains unopened and unread in the hands of men. Endeavour, the counsel is, to inculcate the habit of reading much, thus to inform and guide the seekers on the way. Systematic study of the teachings, and earnest attempts to live the precepts of Maitreya, will give the needed balance and authority with which to teach. Each one, thus equipped, can avail themselves of this opportunity to serve anew. Seize it, the counsel is, with alacrity and humble pride.

August/September 1994

Events without precedent

With every day that passes, the emergence of Maitreya into full and visible presence comes nearer to fulfilment. Ere long, the waiting world will know beyond all gainsaying that the Master of the Masters, the Light and Hope of the world, is now, once more, among men. Little time, indeed, now holds back this culmination of long-laid plans.

These plans have involved the reorganization of the group of Masters of which Maitreya is the Head, preparing Them, too, to take up, again, Their work with men in open demonstration of Their knowledge and power. Much special training has been needed to equip Them for the task. Soon, the results of this effort will awaken men to the new reality in their midst, and point the new direction of the path ahead. Each Master has His speciality, but each embraces the plan for the development of all factors governing the spiritual essence of man. Each, singly, and as members of a group, will stimulate and evoke the spiritual potential latent in all. Thus will it be. Thus will the Elder Brothers of men demonstrate Their kinship and concern, Their love, and knowledge of the Plan.

We are entering a period of profound change. Not all will welcome the direction in which that change must go. Nevertheless, the urgent needs of the time demand the relinquishment of old privilege and power, the acceptance, gladly, of the reconstruction of outworn forms, the better to bring them into line with the true needs of men.

What these needs are will be Maitreya's purpose to elucidate and describe. He will show that without justice for all there is no real hope for man, for without justice peace is an empty dream. He will show the need of men for work, and the self-esteem which stems therefrom. He will draw the attention of men to the special needs of the young, so to foster their latent aspiration and readiness to serve. He will emphasize the role of woman and her need for emancipation, education and respect. He will show that in the years ahead, a vast army of servers will be required to fulfil even the basic needs of a world hungry for food, for work, for education and knowledge; for a chance to demonstrate their humanity and longing for betterment.

In His centre, Maitreya awaits the moment when, under law, He can step forth onto the world's stage and speak thus for all men. In that centre, now, preparations are being made for this imminent event. Few there are whose imaginations can visualize the importance and extent of the happenings of this time; they are without precedent in the history of the world.

October 1994

The doors stand open

Many await the appearance of Maitreya today and confer on Him the attributes of God. True it is that many divine attributes sit lightly on His shoulders, but, for Maitreya, the world of men is His prime concern. In no sense is the Great Lord separate from the sons of men. When, in the fullness of time, men realize this to be so, they will recognize themselves as Sons of God.

Meanwhile, preparations for His open manifestation go forward. Around Him now are gathering those whose task will be to spread far and wide His teaching. Long years of experience as teachers in their own right give these enlightened men the qualifications for this sacred task. Around the world these Holy men will go, bringing the light of Maitreya's thought to all who seek the truth. Many more will follow until this ring of light surrounds the Earth. Thus will it be. Thus does the Great Lord work to bring the light of reason and love to the minds and hearts of men.

Slowly but surely the tide is turning in the affairs of men. Gradually, and in increasing numbers, men are awakening to the dangers in their present ways of life, are grasping the necessity for change, and are electing leaders who are committed to that change. When Maitreya appears before the world, many more such leaders will be found, ready to engage in the tasks of regeneration: the salvage and restoration of this Earth.

With each day that passes, the time comes closer for the final assault on the citadels of mammon. These evil bastions are already undermined, their garrisons in disarray, their leaders bankrupt of hope for the future. In a short time, they will fall before the logic of the Christ, and lose for ever their ancient hold on men. In this way the economies of the world will be transformed. Interdependence and the community of men will replace separation and greed. The new energies of Aquarius, focused by Maitreya, will fuse and blend together into brotherhood the evolving sons of men.

Thus will it be. Thus will the Light of the World send forth His light, and, through that Illumination, rekindle the spark of divinity in the hearts of all men. Available to all will be that light. Each, in his own measure, can partake thereof. Let nothing hinder or inhibit your access to the light of love, knowledge and truth, and, in growing confidence, enter into your divine inheritance. The doors stand open.

November 1994

He awaits your recognition

Speaking figuratively, it can be said that the world now holds its breath. Knowingly or not, many millions now wait for the appearance of the Christ under whatever name or mode. The world is gripped in a tense expectation of deliverance — or further chaos. Many realize that the ways of the past can no longer hold sway nor determine the lives of men; too many suffer under the old dispensation and look to the future to right the present wrongs.

Behind the scenes, awaiting His cue, stands Maitreya, ready to add His unusual insight to the deliberations of men. Soon, the world will know beyond all doubt that the Avatar for the Age now dawning already lives among us, eager to help and guide humanity on its further journey to perfection. Soon, the world will awaken to the mystery in its midst, and take sides for, and against, this unique manifestation of God's Plan.

When men see Maitreya, they will know that the time has come to choose: to go forward with Him into a future dazzling in its promise — or to cease to be. When men weigh the consequences of their action, of their choice, they will surely opt for the preservation of their kind, for the institution of the Law of Love, for the betterment of all men, now and in the future. They will see, with a clarity enhanced by Maitreya's unique status, that the ways of the past must be relinquished, that they have no further value, that they but hold men back in the demonstration of their divine potential.

Very soon now, a most unusual event will allow the world to know that the Masters do, indeed, exist; that Their love and care for humanity is constant and unending; that the Teachers issue from the same spiritual source; and that between Them, and between Them and mankind, no separation exists.

From that time forward, men will address themselves to the issues close to Maitreya's heart: the sharing of resources, justice and freedom for all. In this way, a transformation of life on planet Earth will proceed with the full participation and approval of the majority of men. Naught that is done will infringe the free will of men. Each step of the way will be endorsed by man himself. Thus, and only thus, can men and the Masters, their Elder Brothers, work together for the benefit of all.

Maitreya is ready to appear before the world. The proof of His existence that men seek will be given in large measure. He awaits your recognition.

December 1994

Humanity must choose

With hushed voices and held breath humanity awaits the Christ. Little is it known that millions, consciously or not, feel blessed by His Presence and expect to see Him soon. That expectation will be fulfilled in ample measure. Very shortly, Maitreya plans to make known the fact of His appearance among men; this will enable many to see and hear Him for the first time. Thus will begin the final phase of His emergence. Naught, from then on, will halt the progress of His return. No one, from then, can gainsay His Presence. So will the One for Whom all wait enter the stage in the full sight of men. Before the world, His Plans and Projects will be laid, allowing their full examination and discussion. In the light of their truth, men must make their choice.

The issues are clear: to continue the race to destruction through competition and greed and so remove all sentient life from planet Earth; or to challenge the advocacy of the past and start anew with safer, wiser counsel.

That men will choose for life and further progress is Our earnest hope and expectation. That they will awaken to the folly of their present modes of living is Our heartfelt desire. Our task is but to advise and guide; on humanity alone falls the choice of direction.

Many may imagine that this choice will be an easy one to make but this could well be otherwise: men fear change above all else and suffer needless pain in its avoidance. Nevertheless, the stringencies of the time will focus their attention on the new priorities and galvanize to action a myriad hearts. Soon, the overwhelming mass of men will recognize the need for drastic transformation and an end to the outmoded institutions of today.

Men will begin to breathe more freely, joy and hope will spur them on to experiment with new forms and structures, and from the present chaos will arise a new harmony. Thus will it be. Thus will the old give way to a better, saner rhythm which will evoke from men the divinity that within them lies.

Soon, the long wait will be over, the Great Lord will show His face to the world, and the New Dispensation will begin. Take courage from this fact and enter the ranks of those who, even now, dedicate themselves to the service of their brothers and sisters, known and unknown, throughout the world. Seize this opportunity to affect the issues of the time, and, translating aspiration into action, help suffering humanity to right its wrongs and create the New Era of justice and peace.

January/February 1995

The requirements of change

Before long, men will become aware that the world has changed, irrevocably, and for the better. Despite the many tragic wars and the sufferings of millions, a new sense of realism is entering human affairs, leading directly to *détente*, compromise and co-operation on a scale hitherto unknown. Despite the bellicose stance of a few misguided adventurers, the nations, as a whole, are edging cautiously but surely towards a more satisfactory relationship. A new and unfamiliar trust is growing as the peoples and their governments awaken to their underlying interdependence. Nevertheless, there is a long way to go, and much to do, before such trust can blossom forth as true and lasting peace.

In the meantime, everything that aids this process must receive priority. Above all stands the Principle of Sharing and the redistribution of the Earth's resources. This central need must take precedence in the minds of all who are concerned with the well-being of the world. Without sharing, little can be accomplished. Without sharing, men will know no peace. When this Principle governs, men will have taken the single most important step into brotherhood and right relationship.

Certain it is that men will accept the Principle of Sharing; what remains in doubt is by what means, and at what speed, men will implement this basic law. To aid men to fulfil this urgent need Maitreya and His Group have re-entered the lives and affairs of men. Their counsel, if followed, will show humanity the surest path to justice and peace. Their presence will galvanize and stir to action the slumbering aspiration of millions, and through them change the course of history.

Many now await the sight of the Great Lord. Impatient, and fretting at delay, they know naught of the many factors governing His emergence. Maitreya must ensure that the free will of men be not infringed, that the forces of cosmos act for and not against His appearance, that the readiness of men to accept His counsel is at its most eager.

The economic fabric of this dying dispensation must fray a little more to bring men to their better senses, and to awaken their hearts to their brothers' needs.

Then will Maitreya appear before mankind and offer His solutions to the many problems which beset men today. Taking up His invitation to speak to many millions, Maitreya will outline the dangers of non-action, and show the possibilities and requirements of change. This time is soon; very, very soon.

March 1995

The eleventh hour

Whenever humanity is in trouble, its tendency is to do one or other of two things: to disregard all portents and signs of difficulty and to continue in blind assurance that all will be well; or to make some sudden and uncalculated leap into an opposite direction. For some time, despite all signs of danger, men have opted for the former.

Closing their eyes to the obvious breakdown of their institutions and misuse of resources, and ignoring the warnings of learned men of drastic consequence, they have blundered on, risking the lives and well-being of humanity as a whole.

Gradually, however, it has dawned on many that the future is bleak indeed; that no special preservation surrounds the human race; that without major reorientation the race of men is doomed to extinction. More and more, this truth dawns on the population of a world in peril.

Now, at the eleventh hour, men begin to tackle the manifold problems which await their concern. At last, governments take seriously, and heed, the warnings of planetary dislocation which for long they have ignored. At last, they see the dangers of a burgeoning population amid ever reducing resources. At long last, they recognize the international nature of the many problems and the need for co-operative action in solving them.

A new sense, too, of urgency informs this late approach and augers well for the planet and the race.

Into this more favourable situation the Christ can now emerge. Behind the scenes, He has for long pointed to the newer, better way. Now, in full view, He can add His voice to the growing clamour for redirection. Under His stimulus, men will with vigour create the conditions which will enable humanity to live in peace. Thus will be transformed this threatened planet and thus will begin the ascent of man.

Soon, Maitreya will provide sure proof of His presence, and call for a concerted effort to save this world. Through major television, His words will resound. His message of peace through sharing will galvanize all those whose hearts are pure, and challenge the existing institutions to change. One by one, the decaying structures of the present will fall before the logic of human need and sanity. The greed and corruption of the past will give way to the fresh air of manifested good and, in growing numbers, men will gather around the Herald of the New, the Harbinger of the future blessed time.

Soon, the world will awaken to the reality of its predicament, and, turning to Maitreya, will seek His counsel. That wise counsel will not be withheld.

April 1995

A new Earth

Whether men wish it or not, the world's institutions are changing. Daily, the news of these changes flashes around the globe at lightning speed bringing joy, or sorrow and despair, in equal measure. Never before in Earth's history has man been so conscious of the movement of change or so caught up in its progress. Never, before this time, has the race of men been so focused on itself and its problems and anxieties. Ere long, the speed of change will gain such momentum that only the least sensitive will find it unremarkable. Mass communications have obliterated time and distance, and ensure the engagement of all in the world's transformation. In time, men will come to understand the reasons for these changes, welcome them, and add their willing weight to their implementation.

Meanwhile, many find the speed of change slow beyond endurance. Caught in a quagmire of poverty and disease, millions deplore the paucity of improvement and face the future disillusioned and bitter. All hope gone, they contemplate desperate measures to remedy their fate. Dreams of revolution and revenge rise readily in their minds; only the common tasks of day-to-day survival keep check, for now, on attempts to improve their lot. Millions suffer thus needlessly, awaiting a change of heart in people and countries far away.

Soon, the realization will dawn that their plight need not follow such a painful course, that countless others know nothing of this suffering and grief, that sustenance for all suffices for all, and needs only sharing to prove this to be so.

Then will the demand for justice echo round the world. Central in that demand will be the voice of Maitreya urging a speedy transformation of all that obstructs the true destiny of men. The Great Lord will call for a new dispensation: the creation of modes of living which unite rather than sever the sons of men; the formulation of laws which guarantee justice and freedom for all; the redistribution of resources that the needs of all may be met; the better husbandry of resources that the fulfilment of these needs can be sustained.

Thus will be fashioned a new Earth. Thus will men come to know the joy of right relationship, the satisfaction of service, the truer alignment with the purpose of the soul.

Soon, Maitreya will make heard His voice, and issue a rallying cry to the world's servers. Soon, His voice will galvanize all those whose hearts are alight with the flame of love, whose ardour awaits only His quickening and support, whose best intentions can be blown to the whitest heat.

Soon, now very soon, the Lord and Avatar of Love will present Himself before the world. Be one of those who first respond to His call.

May 1995

The dilemma of choice

Never before in the world's history has so much depended on the decisions now being made, behind closed doors, in the political power-centres of the planet. At long last, the political and economic realities of the present world crisis have persuaded the men of power to address these problems. On their deliberations rests the future well-being of the world.

Until now, the 'first world' nations have taken for granted their favoured position in world affairs, and have organized economic power to their own advantage. For the first time, they turn their attention now to the fact of 'third world' deprivation, and look for mutually beneficial solutions to the many issues which endanger world stability.

Hearkening to the cry for succour from the poorer nations, the rich prepare at last to contemplate the inevitable: the need to share. This represents a vital shift in attitudes and augurs well for the future.

Whether or not these deliberations find expression in concrete actions and proposals, the door to reality and common sense has been opened, a glimpse of the possible, however momentary and imperfect, has been taken. This will lead, in due course, to a ready response to Maitreya's recommendations; willingly and gladly, or not at all, must men accept the needed changes.

That they will accept them is not in doubt: the alternative, terrible to contemplate, would end for ever man's sojourn on Earth. History tells us that man, infinitely adaptable, has survived many crises and dangers — always, however belatedly, his instinct to preserve the race has saved him from destruction.

As he stands at the threshold of the new era, man faces, once again, the dilemma of choice.

In past crises, man has been aided, often from behind the scenes, by his Elder Brothers. This time, a new situation pertains and, in full vision and fact, the Brothers will extend Their counsel and insight. Thus will men be aided in their choices and decisions; thus will they take the shortest path to Truth.

Informed and guided by Maitreya and His Group, men will quickly end the worst divisions in this divided world: mass poverty and starvation will fade from sight and memory; old wounds will be healed, past wrongs forgiven.

Thus will the sons of men recommence their journey into their divinity. Under the leadership of Maitreya and His Brothers, they will know the meaning and purpose of their lives and, dedicating themselves to the establishment of the Divine Plan, will recognize each other as Divine Sons of God. Thus will it be; and thus will the travail of the Great Lord be complete. The timing of His emergence has been determined. The world will see Him forthwith.

June 1995

The unfolding Plan

We are nearing a time of major change in the world: before long, the transformation of all structures will begin, commencing with the dissolution of the stock markets as they now function. This will release the pressures now being imposed on governments by currency speculation, and allow a fair and equitable trading system to be developed. Short-term measures must recognize the special and urgent need of poorer nations for succour. In particular, the problems of hunger and disease must be addressed without delay. New methods of distribution of resources, based on sharing and need, will supplant the present chaotic modes which so divide the world. The blind following of market forces, whose myopic rule causes such misery today, will give way to an enlightened and just consideration for the needs of all.

Very soon, the first steps will be taken. When, in answer to Maitreya's call, the peoples of the world make known their desire for justice and peace, the walls of ignorance and greed which now separate the nations will come tumbling down. The voices of the people, raised in unison, will shake the ancient bastions of privilege and power and crumble them to dust. Thus will it be. Thus will the new thought emerge from the stale confines of the past.

When that time comes, the Masters, too, will add Their voice to the clamour for freedom and justice. Separated no more by the wall of silence imposed by Law, Masters and men will together chart the seas of the New Time, creating a blueprint for change acceptable to all. Consensus will be the guiding rule, each step of the way inaugurated and approved by humanity itself.

In this way, the new structures will be forged, experiments of all kinds undertaken. A new and fresh approach to every problem will release a myriad ideas which, when implemented, will change the face of Earth.

Instant and total change is neither possible nor desirable; too many ancient roots hold, yet, the minds of men. Peaceful and gradual transformation will bring about the desired result: the emancipation of men from the bonds of the past; the inception of an era in which peace will prevail, justice manifest, joyful and ready sharing be the order of the day.

Then will men know the truth for long obscured by selfish greed: that the sons of men are one; that the Father of all cares for the welfare of all and provides adequate supply; that the intrinsic goodness of men shines ever through the mists of ignorance and folly.

Thus bolstered and emboldened in spirit, men will start anew on the long journey to perfection, sure now of constant aid and guidance from their Elder Brothers. We welcome this opportunity to serve the unfolding Plan.

July/August 1995

Maitreya's counsel

Many there are, throughout the world, who now await Maitreya. Under many names do they know and expect Him, and soon shall they see Him. When that great day arrives they will find fulfilment of all their hopes for a better life for men. That sacred day is almost upon us.

Nevertheless, there are many who know nothing of His coming, for whom the idea is remote and unconvincing; who await Him in the far distant future, and look warily on any nearer notion. For them, His appearance before the world is fraught with doubt and anxiety.

Little by little, however, they will come to understand that their fears are groundless, that the advent of Maitreya bodes them nothing but good, that His very presence guarantees their future happiness and the security of this world.

Many will see in Him the answer to their hopes and dreams. Others will go unheeding on their way, unready, as yet, for the changes which He will advocate.

That these will be radical, indeed, we may be sure. That they will entail a degree of sacrifice is very certain. That they will present a challenge to the open hearts of men is beyond doubt. The counsel of Maitreya is for nothing less than the complete reconstruction of human life on Earth.

A mighty programme of change will be proposed, leading, step by step, to a fundamental transformation of structures — political, economic and social — by which men work out their interchange and relationship.

At the present time, men might hesitate before such far-reaching changes, but in response to the advocacy and inspiration of the Christ, and faced with the threat of economic chaos, many will see the need for a new approach and a new urgency in tackling the pressing problems of our world.

These problems, if ignored, would continue to fester, and would erupt in tragic happenings around the world. Pain and suffering for millions would be the inevitable consequence of our present neglect. Thus will speak Maitreya. Thus will He show the need for change.

When men see this, they will gladly replace the present outworn forms with those of better design: an accepted principle of sharing; the creation of justice; the manifestation, therefore, of peace on Earth.

These, the essentials, will transform the world. When implemented, they will bring humanity into right relationship and further, therefore, the Plan of God. The Great Lord stands ready to begin His mission. The world awaits His counsel.

September 1995

The disciples and the Plan

There comes a time in the life of every nation when the soul of that nation seeks expression. This it does in a cyclic manner as the initiates and disciples of the nation respond to soul impression. It is their task to bring into manifestation the underlying purpose of the national soul, and to place that at the service of the race. Each nation plays its part, large or small, in a harmonious interchange which, in its culmination, takes humanity forward on its evolutionary path.

Thus it is today as the world stands poised for change. Little though it may seem to be the case, disciples in every nation are responding to the inner call and making themselves ready for greater service. That greater service awaits them in full measure. Maitreya's voice will echo the aspiration within their hearts and, responding, they will quickly change the world.

Every department of life will feel the touch of Maitreya's hand. When men seek His advice, they will find His hand generous to a fault; naught that His help can aid will find it lacking.

More and more, people are awakening to the need for change. They sense that the old order has run its course and await only a sign of the right direction to take. When Maitreya reveals Himself to the world, He will focus the eyes and minds of men on the essentials: sharing, justice and peace, without which no future for man exists.

Then will the disciples in the nations show their mettle. Then will they come forward, eyes and hearts aglow with fiery aspiration. With clear-sighted altruism, they will present their vision to the nations. With Maitreya, they will align themselves on the side of change, and show how that may best be accomplished. Gathering around Him, they will convey to the people His advice and guidance. Elected to positions of authority and trust, they will carry out the peoples' will.

Thus will it be. Thus will the old order vanish and pass away, overtaken in men's hearts and minds by a truer reflection of God's will for the race. Justice and sharing; right relationship and peace — these are the eternals, the divine attributes without which no progress, for long, is possible.

Man stands now on the threshold of that discovery. A new future beckons, and awaits his transfigured gaze. Entering into and creating that future, man will reveal to himself and his brothers a divinity long hidden and unacknowledged but essentially intact and eternally true.

October 1995

The age of miracles has no end

Increasingly, men are becoming aware that the 'age of miracles' has not ended but, on the contrary, waxes strong throughout the world. Recent manifestations have shaken to the core the complacent certainties of millions. Intensive media interest has guaranteed a worldwide audience for future miraculous events which will astonish, even more, believer and sceptic alike. The door has thus been opened through which Maitreya can emerge — and be accepted as the force behind the miracles.

Thus has been prepared a twofold approach to the hearts and minds of men: modern communications will ensure that the thoughts and words, the ideas and hopes, of Maitreya will reach millions in the privacy of their homes; while miraculous manifestations will engage the attention of countless millions more throughout the world. Already, the name of Maitreya is being linked to recent happenings in temples East and West.

Very soon, therefore, men can expect to hear that the Teacher awaited by all is, indeed, among us. That He lives, and presents His living teaching for the greater livingness of all. Soon, men will know that their long wait is over, that the world has been prepared for an event greater than the mind can contemplate; an event surpassing all in the long history of Earth.

Never before, in the *known* history of man, have the Masters walked openly among men. For the first time in countless ages will They thus conduct Their myriad tasks of succour. In this way, a new link will be forged between the world of men and that of their Elder Brothers. Men will seek to emulate the qualities of these Perfected Ones, and through such inspiration and example the evolution of the race will proceed apace. Thus will it be. Thus will the Guardians bring to bear Their knowledge and experience for the benefit of all.

Those engaged in the work of preparation may take courage from the recent worldwide miraculous events, for they presage the imminent appearance of Maitreya before men. Those who have worked to spread the knowledge of His presence will know that their efforts were not in vain; that the world needed their service; that they gave of their best in answer to their heart's call. They will know, too, that the thanks and love of Maitreya go with them all their days.

Miracles abound, and will continue to astonish; the forlorn hopes of so-called scientists and experts will prove of no avail to discount the evidence of men's eyes. Turning their minds to the hope which these manifestations engender, men will connect them with the wise words of Maitreya, and follow His lead.

November 1995

The day of liberation

With each month that passes, the world is brought nearer to the day of liberation. Countless millions await that day with longing and hope. They look for signs to keep alive that hope and, in increasing numbers, find them. Men everywhere are sensing that the old time is passing, that something strange and new is happening in the world. The old order is retreating, leaving behind its debris, its flotsam of suffering and heartache, division and strife.

Into this arena comes the Christ. What, we may ask, will He seek first to do? His first task, we may be sure, will be to gain men's trust, to engender faith in His advocacy and knowledge, His insight and wisdom. That is no easy task, for many there are who would oppose His views, for whom His very presence is anathema, whose vain hope it is that He will lose heart and return from whence He came.

Many others will wait, uncommitted, until the tide flows strongly in Maitreya's favour. Then will they join the growing multitudes who clamour for change; who recognize the authentic voice of Truth behind Maitreya's words; who see Him as their spokesman and leader, their divine inspirer and friend.

Thus will it be. Thus will men find a leader worthy of their trust, one Who will teach them how to renovate their world, to embrace their brothers in love, to know themselves as the gods they really are.

Gradually, the opposition to the Christ and His ideas will diminish and, finally, end. Eventually, even the most implacable will see that the love and wisdom of Maitreya are divine gifts for the world; that His coming among us is the greatest blessing; that without that blessing the race would surely perish.

Of all the groups, the religious have the hardest task of reconciliation. Deeply entrenched in their ancient dogmas, their divisive doctrines known and taught unthinkingly by rote, they will find it a hard and bitter struggle to renounce these half-truths and rally to the new. Nevertheless, even these earnest but myopic bigots will find, in time, little in the teachings of the Christ to cause them fear. One by one, they will enter, hesitant or not, into the light of the new dispensation.

In that new light, men will find themselves. In its radiance they will see their own reflection and recognize their divinity. Thus will the sons of men follow the footsteps of the Sons of God. Thus will the ignorant become the wise; the wild and violent, tame; the suffering born anew to happiness and hope. Thus, thus, shall it be.

December 1995

The Masters enter man's domain

Whenever mankind is afraid it turns to God or the Angels for help and assurance. Thus it is today, in the midst of man's deepening crisis. On all sides, the cry for help arises and, in answer to that cry, the Agents of God respond. We, the Architects of the New Time, know that deep in the hearts of all men lies a firm belief in higher help and guidance, and it is Our joy and Our age-old duty to provide them. Slowly but very surely, man's awareness grows of the unseen forces which surround him and which are ever ready to succour and aid him. That man mistakes the identity of these forces is not important: Masters or Angels? Few there are who know the truth.

When We, the Brethren, appear as angels, we do so in accordance with the Law of Recognition. In this way, men know that they are not alone. When higher evolution permits, We need no subterfuge and demonstrate Our true appearance. Thus it is that some see angels while others recognize the Brotherhood.

More than ever before, Our dealings with men in daily fashion proceed apace. Whenever opportunity permits, we render service and make Our presence known. In this way, men realize that the time of times is approaching, that the Great Lord is with us, that the isolation of man has come to an end.

Whether men see Us as angels or as men, they will know that help is ever available. They have only to ask. That the help invoked may not correspond to their desires is a lesson which must be learned. We work ever within the Law and the Plan, and fashion Our aid accordingly.

Angels, in myriads, there are, but they touch not yet the lives of men. A time is coming, however, when these unseen forces will offer to men their healing power and knowledge and, safely, enter man's province. Meanwhile, We, the Teachers, the Elder Brothers of men, act to bridge the gulf between the Kingdoms.

Thus can We safely oversee the congruence of men and angels. We are the 'go-betweens'; the willing helpers of both men and the Devic forces; the ever-present Administrators of God's Plan and Purpose; the alleviators of suffering and the Agents of God's Love.

Soon, in large numbers, men will see Us, know Us for what We are. We are your Brothers, gone ahead before you; your willing Guides and Helpers; your Higher Intermediaries; your Mentors and Teachers; your Muses and Inspirers; your faithful Servants and eternal Lovers. We answer your call for succour and enter your domain.

January/February 1996

All will be well

Soon, the whole world will rejoice. Very soon, the face of Him for Whom all men wait will show itself before the world. Very soon, now, the world will know that the Teacher is indeed among men, ready to inaugurate the age of peace.

Clearly, the responses of men will differ widely but one thing is certain: He cannot be ignored. So potent is He, so pertinent are His ideas for the future of the race, that men everywhere will clamour for elucidation and further knowledge of His plans and purpose. Thus, the Great Lord will reveal Himself to men and answer their pleas.

Fortunately, naught can prevent the triumph of His cause, for His cause and the needs of men are one. When men see this, they will rally to His side and demand the changes which He advocates. Thus will be created a spearhead armed with Truth, directed to the decaying heart of the old dispensation. Many will see in Him the Saviour of Old; others will recognize in Him the Exponent of the New. Whatever their stance, men will raise aloft His Banner: Truth and Brotherhood; Justice and Peace.

From simple beginnings, there will arise a flood whose urgency for change will soon engulf the world. Thus shall it be. Thus will the Son of Man return to His people and thus will He renew the lives of men.

Prepare to see the Lord of Love. Prepare to work at His side. Be ready to work with His Brotherhood, for They — the Masters — enter likewise the lives of men. Soon men will know that they are not alone; that the path to the future is encased in burnished stone, hallowed by the feet of Those Who have gone before and know well the way.

Serious problems await His earnest attention; much danger exists in the present affairs of men. Maitreya knows the law and comes as advocate and guide, secure in the knowledge that He imposes not on the free will of men.

Open your hearts to His advocacy and fulfil your role. Take your stand on the side of justice and peace. Make known your stance and attract His energy. Welcome to the Feast; Welcome to your future.

Many will be confused and unable to determine friend or foe. Filled with the old dogmas, they blunder blindly in the dark. But, soon, the old darkness will give way to light and, in growing numbers, they will embrace that light and rally to His call. Thus shall it be. Thus shall the Great Lord guide the footsteps of men and ensure His Victory.

Near, very near, is the time of His open appearance. Never, never before, has such a time prevailed. Take heart and know that all will be well, all manner of things will be well.

March 1996

The domain of Truth

It is with profound joy that We, the Elder Brothers of humanity, watch the events which now unfold. Never before, in the myriad varied crises which have beset mankind in its long history, has the future of the race stood in such jeopardy as has lately been the case. This century stands out as that in which the major conflicts affecting life on Earth have been fought and decided. That they have ended in victory for the Forces of Light is a blessing beyond measure for the human race.

With this thought in mind, let us look at the situation which now pertains on Earth. A new, if tentative, atmosphere of trust is growing among the nations; the threat of global war recedes. A spirit of co-operation, albeit as yet in its infancy, begins to awaken in the minds of many world leaders.

Many local wars still rage and exact their toll of human misery but, more and more, the nations are beginning to accept a common responsibility for their cause and for their ending. Well may it be said that the peoples of Earth are growing into adulthood.

It is fashionable, today, to adopt an attitude of 'cynical observation' of life. It is important, it is thought, to be not involved, but to register, only, the passing panorama of events and stand unruffled before the greatest suffering. Such attitudes limit the value of the incarnation and deny the observer the joy of action.

Major events are under way which, in their manifestation, will present men with a compelling choice. It behoves each and every one to weigh well the nature of that choice and to answer from the heart. No longer may men stand aside and let events take their often tragic course. Now is the time to stand proudly for unity and life, for commonsense and peace. Maitreya is on His way and will claim your choice, your answer to His plea.

Know that you are here for just such a time and doubt not the power of your decision today. Make known your choice for justice and peace and enter the ranks of those on whom Maitreya can rely.

Many today sense that something momentous is about to take place. They know not its nature and fear, often, its portent. They respond to the energy of Maitreya even if, by name, they know Him not. Soon, very soon now, they will see Him. Each can and must make his choice: to doubt and reject and suffer endlessly, or to recreate the future and to enter the domain of Truth.

April 1996

Man's momentous choice

There comes a time in the history of men, nations and races when they must reorient themselves to the reality of the life in which they have their being, and seek to understand the purpose of their existence and the means by which that purpose may better be fulfilled.

Today, the present race of men — the fifth in historical sequence — and all the nations, stand at such a point. Soon, men everywhere will be called upon to weigh heavily the consequence of their actions. On their decisions rests the future of this world.

Very soon, now, Maitreya will present the nations with a momentous choice: to continue in the present fearful, self-destructive mode and perish, one and all; or to follow Him into a simpler, saner, safer way of living which will guarantee a happier future for all the peoples of Earth and link man once again to his destiny as an evolving son of God.

When men understand the nature of the choice before them — happiness or extinction — they will surely hesitate but little in making their decision. To help them in that undertaking, Maitreya will analyse the present problems and show in all clarity the results of the various actions that men might take. Gifted as He is with foresight and age-old experience, He will remind men of their divine heritage, and show them the way to claim their inheritance. Thus shall it be. Thus shall "the Teacher of men and of angels" begin His mission, and thus shall the sons of men restart their journey to become the Sons of God.

Assailed on all sides by the relentless pressure of market forces, men are gradually awakening to its antidote: a truer understanding of the mystery and beauty of all life. Ground down and marginalized by rampant commercialization, men are turning to the nurturing fire of their inner lives, and finding solace therein. A myriad miracles, East and West, remind them of the unseen presence of the divine in life, and hold before them the promise of a better future for men.

Expectantly, men await the Teacher. Knowingly or not, they have called Him forth. Maitreya stands ready to emerge and to begin His call to men: "See yourselves as One and enter your birthright." "Share, and know the meaning of justice and peace." "Learn to love and to trust and know the beauty of life." "See all men as your brothers and become the Gods you are."

Thus shall the Great Lord speak. Thus shall He awaken the hearts of men to the imperatives of the time. The time of decision, the time of all times, is now upon the race. Think well and wisely, and choose "a future bathed in light."

May 1996

Welcome to the feast

In recent years, a new phenomenon has emerged: men have begun to demand of governments their right to freedom and self-determination. Until now, spasmodic attempts to ensure such God-given rights have indeed occurred, and historic revolutions record the perennial longing of men for their divine heritage as free sons of God. Today, however, a new and powerful impulse for freedom spreads across the world: millions demand the basic right to regulate their lives and evolution.

Governments, now, must take stock of this demand, and accommodate their policies to this imperative. Few there are who can with impunity ignore the legitimate cry for justice and freedom which rises from the hearts of beleaguered mankind.

Needless to say, behind this cry for freedom stands Maitreya and His group. For long have They sought to stimulate this demand, awakening men to the necessity of individual freedom, without which the greatest achievements are as naught. Slowly but surely, men have responded to this higher call, and stand now, all but united, to make known their demands and to inherit their birthright as evolving sons of God.

Soon, this cry will break upon the conscience of the world, and a new chapter will open on the evolution of the race. Maitreya will advocate — and millions will respond — that the time has come to recognize the rights of all men for a fair and just participation in world affairs; for a degree of freedom commensurate with natural justice; and for the institution of measures which will ensure the rights of all to the necessities of daily living.

Inevitably, there will be resistance to this call for justice and freedom; many there are who treasure these only for themselves. Nevertheless, the simple truth of these basic needs will dawn upon the world, and, in gratitude, men will turn to Maitreya for

His guidance and succour. Thus will it be; thus will the Son of Man guide anew the sons of men. Thus will men renew their covenant with the evolutionary Plan and begin again their ascent to the highest.

The time is now upon us when all must take their stand: for or against all future progress on Earth — that is the question which each one must face. The future calls you into freedom and justice, and bids you welcome to the feast.

June 1996

A perennial choice

It is near the time for mankind's great decision. Expectant, the Lords Themselves await that decisive moment. Few there are, indeed, among the multitudes who know the importance of this time, the choice for man: to plunge headlong, unheeding, to disaster; or to reorder, and sanctify with justice and freedom, the life for all men.

It is, of course, a perennial choice, focused now as never before. Never before has so much depended on the rightness of man's decision, for today, in man's hands, lies a weapon of uncontrollable power to destroy. Great, therefore, is the need for calm and careful thought.

To enable men to understand the consequences of their actions, Maitreya stands ready to enter the public sphere. He will add His persuasive wisdom to the call for sanity and peace. He will inspire and teach. In growing numbers, men will emulate His actions and manner, and, in time, the world will follow His wise counsel and restore to men their birthright of peace. Thus will it be. Thus will Maitreya fulfil His promise and His duty to mankind.

With impatience do many await this time, knowing little of the many factors, cosmic and other, which must be balanced by Maitreya to fulfil the law. Nothing may be done which infringes the free will of men; naught but the Law, and an understanding of the times, can influence the judgement of Maitreya on the moment of His public appearance. Of one thing you may be assured: not one moment's delay will be countenanced by Maitreya which would, otherwise, allow His open mission of service to begin. He alone is the arbiter of that moment. Await, and trust, His judgement.

That judgement rests on knowledge unknown to men. A cosmic grasp alone permits its correct assessment. Even so,

Maitreya must make weighty decisions on slender — and changing — data. A fine line, indeed, divides the necessary and the possible.

Trust then the skill in action of the Lord of Love. Chafe not at the seeming delay of His appearance — in the all-embracing Now no such delay exists.

Ere long, the Son of Man will assume His rightful place as the Teacher of mankind. Gladly and willingly, the majority of men will follow His advice and take to heart His teachings. Step by grateful step, will they set in place the structures of the future, and, in gathering momentum, the old mistakes will die away, forgiven and forgotten. Thus will it be. Thus will the Great Lord and leader of men fulfil His destiny, and thus will mankind know true joy.

July/August 1996

The end of cleavage

For years, many have awaited a sign that the Christ's return is imminent. On all sides and in many lands these signs have indeed appeared in abundance, but still the doubters doubt. Nothing, it would seem, but the sight of the Christ Himself will shake the scepticism of the doubting Thomases of the world.

Soon they will have no further cause to doubt, no easy rationale to explain away the myriad mysteries in their midst.

Soon, the Son of Man will present Himself and His concerns to millions. News of His appearance will echo round the world and lead quickly to His general recognition and acceptance.

Wherever men now look, they see the necessity for change. The old order is perishing; unstable and insecure, the old is falling apart. Cleavage abounds and competition is the order of the day. The doors stand open wide for the appearance of the Teacher.

Very soon, now, the world will awaken to the fact that a Teacher of immeasurable stature has entered the affairs of men, has graced the world with His presence, and awaits only the assent of humanity to begin His mission of enlightenment and succour.

From then on, the process of change, gathering momentum, will transform the world. All that we see today of cleavage and violence will gradually disappear. More and more, the ways of peace will exert their attraction on men and a new stability will be established in their affairs.

Peace depends on right relationship which, in its turn, depends on justice. Justice will prevail when the basic needs of all are met. The principle of sharing is the key to this divine harmony, and the only forward path for the sons of men.

Thus will speak Maitreya in His approach to mankind. Thus will humanity grasp the importance and necessity of sharing.

Thus will they begin to see the mistakes of the past, and, under His wise direction, remedy them.

The time is fast approaching when Maitreya can present His ideas to the world. His open mission will begin forthwith, and a new and better rhythm will impose itself on the world. Thus will it be. Thus will the "Fisher of Men" become the Teacher of men. Thus will the Great Ones, under His lead, restore to men the ancient Covenants, and thus will a new impetus and direction be given to man's journey to perfection.

Make ready to recognize and welcome the Teacher. Fear not for the future. All will be well indeed.

September 1996

Co-operation — the keynote

As we move towards the century's end, many await that event with apprehension and disquiet. They sense the changes which, tradition holds, accompany such turning-points, and think of the future with fear and dread.

This, it must be said, is a short-sighted view indeed. That there are and will be changes is manifestly true — powerful forces exert their influence on every level and in every sphere; but the cataclysmic chaos so oft heralded today bears no relation to the coming transformation.

Step by careful step, the new forms, as they find support, will alter the shape of societies worldwide. Thus, only, will a new pattern be imposed on the decaying fabric of the past. As men see the logic and experience the benefit of the new ways, the momentum of change will quicken until, on all sides, a crescendo is reached and a new world is born. Thus will it be. Thus will the promise of the new overcome the inertia of the old.

To make this possible have We, your Elder Brothers, taken the decision to work openly among men. This process is now well under way and for many years has Our Brotherhood worked among you. Soon you will see the results of Our work as We prepare Our disciples for service. Soon will they emerge and define the new approaches to planetary living and peace.

Co-operation is the keynote. Today's emphasis on competition, allowed to flourish unchecked, would lead to ultimate destruction. Thus will you see the banner of co-operation raised on every side, inspiring men to work together for the restoration of our world. Naught but co-operation can solve men's problems, manifold and complex as they are; naught but co-operation can heal the old and still-tender wounds inflicted by men on men; co-operation alone can guarantee a sane and peaceful future acceptable to all.

Soon, Maitreya, Himself, will add His voice to the clamour for change. Soon, the world will realize that the New Time has begun: the time of sharing, of justice and peace. Soon, the voice of Maitreya will echo round the world: "Share, and enter into harmony"; "Share, and know the purpose of life"; "Share, and secure the future for all." Thus will He speak, thus will be His Call.

Co-operate, and test the truth of His message. Work together for the benefit of all and know the radiance of His love.

October 1996

The Day of Days

Surely and steadily, albeit slowly, humanity is coming to grips with its problems. Already, a discernible trend for the better can be noted in many spheres: a growing awareness of the dangers to the environment inherent in the present industrial methods; a new understanding of the need for co-operation in solving these global problems; a tacit agreement, based on common sense and mutual trust, that the ancient ways of settling disputes by war are no longer acceptable, and require the vigilant supervision and, if necessary, united action, of the peaceful nations of the world.

This gives much cause for hope that men are awakening to the dangers which beset this generation and are looking for the means of ending their crisis.

Maitreya stands ready to emerge and to add His voice to the growing demand for a different set of values by which to govern men's lives. He knows already the new trend of human thought and seeks to stimulate its expression in every field. Thus does He work. Thus does He inform with His energy and thought the growing number of those who understand the dangers, and recognize the promise, of the time. These are no longer few, and soon, in ever-widening circles, their influence will be felt, their voices heard. Thus shall it be. Thus shall the present destructive actions of men and nations give way to the creation of Earth-centred husbandry and care.

Meanwhile, Maitreya awaits the Day of Days. Already, He knows the time, if not the day, of His first appearance before men. Already, preparations are afoot to ensure the widest possible audience for His words and His advice. Naught will be left to chance. Millions will see Him and take His measure. Only the hardest of hearts will remain untouched by His compassion and insight. Only the truly base will reject His caring love and turn away. Never will men have heard better or truer words so simply uttered or so deeply felt. Thus will the Lord of Love introduce Himself to the world, and thus will men benefit and respond.

From that time onwards, the men of action, waiting in the wings, will come forth and guide the affairs of men. Not alone, but speaking for the massed intent of millions, they will utter the demands of men of goodwill everywhere: for justice; for sharing; for peace and right relations.

Thus will it be. Thus will the stage be set for the open Declaration of Maitreya before the world. And thus will this Great One, this Titan, this bringer of God's Treasures, begin His Mission.

November 1996

The Masters emerge

The Vanguard of the Masters, in Their various cities and focal points, are preparing Themselves for immediate emergence into the open arena of the world. The time has arrived for Their acknowledged participation in the affairs of men. They know, too, that Their task is not an easy one. Each Master is a man but has long outgrown the human state of consciousness with its limitations and illusions. They understand well the suffering which these limitations and illusions confer on men, and seek in every way to alleviate their lot — They, too, in Their long sojourn on the Path as simple men, knew well and keenly felt that selfsame anguish.

But now They must work with men as equals, tackling together the myriad problems which beset men's lives. This They must do in such a fashion that the free will of men is not infringed: aiding, and blessing with Their energy and insight, each tentative plan put forth by humanity itself. They await with ardour the challenge of this enterprise, firm in the conviction of its eventual success.

When men see their Elder Brothers, they will see, too, their birthright, witness their divine heritage. Each man is a Master in the making. Naught do We have or know but which one day all will achieve; We are yourselves gone before.

This being so, We can act as a light to guide your way, and to prevent many false steps or wrong turnings.

The time is now upon us all when men and Masters will meet and begin their mutual task — the transformation and rehabilitation of the world.

Whether men know it or not, We, your Elder Brothers, have for long been at your service. Little there is, in the multi-coloured fabric of man's experience, which has not felt the caring hand of Our Brotherhood. Little is there, in the long history of man's discoveries and achievements, which owes nothing to Our inspiration and guidance. Thus have We sought to teach and to protect, until such time as man can travel the Path alone.

From now, in your midst, shall We openly work, to create with you the new civilization, conferring on you the benefits of Our long experience. Much time and heartache can be saved, therefore, by this, our mutual endeavour.

First will you see Our Master, Maitreya, the Great Lord. Then shall We reveal Ourselves, one by one, until all the Vanguard are known by name. Gradually, as circumstances permit, yet more of Our Brothers will add Their weight to the work of succour, the salvaging of a planet, the restoration of the Plan.

December 1996

The century's end

Men are becoming increasingly aware that we are fast approaching the century's end. In such a situation, they also look for signs and portents, warnings and revelations. The communication networks merrily ply their trade, combining truth with fantasy, fact with fiction, hope with fear. In the wings, Maitreya stands ready to emerge, to end the speculation and to renew men's faith in their own divinity and worth.

On all sides, the signs are indeed in evidence, clear indications that the 'age of miracles' has no end. Few can deny the profusion of signs which, daily, occur, pointing, however obliquely, to the miracle in our midst. Soon the world will know for certain that the Son of Man is indeed among His people, that the long wait is over, that the Teacher is ready to begin, openly, His Mission, and that a new way beckons men forward to their destined future. Very little time now separates men from their recognition of the Teacher's Presence. Theirs is the task to evaluate His worth to their cause, and to align themselves with His endeavour.

That humanity will not be found wanting is not in doubt. Despite all evidence to the contrary, men are ready — indeed, longing — for change, for a restatement of the reality of Brotherhood and Justice, for the necessity of Harmony and Peace. Thus will men respond to the call of Maitreya for these ancient symbols, now translated into practice.

Naught, then, can halt the progress to the future, the establishment of right relations between the peoples of all the nations. Then will unfold a Plan, daring yet simple, complex yet clear, ancient yet radiantly modern, for the restoration of men to their predestined path to perfection.

Many of Those Who have trodden this self-same Path are now among you, ready to assist and guide to the limits of the

Law. We know well your problems and fears, and seek to comfort and inspire. When men see Us, they will see Those Who have known, too, men's every anguish and pain, humiliation and joy, yet Who have succeeded in surmounting these perennial obstacles on the Way, and are the guarantors of men's equal achievement.

Give Us your trust and allow Us to aid and guide you. Learn from Us the ways of God which can become the ways of men. We are your brothers; older, wiser, but otherwise the same.

We have come into your midst as brothers and friends; see Us thus and let us journey together into the golden future which awaits our fashioning.

January/February 1997

The end of conflict

Within each individual is the simple desire to live in peace. That millions do not do so is a major blight on today's civilization. What, then, prevents the manifestation of man's deepest desire and hope?

To be sure, many factors play their part in the failure of nations and communities to live together in harmony: poverty in the midst of plenty must be seen as playing a powerful role in dividing man from man; but ancient hatreds and prejudices, their origins lost, often, in dim memories of the distant past, have an overwhelming influence on the lives and actions of many peoples. Beneath the surface of modern life, the ancient racial and tribal divisions exert, still, their power and sway.

Powerful political and economic forces, now global in their effect, but hide, and oft exacerbate, the tensions, East and West, North and South, which reflect the racial confrontation persisting for countless centuries.

Today, where the conditions exist for that catastrophe, these tensions explode into open warfare. Political adventurers, hungry for power, cynically exploit the legitimate aspiration of people for freedom and cultural identity. Vast sums are needlessly wasted on the purchase of arms, and the ensuing wars take their inevitable toll. Thus it is today in Africa and South America and, until recently, in the Balkans. The rape of Bosnia and Croatia, initiated by the Serbian leadership, reflects the latent hatreds which so cruelly surfaced in that turbulent area.

The conflicts in the Middle East and Ireland bring yet another factor to this age-old problem: religious intolerance, from the earliest times, sows in profusion the seeds of chaos.

Meanwhile, Maitreya awaits His opportunity further to turn the tide. Already, the energy of Equilibrium, focused through Him by the Spirit of Peace, is driving these destructive forces into the open. There they can be resolved and so lose their ancient hold on men.

Slowly but surely, despite all evidence to the contrary, the tide is turning. These powerful cosmic forces, under the great Law of Action and Reaction, are purifying the hearts and minds of men. A new dispensation is being built in which a new harmony will prevail. *In equal measure to the present discord so will be the peace.*

Stand ready to see the Great Lord, for the time of His emergence is nigh. Respond quickly to His call to aid Him in His task and end for ever the hatred and intolerance of men.

March 1997

The recognition of Maitreya

Very soon, the world will see the Teacher. The question arises: will people recognize Him? For the vast majority, recognition will not be difficult: seldom, indeed, does a man of His stature — demonstrating, radiating for all to see, the Love, the Wisdom, the Purpose and the Grace of God — come openly into our lives. Millions will respond and rally to His side, eager to implement the plans which, He will advise, are essential for the regeneration of life on Earth. Many will brook no delay, and catapult themselves into groupings and formations through which to tackle the manifold problems and needed changes which beset men today. Like men inspired — as indeed they will be — millions will begin the task of transformation — certain in the knowledge that they work towards the fulfilment of God's Plan for this Earth. Thus shall it be. And thus shall men begin to see themselves correctly, as brothers, working together for the good of all.

Not all men, however, will recognize Maitreya as the One awaited by all the nations. Steeped deeply in the world's scriptures, however fragmented, and however discoloured by time, many will turn away, at first, from this latest manifestation of God's continuing Plan for the world. They will find it hard to reconcile Maitreya's simple and practical approach with their mystical expectations and dogmas. Do not be surprised, therefore, by their angry and anxious rejection. Thus it was in Jesus' time. Thus, also, when the Buddha began His work. Thus, too, did Krishna know dissent and condemnation. Thus has it always been when the New has presented itself to the Old.

Be not afraid, therefore, when the "men of cloth" raise their voices against the Great Lord, naming Him Antichrist and arch-deceiver, for they know little of the laws which underlie their faiths and act and speak from ignorance and fear. They, too, are tested in this fashion.

Maitreya knows, already, those on whom He may count. Their numbers and their conviction are equal to the task. Within them shines the light of recognition and of hope, and their hearts' ardour guarantees success.

Soon, Maitreya will call men to His side, offering to lead them into a new and better world. Soon, therefore, will men be called upon to recognize the Teacher in their midst, and to take their stand on the side of truth; it is the truth of God's continuing concern for the needs of all men that Maitreya demonstrates. It is that which has brought Him, at the head of His illustrious Group, among us.

April 1997

Coping with change

When Maitreya comes before the world there will begin for men a period of intense heart-searching and reflection. It is only to be expected that for many it will be a painful, even traumatic, one. So steeped in the ways and ideas of the past, so fearful of a future unknown and strange, are millions today, that men will want to take stock of the new situation which will then pertain.

The necessity of change, radical and fundamental, will soon engage the minds of a growing number of statesmen and politicians, eager to add their voices and to put their stamp on the time. Far-reaching though they must be, the changes, it will be realized, must proceed at a pace commensurate with men's ability to adapt. Naught will be served by a too eager attempt to force the pace of transformation. Radically but logically, step by tested step, must the new foundations be built. On such firm rocks alone can the future stability of society be assured.

When Maitreya first announces His plans and hopes for the rehabilitation of the world, His energy of Love — the Sword of Cleavage — will further delineate the divisions which now exist. Men will take sides — for or against the new principles that He will present for the betterment of all. Thus will it be. Thus will a period of discord and discontent precede the acceptance of the new. Gradually, however, even the least sanguine will acknowledge the need for a reconstructed world and add their weight to the task.

There will begin a time unlike aught seen before on Earth. On every hand and at every level the changes will pursue their logical course, cementing in law and principle and form the aspirations of all. Thus will men regain a hold on their destiny and turn away for ever from the abyss. Not all men, of course, will view the future with equal pleasure. Diehards abound in every field and must be cajoled and humoured into compliance.

In time, even those who most oppose will renounce their intransigence and enter the field of labour for the common good.

A simpler and a better life awaits the builders of the new time. This is the time of test and choice. When men realize this they will gather round Maitreya and seek willingly His guidance and succour, glad to be of service and to confirm their identity with His aims.

May 1997

Synthesis

Wherever one looks, today, the signs of change become increasingly evident. Nowhere, it would seem, have the new energies failed to penetrate and make their presence felt. The turmoil and turbulence, now so widespread and severe, bear witness to their effect. Thus do the fires of purification perform their salutary task. All is being renewed, and cleansed of ancient wrong. Many misunderstand these signs of change and misinterpret their meaning, seeing only the breakdown of the familiar and the loss of icons on which they could rely. Thus do they fear for the future and regret the fading past.

From now on, a different vista will meet the eyes of men: a growing sense of order will colour man's affairs and lead eventually to an established synthesis. Thus will it be. Thus will men grasp the nature of the New and seek to implement its forms.

Frequently, men try to impose their own idea of order on disparate groups. Thus do the ideologies of hate and division cause havoc for the people. Inevitably, these fragile forms disintegrate for lack of wide support; dogma and doctrine cannot for ever rule the lives of men.

More and more, the quality of synthesis will engage the minds of men. More and more, they will discover its true meanings: a meeting of minds and hearts; identity of purposes; a fusion and blending in the experience of union with each other and the Source of all.

Thus will men learn the secret of life and love and thus will they become Gods.

When Maitreya appears before the world He will encourage men to explore the nature of these relationships and to seek to give them expression in the building of the new institutions.

Only thus can these structures embody the needs of all, and the new culture foster the spirit of inclusiveness.

Men must learn to live in harmony and mutual respect. The spirit of goodwill must underlie their thoughts and actions, and end for ever the competition which so drives men today. Only thus can the underlying synthesis bear its unique and proper fruit.

Soon, men will hear the words of Maitreya and be challenged to respond. They long to hear an appeal to their highest good, and when they do they will not be found wanting. Thus shall it be. Maitreya will invoke man's fundamental aspiration for Brotherhood and give it form and focus in the restructuring of the world.

June 1997

The future is assured

Conditioned by religious dogma, millions await the millennium as a time of cataclysm — indeed, many believe, the time for the ending of the world. While much destruction does occur as man upsets the natural balance of nature, the expectations of those who consult the scriptures in fear and trepidation will not be fulfilled. Eventually, even the present perturbations will subside.

New energies engender new possibilities, and today the world receives them in abundance. The present violent discord will soon give way to an established equilibrium, preparing the world for a further advance.

When conditions are more settled, men will be able more correctly to assess the true state of Being of mankind. This, they will find, is not so bleakly God-forsaken as many think today. There are, of course, many pockets of darkness, and hate and separation still rule the lives of countless groups of men. However, from Our point of vantage, We see the Light which ever stronger grows among those who aspire to express their true potential.

It is upon these that We turn Our Light to stimulate and sustain their efforts. Meanwhile, Maitreya's mighty ray enlightens the hearts of millions and turns them to the good.

This being so, We are not disheartened by the chaos which appears to threaten the future of mankind. Not all is well in man's abode but everywhere Our gaze alights We see the evidence of regeneration.

So do We joyfully await the day when, openly, We may walk among men once more. This time is almost now upon Us. We listen for the call. Then gladly will We advise and teach men from Our ages-long experience. Naught that We have to give will be withheld which safely may be given. Men themselves command the speed and scope of Our response.

When Maitreya appears before the world a new situation will develop: the old certainties will quickly disappear, to be replaced by a surge of hope in the New. A sense of life's adventure will enthral the young and prepare them for a life of service. Thus shall Maitreya, moving among men, inspire the creation of the New Dispensation. Man's long dream of Brotherhood will gradually become a fact, and, uplifted and inspired by this experience, men will surpass, even, their highest expectations. Have no fear, therefore, for the future is assured. The way back to the Source is plotted and planned. We are the guarantors of its reality.

July/August 1997

A time like no other

In normal times, it can be assumed that changes will take place slowly, if at all. Humanity needs much time to contemplate, to measure, and to respond to, all manifestations of possible change presented to it. Thus has it been and thus, it is expected, will be the future.

However, these are not, by any reckoning, normal times. Thus it is today that the speed of change accelerates, and out-distances by far, the capacity of many to respond and understand. They are left rudderless, without compass in the storm, and seek only to cling to the old certainties, which, sadly now, have left them unguarded and alone.

For many, this is a time of major confusion and fear. Little, it would seem, is there to change their apprehension that the long-expected Armageddon is soon upon us, that humanity is doomed, that the millennium heralds the end of all life as we have known it, and that we must prepare for the "end times".

Such is the view of so many today that it behoves those who know otherwise to raise their voices against these destructive thoughtforms; to raise, instead, men's hope of a better life for all.

This better life will be man's, beyond question. Maitreya and His Group are pledged to aid, in every possible way, man's further progress; all that the Law allows will be given — men cannot imagine the gifts which lie in store.

Sooner than many may think, the Great Lord will appear before the world, and, offering Himself in service to all, will create a new dispensation in which each will know and demonstrate his worth; each will see his brother as himself; his goal the establishment of true and lasting peace.

Thus will it be, and thus will a new and thrilling passion for life replace the present cynicism and distrust. Have no fear, the

Earth is not doomed nor about to end in chaos. On the contrary, plans are in hand for its regeneration and that of all its kingdoms.

Men will soon know that this is a time like no other before. Never in man's long history have the opportunities for such rapid progress as now pertains been his. Seize then this special time as the divine blessing which it is and move boldly forward into the future. Take heart from these words from One Who knows the Plan and Who calmly awaits its manifestation by the hands of men. Your Elder Brother knows that man will triumph.

September 1997

A nation mourns

When a nation loses a major representative, the people, as a whole, suffer trauma and shock. Thus it is today in the United Kingdom. The death of Princess Diana, the "People's Princess", has wrung the hearts of millions, and an unprecedented display of "People's Power" has conditioned the extent and the nature of her mourning.

That the people loved her is manifest and not in doubt. That she, in turn, loved them and sought to serve them has evoked the aspiration of millions and shown their readiness for the message of Maitreya — the Lord of Love. It was the love, the concern and caring, of Diana which won the people's hearts.

Nations, of course, are complex entities, and many and various are the strands which together form their nature. Britain now, however, is one whose soul is somewhat manifesting, and it is, indeed, the soul's love, of Britain, that the world is witnessing today. Nor is it by chance that Maitreya, the Embodiment of Love, resides in Britain's capital.

When Maitreya appears openly before the world, He will likewise stimulate the love nature of the people of all the nations, thus creating a vortex of love whose radiance will transform the lives of men. In this way, through man himself, the Great Lord will work to complete His mission: restoring Divinity to Its true place in the hearts of men.

From now on, a new mood will prevail around the world. The great ideals: Tolerance and Sharing; Justice and Brotherhood, will imprint their message on the minds and hearts of people everywhere, and into that atmosphere of heightened aspiration Maitreya will emerge.

The time of Emergence is now upon us. Naught can now delay the open appearance of the Great Lord. Before long, the world will know that succour is at hand, that the problems pressing today on the minds of many are solvable and transitory, and that their solution lies unused in the hands of men. Thus will it be. Thus will Maitreya hearken to the need of all men for participation in their destiny; an opportunity to express their heartfelt longing for justice and peace; the manifestation of their intrinsic divine nature; to show their readiness to follow His lead and to create a world in which separation no longer rules and divides the peoples of the Earth. The Lord of Love comes forth. The Christ, the Eldest of the great family of brothers, emerges forthwith.

October 1997

The choice is man's

The importance of being alive at this time is that it provides to all the opportunity to serve the Plan and the planet as never before. No one, today, should feel excluded from this unique opportunity, however humble or restricted their circumstances — the planet belongs to all and the Plan involves all.

More and more, the planet's precarious state of imbalance, created by man's misuse, sounds a warning note which men ignore at their peril. The very breath by which men live is threatened, the air, polluted and poisoned, wreaks havoc on the lives of many millions.

Into this crisis has come Maitreya. He knows the dangers better than any man. What can He do to help men save themselves from further suffering, and to restore the planet to full and vibrant health?

The Karmic Law controls the nature and the scope of the aid that He may give. Advice and guidance will be man's for the asking but men must be prepared to change the present modes of living to ensure the planet's future and the future of their children. The resources of the Earth are finite but with good husbandry and sharing, adequate for the needs of all.

Men must, therefore, redefine these needs, and enter into a new and truer understanding of the meaning and the purpose of their lives. This will come when a measure, even, of sharing has replaced the present destructive competition, and led man away from the precipice edge. The choice is man's: to share and flourish, or to continue in deadly competition and together die.

That men will choose the way of Life is not in doubt — the hearts of men, when tested, are found ever to be sound.

Thus will men be readied for the next phase of the Plan: the establishment of Right Human Relationships, the expression through men of the love nature of God.

Many, today, doubt that such an ideal is capable of fulfilment, given the manifested selfishness and greed of humanity today. Nevertheless, We know that within the hearts of all men burns the same aspiration for Justice and Brotherhood, the same hope of ending the fear that underlies the selfishness and greed.

We, your Elder Brothers, have known that same greed, that same selfish desire and fear. That We have conquered is the guarantee that all men can do the same. We do not doubt. We *know* that man will rise to the test — and triumph.

November 1997

The time has come

No longer must the world wait for the public sight of Maitreya. Soon, before the nations, the Great Lord will appear, and, addressing them as an Elder Brother, make known His hopes and plans. He will, of course, emphasize the need for sharing, the key to all future progress for the race. He will, too, show that sharing of resources is the simplest to achieve of all the many changes required to steer men back from catastrophe. When men share, He will say, they will renew their faith in life.

Soon, very soon, the media networks will carry the news that a new voice speaks, a new vision presents itself to the people, a new concern demonstrates its compassion for the suffering of millions and calls forth the heart's love of men. Thus will it be. Thus will Maitreya awaken the conscience of the peoples, and thus will the people awaken to their opportunity to serve the Plan and their destiny.

When Maitreya appears, He will address the major problems which now beset humanity: the misery of the starving — the dire poverty of millions condemned to living hell; the many wars now raging, known or unheard; the vast army of refugees, displaced and discarded; the prisoners of conscience whose voices are muted in pain. Maitreya will call for a greater responsibility for the planet's health: the creation of an economy sustainable and fair; the husbandry of resources to safeguard future generations; the purification of the environment — the air, the soil, the waters, on which all life depends. These Maitreya will address and offer His solutions.

Unknown, as yet, to all but a few, Maitreya must now enter the world stage and present His ideas to all. Many will see the normality and justice of His views but others, sadly, will resent His intrusion into man's affairs and will call for His exclusion. Thus will the Sword of Cleavage present to men their choice: to continue on the downward slope to unrelenting suffering and pain — or to remedy the ills of the past and enter into their birthright.

Maitreya will call for everyone to join His army of helpers — to sustain and purify the environment; to galvanize the peoples into action on their own behalf; to cleanse the planet of polluting toxins and to re-establish harmony among the nations. His task is not little but He stands ready to fight the present evil — and to conquer.

December 1997

Man's essential choice

When man awakens to the knowledge of his true nature a profound transformation will take place on Earth. That event is not so far distant, as many might assume. Even now, the signs are appearing that show Us, your Elder Brothers, that many are awakening to this blessed truth. The Magnet of Evolution, God's spiritual engine, draws forward and upward many now ready for this revelation. Many stand at the portal, ready to know themselves as Gods. In time, so many will have passed through the gate that the divinity of man will become acknowledged fact. Thus will it be, and thus, too, will men recognize their Oneness.

To aid this process, Maitreya and His Disciples stand ready to emerge, adding Their gifts of love and experience to man's endeavour. Without Their Presence, man's progress would indeed be slow, hazardous, even, in the extreme.

Today, the world awaits, knowingly or not, the manifestation of Maitreya, openly, in men's midst. Likewise does Maitreya eagerly await the moment when His face can be seen by all, His words resound in expectant minds and His love penetrate the open hearts of all who love their fellow-men. Recent events encouraged the hope that His emergence might begin ere the close of the year now ended but, with Us, plans are made — and discarded — as circumstances dictate, and no single date is irrevocably set. Essentially, however, that moment is now upon us, and men may expect to see the Great Lord at any time.

When, soon, that day arrives, many will experience the extraordinary potency of Maitreya's love, the profound knowledge of the human situation which is His, the practical steps to remedy that situation which He will advocate. Theirs will be the task to measure, to assess and to make their choice: freedom and justice for all, and an end to human misery — or an end to man's sojourn on Earth in humiliation and defeat.

325

Maitreya knows that men will rightly choose; that He has not come in vain. He knows that burning brightly in men's hearts is the aspiration, the longing, for brotherhood and justice, for right relationship and trust. Maitreya's leadership and love are the twin keys to unlock the hearts of men.

Readers of these pages will know what to expect, will sense how to react. Take this opportunity to serve your brothers and sisters throughout the world by telling them the glad tidings. Awaken them to the priceless experience and choice which will soon be theirs. Encourage them with hope and expectation of a better, happier future and open, thus, their hearts for Maitreya's love.

January/February 1998

The seeds of wisdom

Never before in the history of the world has so much depended on man's decision and choice. Man is now the chief arbiter of his fate. His nursery days are over and he is capable, at last, of rational thought and action. Very soon, his insight and common sense will be put fully to the test.

Emerging from his long dependence, man, himself, takes the helm and guides his life to victory or perdition. This is, in every sense, a turning-point in history. What, we may ask, will man decide? The choice is clear, the future, if he fails, is bleak indeed.

Men must come to see all men as One, brothers all in infinite variety, requiring, each, the wherewithal to live. This simple realization must find its place in the hearts of all to guarantee the future of all.

To help men to see this, Maitreya has set His sights on early emergence. He knows that many will find His teaching unpalatable, that many vested interests stand in the way of ready acceptance. He knows, too, that men essentially long for justice and peace, that only a small minority dream otherwise and cannot be won over. His task is not an easy one but neither does He work in vain.

Already, the signs of a new awareness by men of the peril in which they stand are clear to see; slowly but surely, the lessons of life are being learned. Many, if only in their thoughts, are turning away from the crude and cruel competition which dominates today. They look for new and better ways to earn their livelihoods and to relate to others. The soil is, therefore, fertile for Maitreya to plough and sow.

The seeds of wisdom and truth which He will sow will generate in men a new depth of focus, a new and serious assessment of man's predicament, and a realization of the pressing factor of time in the healing of Earth's ills.

Those who respond will flock to His banner and engage in the tasks of education and action. Thus will it be, and thus will men themselves heal the wounds of the past and enter into their birthright as free agents of the divine. Gone will be the old certainties and gone the old conditioning. A new, fresher and more wholesome stance of independent thought and practical consideration will replace the present doctrines.

A new clarity and insight will replace, too, the present ignorance of vast areas of consciousness and life. The tentacles of materialism will release their hold on men's minds, and a broader, more inclusive realism will fashion the forms of the new civilization. Thus will it be.

March 1998

The blueprint of the Divine

We, the Elder Brothers of the race, stand ready to emerge from Our ancient retreats. Already, a considerable Vanguard have prepared the way. Their presence, albeit unknown to all but a few, has made deep inroads into the ignorance and superstition which still condition vast numbers of men. Their disciples, men and women of high calibre in the various countries, dispense, daily, the essence of Their teaching. In this way, men are being made ready for the historic days ahead.

When the time is right, these disciples will come forward, trained in the ways of the future, and, by dint of obvious knowledge and integrity, will be elected to positions of influence and power. Thus will it be. Thus will the Masters, effectively but under Law, work through Their representatives in the world. The time of this event draws ever nearer.

These working disciples, men and women of different nationality and background, have in common a deep love for their brothers and sisters wherever they may be, an altruistic concern for the good of all and a proved ability to implement their will and aspiration. They will set in motion the changes which, in gathering momentum, will lay the foundations for the structures of the New Age.

Behind the scenes, groups of Masters will continue the work of stimulus and teaching until a vast network of educated and inspired disciples has been formed — all dedicated to the task of transforming, for the better, the ways and ideas of men. Thus, gradually, a new world will be created by man himself, aided by Us, your Elder Brothers and Mentors. Thus will the tasks of reconstruction and succour be accomplished under Law.

Many await this coming time with fear, cognizant of the far-reaching changes which must take place to purify and render harmless the wayward actions of men. When, however, the necessity of change is grasped and understood, the majority will gladly lend their weight to its implementation.

When Maitreya appears before the world the signal will be given for this work to begin. Each will choose his part, large or small, and each will know his contribution is vital to the whole. Thus will men, together, work for the good of all, and thus, together, will they find themselves in each other's hearts.

Thus will men learn to love and to know the joy of brotherhood and justice. Thus will they demonstrate on every hand the blueprint of the Divine.

April 1998

Unique is the time

For many today there is every sign that the world is moving headlong to destruction. On each hand they see their icons fall, their hopes fade, their future threatened. Lost and bewildered, they cast about for succour, unable to withstand the impact of the new. Few are the signs, they believe, that good can come from the current speed of change, nor, can they hope, that they will benefit. Locked thus in fear, the future for such looks bleak indeed.

How mistaken are they, if only they did know. How far from the truth is their concept of the future.

Could they but catch a glimpse of the wonder which awaits them, their fears would turn to joyful expectation, their hearts aglow with the fire of aspirations fulfilled.

Marvellous are the possibilities which demand the attention of men; unique is the time for the enlargement of man's consciousness: a time like no other in the history of the world. Why should men fear with such a prospect?

When Maitreya and His Group emerge, men will realize that their fears are groundless, that naught but good awaits the sons of men, bolstered in faith and courage by the presence of the Sons of God. Thus will it be, and thus will men awaken to the possibilities which the future presents to rise in stature and scope; to take up their predestined role as the Keepers and the Nourishers of the lower kingdoms; to harness the forces of the universe and to use them for the good of all.

Naught but man himself can prevent man from fulfilling his destiny.

When men are ready to accept the principle of sharing all things become possible. The ties of trust and respect thus engendered will release mountainous waves of energy which, focused and controlled, will transform the world. Nothing then can halt the forward march and progress of man. Nothing then can daunt the fiery spirit of awakened man. Claiming his birthright man will become a God.

The presence of the Sons of God is the guarantee that man will indeed inherit his birthright, and take his place beside his Elder Brothers — caring and comforting, teaching and counselling, revealing and inspiring, those who follow after.

Man stands at the threshold of great things. Naught can deter or limit him if he follows the example of the Brothers — and wills it so.

May 1998

The reception of Maitreya

Maitreya knows that when He steps forward into the world arena a mixed reception will be forthcoming from humanity. There are many who look forward to that moment with joyful expectation, who will see it as the beginning of the New Time which awaits the sons of men.

There are others, however, understanding little of the meaning and process of His advent, who will look askance and doubt His credentials, fearfully aware of scriptural warnings which they all too readily misinterpret.

Others, too, will simply watch from the sidelines, awaiting a lead from those they hold in some esteem.

Thus will humanity range themselves on one side or the other: those who welcome the Teacher with open arms, eager to follow His precepts and advice; and those who see Him as the embodiment of evil and all that they distrust.

Thus will the Sword of Cleavage do its work, revealing those who stand for freedom and justice, for practical goodwill and love; revealing also those whose suspicion and fear, prejudice and hate prevent their recognition of the truth of Maitreya's message of compassion and love. Thus will it be, and thus will men be tested as guardians of their future.

When the initial shock of Maitreya's presentation calms, people will see that within much which to them is mysterious and new, much remains logical and practical, self-evident and true. Ancient truths re-uttered will echo in their minds as long-remembered certainties, upholding their faith in life. The aspiration lying at the heart of human evolution will assert its beneficent power and awaken men to the opportunity to serve as never before; to find a new hope and purpose; and to create the outer forms of the new civilization. Thus will it be.

Look forward to this time which is near at hand; Maitreya stands on the threshold of His emergence, ready to do battle with separation and greed. Rally to His call for justice and freedom, reconciliation and peace, and place your all at the service of the race. This is a time like none before. This is a time which will never be repeated. Look deeply into your hearts and make your choice: a future bathed in light and love — or a denial of your destiny.

Maitreya knows the time is ripe for change. He knows humanity is ready for the test. He stands ready to emerge and begin His mission.

June 1998

The coming century

When mankind nears a moment of major crisis it reacts in one of two ways: either it falls into apathy, awaiting, fatalistically, the inevitable, or else it is galvanized into indiscriminate action and runs in all directions without sense or purpose. Today, at this time of change, it is the latter reaction which holds sway. Everywhere, men act as if the future no longer exists, as if they represent the ending of meaning and value on Earth. Greed has taken hold of their hearts and senses, and, as if in dream, they walk wild-eyed to the precipice.

Thus it is that men approach the coming century: many in fear and most in doubt. They know nothing of the marvels which await mankind's astonished eyes. They know less of the wonders which they, themselves, will one day perform. Ignorant and afraid, they grasp blindly at all that they can hold in greedy hands, thinking that thus they may be safe, and secure from future loss.

While many live thus, there is a growing number who are awakening to a different view, who see the possibility of undreamed of harmony, and who resist both apathy and chaos. As yet, they are the minority, but soon the forces of chaos will succumb to their vision of justice and peace; a new world will be born from their fearless hold on life and creative action. These men and women of goodwill will challenge the old concepts of division and strife, and, stage by stage, will reconstruct the world. Thus will it be. Not alone but guided and inspired by Maitreya and His Brothers, this group of stout hearts will wax strong and influential, eagerly encouraged by the following masses.

In a short time, major inroads will be made into solving the many problems which afflict mankind today: hunger and oppressive poverty and the denial of basic rights; destructive competition among the nations and environmental decay; ethnic bigotry and the army of refugees which results; above all, the scourge of war.

When men realize that these problems are solvable naught will for long delay their ending. With a will, men will tackle them one by one, with growing understanding of the urgency and the means.

Maitreya and His growing group of Masters will show the way, outline the possibilities and pitfalls, encourage and inspire. Men, themselves, will set in place the framework of the new world, born out of necessity, out of a longing for justice and peace, for the establishment of brotherhood and the rule of divine law.

July/August 1998

The world, today, is One

Maitreya stands ready to emerge. Recent events in the 'gambling palaces', East and West, encourage the expectation of an early approach to humanity. Not for long can the Western economies withstand the contagion which has brought the Eastern nations to their knees. The world, today, is one, and slowly and painfully the nations are awakening to this fact.

That said, there is little doubt that the major Western powers will seek to ensure their own survival at all costs. Self-interest will (as always) be the order of the day, and gone will be even the semblance of altruism in dealing with the world crisis. However, so interconnected is the present world economy, so various and so widespread the investment in each other's industry and financial structures, that soon these shaky structures will themselves collapse, leaving the world ready for the new.

It is to encourage the acceptance of a new approach that Maitreya will work, exhorting the nations to accept that sharing alone will solve their problems, that without sharing and justice, peace will elude them always.

Gone for ever must be the reign of the freebooters, the cavalier disdain for the rights of others. No longer must the exploitation of millions be the source of corporate wealth, and be acceptable as the norm.

When Maitreya speaks, He will draw attention to these major ills of present society and sound the call for change. The collapse of the stock markets will awaken men to the disease of speculation which is destroying the very fibre of men's lives.

Thus shall Maitreya become a central figure in the period immediately ahead. Thus will men find a leader of thought, a spokesman for the oppressed, and thus will men awaken to the new light which Maitreya's teaching brings — the light of wisdom and truth.

Perhaps, at first, men will doubt the efficacy of Maitreya's plans, but in time they will see that no other course will bring relief to the poverty and pain suffered by half the world. The downward-spiralling stock markets will signal the end of an era of rampant greed and a new realism will replace the present chaos. Men and women everywhere will rally to Maitreya's side, their aspiration awakened as never before, their hearts aglow with the opportunity to serve a most worthy cause: nothing less than the recreation of this world.

Soon the call will ring out: Share and save the world! Justice alone will bring us peace! Men everywhere are brothers!

September 1998

The restoration of the Plan

For the first time in recent history humanity is beginning to realize its interdependence. For many centuries, the nations have fought and pillaged one another, leaving in their wake untold misery and despair. While many pockets of such violence still persist, the peoples, on the whole, have renounced — at least in theory — this unholy practice. The last two major conflagrations have purified the race and made possible a new approach to life.

This also makes possible the return to the world, in open view, of the World Teacher; this time not alone but together with His disciples, the senior members of the Hierarchy of which He is the head. The Kingdom of God will thus be made manifest, openly, among men. This is a return to the conditions which prevailed in ancient Atlantean times, one hundred thousand years ago. Then, the Masters walked among men and were known for what They are, the Guardians and Teachers of the race.

Now, as we enter the Aquarian Age, the spiral of history unfolds a new possibility of progress for humanity and the Plan. The Presence of the Masters will act as a galvanizing magnet, stimulating millions into action to restore to equilibrium this world. Thus will men renew their association with their mentors and Elder Brothers, and thus will they move forwards and upwards at accelerated pace. The time has come for this happy and holy reunion.

Behind the scenes, the Masters have prepared Themselves most arduously for this time, and welcome the opportunity to serve in more open fashion; They, too, have longed for closer contact with Their younger brothers. From now on, that contact will increase, leading to a time of mutual interdependence in which mankind will itself assume responsibility for the furtherance of the Plan.

We are nearing a time of transformation extraordinary in extent. Soon, very soon now, the world will awaken to the reality of economic collapse. The financial structures of the present will be exposed as the shameful mechanisms which they are — condemning millions to poverty, starvation and want while others "parade their wealth before the poor".

Soon, Maitreya will step forward and make known His voice. His precepts will resound: "Only Sharing will save the world." "Make Sharing and Justice your banner and know true peace." "Have faith in Sharing and transform life on Earth. There is no other way."

Thus will Maitreya galvanize and inspire the creation of a new approach to living, and thus will men, themselves, open their hearts to the possibility of the New, and restore the Plan on Earth.

October 1998

The New Age is upon us

For many years, it has become natural and usual to speak of the New Age and what it means for humanity's future. Few recognize or understand the changing astronomical relationship which makes a New Age possible — and inevitable. For more than two thousand years, the major cosmic energy conditioning life on Earth has streamed to us from the constellation of Pisces. That influence is fast waning as our sun moves away from relationship to Pisces and into that of Aquarius.

The new energies of Aquarius, mounting daily in potency, are already making their presence felt, and lie behind the changes, in every sphere, which are now occurring on a global scale. These changes must, and will, reflect the quality, the inner nature, of the Aquarian energy — namely, Synthesis.

These energies of Synthesis, fusing and blending the different strands of our multifaceted life, have the task of bringing humanity to an awareness of its Oneness, an appreciation of its part in the Great Plan, and an ability to manifest that Plan in right relationship on the physical plane.

The first steps are being taken now as the nations wrestle with the problems of a dying economic structure and changing political affiliations. The early signs of a new global consciousness can be seen as men realize the need for co-operation in dealing with their environmental problems. This augers well for the future and shows correct response to a major danger facing the race: unless the damage now being done to the environmental balance of the planet is quickly restored, the life expectancy of many will dramatically decrease. No one, rich or poor, is totally free from this insidious breakdown of the human immune system. Men tamper with that system at their peril.

Notwithstanding the seriousness of these and other problems, much progress is being made in tackling them, and many groups exist, worldwide, whose main concern is to bring these hazards to the notice of the governmental agencies in every country.

That being so, there is every expectation that the nations will emerge from this period of trial with a new confidence in the future, and in the benefits of co-operation and mutual help.

In this way, the energies of Aquarius are, indeed, bringing the peoples together, creating the ties of co-operation and understanding, and, albeit slowly and gradually, welding the disparate forces of the present dispensation into a synthetic whole.

The New Age is truly upon us. The imminent advent of Maitreya and His Group will signal its inauguration.

November 1998

Prelude to change

Throughout the world there is a growing sense of impending change. The collapse of major currencies and financial agencies has shaken the fabric of the world economy and initiated attempts to shore up, and rectify if possible, the crumbling edifice of the global economic structure. These last-minute attempts will not succeed. In the short term, they may but delay the ultimate collapse of a system no longer viable, or useful to the vast majority of men. As the millennium fast approaches, the old, outworn structures are losing their stability and coherence, thus clearing the ground for the construction of the new-age forms.

These new forms must embrace the ideals and aspirations of *all* men for a more just world, a world no longer torn and divided into rich and poor, powerful and weak. They must, above all, embrace the idea of synthesis, the inner, spiritual intention of the Aquarian dispensation.

When Maitreya emerges into full public work, He will lay the foundations of these new approaches to living: He will emphasize men's Oneness and the need for sharing, justice and freedom as the only guarantee of peace; He will call on all men to forgive and to forget the wrongs of the past; He will sound the clarion-call to work together for the good of all.

Thus will the Great Lord show the way ahead for all who are ready to begin the journey to the future. Thus will He indicate the steps which must be taken or avoided if the race of men would survive and prosper.

It needs little imagination to see how potent will be the effect of Maitreya's words and presence. Never before in man's history has a man of such stature and accomplishments offered His unique service and knowledge to the world. With Him, too, are

His Disciples, Themselves perfected Masters, ready and eager to begin Their work of salvage and succour.

Despite appearances, the world is changing for the better; the present collapsing structures are but the essential prelude to a much-needed sense of realism by which man can readjust his values and bring new meaning and purpose to his life. Maitreya and His Group are here to stimulate this process, to aid in every situation, to act as the Elder Brothers that They are. Soon, They will be known as the Advisers and Keepers of the Truth, the Mentors of those who would learn the ways of Right Relationship and who are ready to work for their brothers and sisters throughout the world. These are many and are known already. Add yourselves to that growing number and show *now* that you are one of His people.

December 1998

The common good

As the millennium draws ever nearer, it becomes increasingly evident that new values are gradually entering the minds and hearts of humanity. No longer are millions, erstwhile all but slaves, prepared to tolerate their lot; they rise against the tyranny which oppresses them and demand a better life.

Elsewhere, a new concern for honesty and the rule of law calls into question and condemns the corruption and *laissez-faire* of the recent past. A new sense of responsibility for others grips the conscience of many who seek to serve their brothers and sisters around the world. From whence comes this cleansing power, this salutary Grace?

For many years now, Maitreya has focused in the world the energy of the Spirit of Peace or Equilibrium. This mighty, cosmic Avatar is changing, under our eyes, the fabric of men's lives. Through His beneficent power, that which destroyed and tore apart is rendered harmless and benign; that which separates and divides now seeks to bring together. In equal measure, in opposite balance, Action and Reaction impose their restoring rhythm, and bring harmony to the world.

When Maitreya works openly, men will see more clearly the working of this great Law.

Meanwhile, the old order crumbles, driven to the edge by its own extremes. Men are witnessing the collapse of the Empire of Greed, the tyranny of market forces, the freebooter's heyday. From now on, the tendency in all affairs will be towards the Common Good. That which works for and upholds the Common Good will flourish; that which works against will wither away. Thus will the new forms and institutions fulfil the needs of all men.

The time is soon coming when the Common Weal will be the benchmark by which all actions are judged. Thus will be safeguarded the integrity of the new.

Many are clamouring for change yet fear its advent, so influenced are their minds by established institutions and media. When Maitreya, soon, emerges, men will realize that the changes which He will advocate are for the betterment of all men, that no group need fear the future. Thus will the Great Lord work to unite the forces for Good, to invoke the latent Goodwill in all.

Soon, Maitreya will begin His process of Emergence, appearing before the people in many public broadcasts. Thus will He gain the interest and attention of the masses whose voices will call for His Declaration.

Thus will the Teacher fulfil His pledge to return among men and to lead them into a new and higher light. Thus will it be, and thus will men begin again their journey to the stars.

January/February 1999

Inclusiveness the key

At present, a lull has occurred in the international financial collapse. The economies of several nations, tottering on the brink, have been shored up by the international banks and agencies to a greater or lesser degree. This effort to avoid a total breakdown of the present economic system is doomed to failure and cannot for long endure.

So great are the tensions inherent in the vast differences in economic power wielded by the various nations that true stability is impossible to achieve. This being so, it is only a question of time before the whole shaky edifice collapses ignominiously.

This will be the signal and the opportunity for a complete reappraisal of the economic priorities of the world. The needs of all peoples are the same: adequate food, housing, education and healthcare are the essential requirements without which men cannot reach, nor render to society, their full potential. Millions, today, are denied these basic rights.

When Maitreya emerges, His first priority will be to address this fundamental problem, to show how simple it is to change the *status quo* when men see themselves as brothers. He will advocate, as a matter of urgency, the sharing of the necessities of life more equitably as the prerequisite for a stable world society. Thus will He draw the peoples together and commit them to transformation. When men see the need, and recognize the possibilities thus revealed, they will gladly adhere to Maitreya's recommendations and implement the needed changes. Thus will men, themselves, construct the foundations of the new world. Eagerly, they will seek the advice of Maitreya and His group of Masters, thus avoiding the pitfalls which might otherwise nullify their efforts. That advice will, graciously, be given, so steering men into safe and welcoming harbours.

Naught but that which fulfils the needs of all will Maitreya advocate. His inclusiveness, therefore, will determine the nature and the form of all transformations. Thus will men learn to see the higher vision, the reality of a world shorn of division and selfish greed; of power-hungry domination of the weak and poor; and, in growing unison, of the possibility of a world without war or want, without competition and the needless sacrifice of the many for the few.

Thus will it be. Thus will Maitreya inspire the creation of a new and better world. Thus will He invoke the innate Good in all men, and show them the way to fulfil their divine destiny as Sons of God.

March 1999

The end of the 'barbarian age'

There will come a time when humanity will look back on this time as the 'barbarian age'. So far from the possible ideal is the present dying civilization that future men will wonder how, and for so long, were we able to sustain it.

There are many causes and factors involved in this sad situation: the long, slow, decline in man's relation to man runs parallel to, and reflects, the growing sophistication of his weaponry. His present, triumphant ability to kill from places continents apart sets the seal on his progress to self-destruction. War has been made clinical and impersonal: no longer need the warrior witness the look of terror on his victim's face.

In this situation, it is small wonder that man's institutions, political and economic, reflect, in their turn, this growing alienation of men from the wellsprings of their lives. Commercialization, that burgeoning but stealthy and often hidden menace, controls now the lives and destiny of countless millions, and reduces to a cypher the God-given individuality of man. People are now statistics without purpose or needs, pawns on the chessboard of market forces and company profits.

The arid desert which we call the modern world leaves men bereft of that which makes them human: happy, creatively fulfilled, quick to respond to each other's needs, and free. Deadly competition corrodes the human spirit and now sits in judgement on the 'battle' of life. Life, the Great Adventure, has been corrupted and replaced by an agonizing and unfair struggle for mere survival.

To be sure, these dire conditions are not everywhere and uniformly present but for vast numbers they represent the reality of their lives, and, unless men change direction, they can only worsen.

When Maitreya enters, openly, the world arena, He will show men that such a life of pain and struggle is not inevitable, is not their only option; that another way is theirs by right if it is their will.

He will show that already, amid the chaos and mounting greed, men are reacting against such weakening of the sacred ties of life; that great new forces are generating a new beginning, and that out of the present turmoil is gradually emerging a higher, truer demonstration of the inborn capacity of man to meet the challenges of his time and to overcome his difficulties.

Maitreya will remind men of their own high origin and destiny, and will inspire the creation of a new way of living: in harmony, in right relationship, without recourse to war or competition, in the fullest co-operation and mutual respect. Thus will it be.

April 1999

All things new

For many centuries men have awaited the events which are now coming to pass. Consciously or not, they have sensed the possibility of planetary renewal and looked forward to the presence of a teacher or saviour to point their feet in that direction. Notwithstanding their beliefs and actions to the contrary, men have always known that evolution proceeds according to plan, that naught can halt that process, and that only ignorance and neglect have alienated them from their experience of many lives ago.

Today, around the world, a new and vibrant expectation heralds the arrival of the Teacher, albeit in a manner and guise unusual and unexpected. For many, it denotes the fulfilment of their cherished doctrines and prophecies, for others it is the answer to their prayers for succour and guidance.

To humanity as a whole, it offers the possibility of a complete change in perception of life's purpose and meaning, and the opportunity to contribute their individual gifts of talents and energy to the transformation of this world. That is no small task and will require the concerted dedication, skill and, above all, goodwill of all men to accomplish. They will not act alone nor without guidance. In every endeavour, men can expect to receive the help and encouragement of their Elder Brothers, Those Who have gone before and Whom men call Masters. We stand ready to inspire and to assist in every action which benefits and unites the race of men. Fear not, therefore, the awesomeness of the task, for help will be yours on every hand.

There are many actions which, as yet, men are unable to perform, lacking not only the means but the awareness of the need. These, where possible within the Law, We shall accomplish for you. Thus shall We lead you, step by step, along the Path of Achievement, saving you much hardship and many false starts.

Today, Maitreya, Our Master, performs many tasks which only He may do as the Agent of Divine Intervention. Thus does He speed the day when all may see Him. That day comes ever closer and will be the signal that the New Age has begun; that the New Livingness which He embodies is being spread abroad; that humanity has within itself the means to right the ills of the world, and needs only courage and the trust in its own Divinity to make all things new.

May 1999

The rule of Law

Since mankind has, for the most part, rejected the rule of Law, it has experienced a series of disasters which it has interpreted as 'acts of God'. These 'acts of men' bear little resemblance to the planned evolution of this Earth. When men realize this, they will make a concerted effort to readjust their thinking and actions, and thus set to rights the 'rule of Law'. Gradually, the rhythm of the Law will impose itself on life and a new harmony and greater equilibrium will result.

To aid this process, a mighty Avatar stands behind Maitreya. The Spirit of Peace or Equilibrium, through the Law of Action and Reaction, pours His cosmic Presence upon the chaos of this world. Men do but dimly, so far, register the impact of this transforming force; nevertheless, the energies of Equilibrium now saturate the Earth. This being so, men can look forward to an extraordinary era of calm, different, indeed, from the turmoil of today.

Within that unparalleled era of peace and calm the new civilization will grow to ever more glorious heights: reaching for the stars, man will conquer space and destroy the illusion of time. The energies of cosmos, today unknown, will be harnessed and put to use. A growing sense of his divinity will drive man to look deeply within, finding thereby the essence of his true identity and his oneness with nature and God. Thus will his environment, no longer abused and prostituted to his ends, flourish and render back the sustenance for all his needs.

Thus will the new civilization represent the next great step in the unfoldment of the Plan. Thus will man regain the momentum of his evolution, lost so long ago. And thus shall We, your Elder Brothers, watch and encourage, warn and protect, and experience the joy of man's return to the fold. Thus shall it be.

As Maitreya has so often stated: "men must see themselves as One." This is the essential first step to all future progress; on the fulfilment of that condition everything else depends. The first task of Maitreya and His group will be to show men that this is so, that only then can self-destruction be avoided, that only then can the sleeping potential of man be unleashed for its next and great achievement.

We do not doubt that men will awaken to their Oneness. Underlying all man's restless striving is the dawning awareness that all must share in the solving of the huge and manifold problems which beset them today; that the responsibility, like the problems, is global and indivisible, and that only through co-operation and self-denial can they adequately be met and overcome.

Maitreya, soon to appear before the world, has the task of opening men's minds to these truths. Do not doubt His ability and success.

June 1999

A hard lesson

Rarely does man see beforehand the consequences of his actions, and rare it is, indeed, even if he does, that he allows such knowledge to inhibit his activity. The pull of desire is so strong that, for most, its demands are all-compelling.

Thus it is today in Yugoslavia where the desire for power of one weak and wilful man has caused untold misery and death to many thousands. Those nations now in contention with this ruthless adventurer ignore at their peril the brutal history of this reckless man. The United Nations, standing and sounding as one, must indict and try him as the criminal he has shown himself to be. Otherwise, peace in the Balkans — and, by imitation, elsewhere — is a forlorn hope.

Naturally, the nations are divided in their response to the actions of the NATO forces. They have each their various reasons for hesitation and criticism, but without such action the tyrants of this world would cause ever greater mischief and suffering to their peoples and imagined foes.

We, your Elder Brothers, are never advocates of war but neither do We advocate a lame acceptance of genocide and human degradation; the world, today, is too fraught with dangers for such appeasement.

From now on, the nations must plan ahead for such contingencies, and let be known their will to act. The sentimental call for peace at any price is not Our way; the Path of Love must also be the Path of Justice and Sanity.

The question arises: how to proceed to end a tragic episode in recent European history? Nothing less than the complete abandonment of this cruel endeavour of separation by the Serbian leadership should be acceptable under the rule of law. Otherwise this evil adventure will inspire others to emulate its ambition and prove a constant threat. The return of the refugees and their rehabilitation is a major priority; the reconstruction of their torched and pillaged villages a daunting task. The Serbian people should be held responsible for the reparations required and thus, in some measure, assuage their guilt. Huge loans will be needed by the Yugoslav Federation to enable them to meet these obligations and to rebuild their own war-shattered homeland. They must be made to see the unacceptability of their nationalistic ambitions and the need to abandon a leadership which leads them so astray.

This is not the first time that the bitter ferment of the Balkans has erupted in war. The world is now too small and too interconnected to allow this age-old separation to do its destructive work. Wise diplomacy, broad vision, and the threat of force of arms must together calm the fires of territorial ambition and ethnic pride.

We, the Teachers, watch closely this hard lesson for humanity, and, in the present situation, are not discouraged.

July/August 1999

A testing time

Without doubt, this is a most testing time for humanity. All await a sign, a signal, that the time ahead bodes well, that the much prophesied Armageddon is not the nemesis foretold, but a figment, only, of man's fear and imagination. Nevertheless, many continue to hold to that sad conclusion to man's sojourn on Earth and poison, therefore, the atmosphere of hope. Certainly, signs of hope abound but man's doubts prevent his correct assessment and understanding.

With the advent of Maitreya all of this will change. His presence will reassure the masses that their future is safe, that a new light shines in their midst, and that the era of Brotherhood beckons them into its creation. They will know beyond doubt that their needs can and will be met, that they matter and have meaning and purpose. In a new experience of self-worth they will gladly adopt the methods of self-transformation. The ancient dogmas and fears will lose their tenacious hold and in that unaccustomed freedom men will renew their joy in life and welcome change. Thus will it be, and thus will the Great Lord inspire and attract the love and devotion of countless millions.

As a Teacher, Maitreya is beyond peer; We, His immediate disciples, know this to be so. Ages-long experience has taught Him the Wisdom, the loving understanding, to enter into the hearts and minds of all, and thus to inspire all to emulate His attainment. Even today, many are beginning to respond to His unseen presence and are finding within themselves that this is so. When Maitreya emerges fully and openly, this process will quicken dramatically until all will know that the Christ is once again living and teaching among men.

At first, Maitreya will concentrate on the major problems — political and economic, ecological and social — which threaten the stability of the world and the well-being of men. As these problems begin to find solution, His attention will turn to the inner constitution and psychology of man; the causes of disease and its prevention and cure. He will reaffirm the great and basic laws which govern life on Earth and our connectedness with all Cosmos. He will show that Right Relationship is central to any understanding of the meaning and purpose of our presence on this planet and that Right Relationship is the destined next achievement of man.

Many, therefore, are the tasks which await Maitreya as He waits in the wings, ready to emerge into the full light of day and the full glare of man's curiosity and hope. The Great Lord is not daunted by the immensity — as only He understands it — of these tasks; He knows that all is well planned and understood and that man, himself, is ready for the new life ahead.

September 1999

The Blueprint of the future

When men see Maitreya in full and open view, they will find much to admire: His grace and joy; His modest wisdom and all-inclusive love; His readiness to share all that He has and is with men of every station. His humility will astound, His knowledge, vast and deep beyond measuring, will reveal to men the paucity of their own. Thus will they turn to Him for guidance and, sure of His concern, become again the students and earnest seekers they once were. Thus will it be, and thus will the Great Lord present to men the Blueprint of the future. That future holds for men such wonders that few today could comprehend them.

Imagine then a future where no man lacks for aught. Where the talents and creativity of all men demonstrate their divine origin. Where war has no place in their thoughts and where goodwill casts its benevolent net over the hearts and minds of all.

Imagine cities of light lit by Light Itself; nowhere to be found the squalor and deprivation of today; imagine transport, fast and silent, powered by light alone, the far-off worlds and even the stars brought within our reach. Such a future awaits the men and women who have the courage to share.

Such a future awaits those brave ones who love Freedom.

Such a glorious future awaits those who long to understand the meaning and purpose of life.

Maitreya, too, awaits His opportunity to emerge and to begin, openly, His Mission. He, too, grows impatient with the long wait. But the Law rules all and Maitreya abides lovingly by its wisdom. Nevertheless, the time is very near when the Great Lord can emerge and speak directly to men. This being so, those whose task it is to prepare His way have but little time in which to do so. Make that then your *first priority*, leaving all else aside.

As always, the free will of men may not be jeopardized. Thus it is that His name will not accompany His first appearances, allowing men themselves to ascertain His worth. As a man among men will He appear, voicing aloud His brothers' needs and thoughts.

In time, so many will respond that His true identity and stature can be confirmed. This time is expected to be short but the pace of recognition lies in the hands of men themselves. The present phase of miracles, now worldwide, will continue and accompany this process until no one can deny its significance at this time.

Thus the world will be won over and prepared for change. Thus the call will go out from the people of all the nations for the Avatar to speak, and thus will Maitreya answer that call and declare His mission and purpose.

That silent declaration will announce the start of the New Era: of peace, of sharing, justice and freedom; the awakening of men to their divinity, and the creation by men of a civilization wrought in the form of God's Plan.

October 1999

The Laws and Rules of Life

Since time immemorial, men have known of, and expected the coming of, a great Teacher, an outstanding man of wisdom and revealed truth. Cyclically, age after age, have these Great Ones come forth. Today is no exception to this cosmic law. As the new era dawns, men stand expectant as never before for a sight of the Great Teacher Who, though they know it not, is already in men's midst.

Throughout the planet, old and young, poor and rich, make ready for His Announcement, His Declaration of Mission and Purpose, His tryst with mankind. As the old century and era wind to their close, men's minds are quickening to the new energies which will fashion the forms of the new civilization and impose their qualities on the consciousness of men. These qualities — of synthesis and fusion, tolerance and goodwill, harmlessness and brotherly love — will, in time, bring the race of men to the manifestation of its destined glory. Thus shall it be, and thus shall men enter again into their age-old Covenant with the Divine.

Little though they may know it, men are on the threshold of a reawakening to the very meaning and purpose of their existence.

It is, in part, to see men safely through this period of trial and test that their Elder Brothers, the Masters of Wisdom, are returning openly to the world. With Their great leader — Maitreya, the World Teacher — at Their head, They will inspire the creation of the new, more appropriate structures which will allow men to live and work together in peace. From that peace will manifest a creativity and resource unlike aught seen before.

Men will learn and understand the subtle laws which govern their lives: the basic law of life, the Law of Karma, of Cause and Effect, which controls the destiny of all; the related Law of

Rebirth, which makes possible the journey of the Soul in matter; the Law of Harmlessness, which governs right relationship, and the great Law of Sacrifice by which all evolution proceeds.

Through an understanding of these laws, men will come to resemble their Mentors, their Elder Brothers, and to demonstrate the Divinity shared by all. They will hearken to the teaching of the Wise Ones and, step by step, inherit their Birthright. Men are born to become Gods and nought can change that destiny; the timing, only, lies in men's hands.

Soon the world will know that the One for Whom men wait is now among us. Soon, indeed, will He show His face and beckon men to His side. Calling for justice for all will the Great Lord stake His claim to the right to teach the Laws and Rules of Life, the Sacred Path by which men become Gods.

November 1999

Humanity's response to Maitreya

Preparations for Maitreya's emergence are well under way. Naught can halt this blessed event; the timing, only, remains to be decided. This timing is more complex and difficult than men can know, based as it is on knowledge of the Law and on calculations beyond man's ability to comprehend. Notwithstanding these difficulties, it can be stated that the moment of the Great Lord's first appearance — which will allow Him to speak to millions though not by name — is near indeed. Despite the anonymity which the Law requires, there is little doubt that vast numbers will hearken to His words and align themselves with His cause. His message will touch and open the hearts of many who, knowingly or not, but wait for His appearance. Thus will He focus their aspiration and galvanize them into action for the common good.

To many, His words will come as no surprise for they have long held to their meaning and sentiment. To hear them stated so simply from the heart will renew their hope and rekindle their ardour for change. Others will find in Maitreya's words a programme for disaster: all that they hold dear will feel threatened by His advocacy of sharing. Not for long, however, will they withstand the logic of His persuasion; in ever growing numbers they will come to see that sharing and justice alone will right men's ills and solve the manifold problems of the time.

More and more, the simple sense of His ideas will penetrate the hardened hearts of those who now know little suffering; for whom all is well in the world. Their blinkered complacency will be shaken by the outer changes which their greed engenders. Their failing fortunes will bring them to their senses and, in time, to Maitreya's side.

Already, the cult of money and greed is beginning to be questioned at its source: the market worshippers grow hesitant as their games of chance reach new and dizzying heights of reward. The 'man in the street' is awakening to his insecurity in the economic turmoil, and recognizes that he has been hoodwinked to comply.

In the poorer nations, too, a new mood is beginning to prevail: the call for justice is rising and can be heard with a new urgency. Not for long will the impoverished millions suffer their lot in silence. They, more than any, will welcome Maitreya's call for justice and sharing and see it as their own. They, more than any, will see Him as their Champion, their Voice, and give Him their allegiance. In time, men will rise with one voice and call for His establishment as Teacher, as Wayshower, as Mentor and Guide to the New Time.

Thus will Maitreya channel the energies and aspirations of men into a new and better direction, one that will fulfil the plan of God and the destiny of man.

December 1999

The New Millennium begins

It is with baited breath that men await the appearance of Maitreya. 'Millennium fever' has now reached the point of 'auto-combustion' and men, like impatient horses champing at the bit, grow restless and ready for action. What form or direction that action must take is still unclear to most but the sense of impending, far-reaching change is now uppermost in men's minds.

Throughout the world, the desire for peace has been expressed by young and old as their dearest wish. They recognize, better than the politicians, the imperative for peace. A new sense of human unity, if only briefly, has shown men the possibility of lasting peace and practical goodwill. This, alone, augurs well for the future.

Throughout millennium celebrations, a growing realization that an era has ended and a New Age begun imposed itself on men's minds and hearts. New hope and aspiration has replaced the former apathy and set alight men's expectation of a better life for all. Plans for further aid for the dispossessed are already under way, and reflect the growing sense of responsibility now felt by many — young and old alike.

Men need now only the inspiration of Maitreya to unleash their readiness to act and serve. The taste of Oneness has opened their hearts to the beauty of love and sharing, and ripened their readiness to create a better world.

The leadership given by Maitreya will not disappoint. He will raise the hopes and aspirations of all, and set loose the highest that men have, albeit hidden now and unexpressed through fear and ignorance of its existence. He will conquer men's fear and establish, in truth, a new humanity.

Thus will the Great Lord pave the way for the next phase of His Mission — the establishment of the Kingdom of God among men. This is not the ethereal kingdom beloved by the average religious person but the Spiritual Hierarchy of Masters and initiates of which Maitreya is the head. His is the task to create a reflection of that divine expression in the outer, physical world, a kingdom which all men can see, and to which, eventually, all will be drawn on their path to perfection.

Through the doors of Initiation the disciples will pass into the Halls of Wisdom, and take their places as conscious Servers of the Plan. Thus will it be and thus will the Great Ones lead the new humanity into their destiny as Sons of God.

Maitreya is about to knock loudly on the doors which lead to freedom and justice and peace. Listen and recognize His knock and be prepared to act boldly and wisely under His lead.

January/February 2000

The voice of the future

Since the beginning of the new century, a noticeable change has taken place in many parts of the world. On the one hand, many important steps have been taken to alleviate the suffering of the developing world; while on the other, mischief has arisen once more in middle and eastern Europe, adding to the social and political tensions to which that area is so prone. The New Year Blessing of Maitreya, poured out for all, has quickened the aspiration of many, and lightened the hearts of countless seekers, knowingly or not.

Much has been written about Brotherhood, that sacred state of Oneness to which all men aspire. Under the influence of Maitreya's energy of Love, many have received the experience, directly, of that blessed state.

Meanwhile, the 'gambling casinos', the world's stock markets, continue their dizzy climb to a still higher platform from which to fall headlong into chaos.

The marvel is that many wise heads shake and warn, but in the excitement of greed few hear the warning voices. Thus the stage is being set for the collapse of the present economic disorder. Thus men stoke the fires of their own undoing.

Into this turmoil will step Maitreya. Men will turn to Him for answers to their dilemma. When all that men value and hold dear has turned to naught the future appears forbidding indeed. How then to proceed and prosper once more?

Maitreya will show the answers are simple but until then difficult for all but a relatively few to accept: that sharing is the natural, if untried, way for men to live together. That thus will begin the end of men's major problems.

Of necessity, men will find themselves looking with fresh eyes at the possibilities of redistribution and the justice which will ensue, and find them good. In this way, stage by stage, men will transform their broken edifice, built from greed and exploitation, into a thing of beauty answering the needs of all. Thus will it be. Thus will Maitreya prepare men for a spiritual journey unlike aught seen before, a journey which will turn men, in time, into the gods they are.

Little time remains of the old order. The forms of the New Millennium await, impatiently, their precipitation, revealing to men the beauty which lies ahead. Knowingly or not, men lift up their heads, sensing a new light and, soon, a new voice. That voice is the voice of the future, the voice of Maitreya.

March 2000

The requirements of the future

Within a short time, men will begin to recognize that truly significant changes are taking place in human affairs. Almost without notice, far-reaching changes in how men relate to each other — communally, nationally and internationally — are already accepted as the norm. To be sure, many are the transgressions on human dignity and free will which stain and dishonour the actions of both governments and individuals, and sad it is to contemplate these cruelties.

But, imperceptibly, a new spirit of tolerance and understanding is making itself felt. At the same time, less tolerance than hitherto is shown to those who flout the rule of law, who work against the Common Good and foster violence and misrule. This bodes well for the future of the race. Tolerance of evil is not Our way.

Essentially, all men are One. The time is soon coming when men will realize this to be the case. When that day dawns, great indeed will be the joy which all men know.

Meanwhile, a new phase in man's history begins. Step by step, men will set in motion the requirements of the future. These must respect the destiny and free will of all. The right to the essentials of life: food, shelter, healthcare and education, must condition the direction of all governments' actions. The safeguarding of the environment — with all that that entails — must become a sacred duty which will allow men, in time, to nurse this planet back to health. So must it be if men would inherit their birthright and find, again, the path to God.

To aid men to do this, Maitreya will soon announce His presence and show His concern for all. Daunted not at all by the magnitude of the task, Maitreya will take humanity in hand and gently guide its ship into safer waters, far from the treacherous rocks on which men seem bent to founder. Maitreya will show the way back from that danger and pilot men to harbour. Thus will He ease the entry into the New Age and save men much suffering and heartache. Many there are who accept and believe that the Christ is in the world, who await impatiently His emergence into the open, yet who do no more than wait and wish, leaving the work of preparation to others. Sad it is that thus they waste the opportunity to serve uniquely at this unique time, a time like none before and none to follow.

My earnest wish for these is this: that they seize this opportunity to be of service to the Christ, and to their brothers and sisters who know not yet that He is among us. Tell them what you believe: that the Great Lord is here; that Maitreya knocks loudly upon the gate. Very little time remains to do this and prepare them for this precious experience. Seize the time and *act*.

April 2000

The end of chaos

When one looks at the world with the clear eye of knowledge, there is revealed to that discerning gaze a view altogether different from that held by most observers. To the vast majority, this is a world in chaos, characterized by war, flood and pestilence. Terror reigns in the hearts of millions. To be sure, the world today knows all of these catastrophes — and many suffer grievously as a result — but behind the terror and the pain there is a growing sense of hope that things will change for the better, that this period is interim and will not last for ever. Thus it is in many areas where the turmoil is greatest, the hardship most acute and most difficult to bear.

Behind it all, behind the endless and mindless destruction, this world is emerging from a dark and dream-filled sleep, the awakening from which is difficult and traumatic in the extreme. New and powerful energies are stirring humanity to action as never before, and, as always in such a situation, the first responses are mixed: chaotic and destructive, followed by a new and higher rhythm which gradually imposes itself on the whole.

We Who look at life beyond the outer forms and events know with certainty that this difficult period has all but run its course, that the stability and calm yearned for by so many is almost at hand, and that humanity is wakening, refreshed and renewed, from its long, dark night.

Thus is the world now ready for the reappearance of the Christ. Thus are men now ready for what He has to give.

When He came before through His disciple Jesus, men were unready to respond to His teaching. Today, through centuries of suffering, education and experience, are men prepared to understand and *act upon* His precepts. As Preceptor does He come; as Teacher, not saviour, does He fulfil His mission.

Soon, the One for Whom the world waits will emerge and present Himself for all to see. Soon, men will engage in a dialogue with their Higher Selves and make their choice to live or die. Thus is being enacted the great drama of this time.

Little though men may know it, the end is known from the beginning, and they may be well assured of the final triumph of Reason and Truth.

Maitreya will use as signal the collapsing stock markets, the gambling halls of greed; then will He enter, openly, the arena of the world and state His case for justice and freedom, sharing and common sense.

Well may men take stock of themselves and their priorities, their aspirations and values, for on their coming decision lies the future of the world, the well-being of humanity and their immediate role in the Plan of God.

We, the Watchers, your Elder Brothers, await with confidence and joy your just decision and future glory.

May 2000

A new Freedom

With wonderment, We, your Elder Brothers, watch the extraordinary spectacle now being enacted by those who administer the economic and financial affairs of the nations.

As the stock markets teeter uncontrollably under the twin onslaught of greed and fear, the 'men of money' now seek to bolster their power by combining the major markets into one. This, they assume, will strengthen all.

In Our view, this will but hasten the total collapse of these 'gambling casinos' of the world. Now, as one, the bourses will react to the winds, blowing now hot, now cold, which fan the fever of the speculators and drive them to the edge. The 'buffers' of dispersion are being abandoned and naught, then, can halt the spiralling fall.

When that happens, men will see the folly of this tawdry enterprise and turn to face reality for the first time. When, too, that happens, Maitreya will begin the process of His open emergence and speak directly to the people in their confusion and despair.

He will show men that, far from losing all, they have gained a new freedom: the loss only of the glamour and lure of riches and power. When men hear Him speak, they will realize that right relationship is the true reality they seek, and, emboldened and purified, they will set in motion the process of sharing and justice. Thus will they guarantee the peace for which men yearn and which, for so long, has eluded them.

Maitreya will show that when men act from the heart they act according to the Plan which, did they but know it, directs all lives. When men see this, they will gladly forgo their former follies and misdirections, to set in place the new and better relations, one to another, which will characterize the coming time. Thus will it be. Thus will men, step by step, awaken to their role in fashioning the new civilization.

With Maitreya and His group in the lead, guiding and advising, no time will be lost in furthering the plans and blueprints which await implementation. In due course, all will be transformed and changed for the better. The outlines of the new dispensation will quickly emerge, and inspire men to even bolder measures. Thus will it be. And thus will the Great Ones, your Elder Brothers of old, enter once more into the lives of men; and thus will men themselves take the next step on their path, a path which, slowly and surely, will take them to their Source.

June 2000

Moving into Divinity

Throughout the world, men are beginning to realize that their long-held beliefs and certainties are less certain than they had supposed. The breakdown of their social and political institutions calls in question the value of their established ways of thinking, and presents men with a dilemma: the current modes of thought and action no longer seem to work; the future modes are, as yet, unclear. Thus it is that men stand undecided, awaiting guidance, lost in a vain attempt to maintain the past or to predict the future. In such situations, men are ripe for change.

Few there are who know the direction or the extent of the needed changes, nor how they may be accomplished, but, gradually, it is dawning on many that the present ways of living are bankrupt of meaning and lack all potential for human happiness. Large numbers thus 'opt out' of the struggle and seek solace and equilibrium in the growing number of religions, philosophies and 'cults', ancient and new. The changes needed seem too vast, too radical, for human hands or minds to set in motion, and they turn inwards to the God Who, they suspect, controls the affairs of men.

Did they but know it, they, themselves, are that very God, awaiting an opportunity to manifest. They, themselves, control their lives, for good or ill. It is they, by their actions, who turn the wheel of events, who engender conflict or peace, who sow mischief or goodwill. Men must learn their role and innate power in life and take, thus, responsibility for its quality and direction. Unless they do this they will never leave their infancy behind.

Maitreya enters now the world arena to teach men that they are Gods in potential, that they are powerful, indeed, and that conditioning, alone, holds them in thrall to superstition and fear, competition and greed. He will show men the way to renounce the past, and to construct, under His wise guidance, a civilization worthy of men who are moving into their Divinity. The day is not far off when men will hear His Call, and hearing, respond. The day is not far off when men will know that the long dark night is over, that the time has come to welcome the new light which has entered the world.

Thus will men begin the task of reconstruction, a task which demands the strength and will of all. All must see this time as an opportunity to serve and grow, to fulfil the destiny which has brought them into the world now.

When, in future times, men look back to these climactic days, they will wonder with astonishment and disbelief at the ease with which we tolerate the iniquities of the present: the cruelty and pointless suffering which so besmirch our lives. Maitreya comes to do battle with this ancient wrong and to lead men into the Era of Light. Give Him your welcoming hand and let Him guide you to your Self.

July/August 2000

The art of co-operation

More and more, men are beginning to understand the severity of the problems which face them today. On all fronts — political, economic and social — these problems multiply and cause much heartache and sad shaking of heads. Add to these the environmental problems which man's cavalier attitude to nature and its resources has engendered, and the future for mankind looks bleaker still. The realization is dawning that mankind's life is in crisis and that something radical must be done before it is too late.

What, indeed, can man do to save himself from disaster? What steps can he take even to mitigate the threat to his well-being?

The answer is relatively simple but, it would seem, difficult for men to grasp, caught, as they are, in the net of their own conditioning.

Men must release themselves from the poison of competition, must realize it for the glamour which it is, and, seeing the Oneness of all men, embrace co-operation for the General Good. Only co-operation and justice will save men from a disaster of their own making; co-operation and justice alone will guarantee their future. Considering that this is so, man has little option but to accept co-operation as the key to his salvation.

When men co-operate rather than compete, they will find a magic potion entering their lives. The ease with which long-lasting problems will be solved will astonish, the impossible will yield to the lightest touch, and, through co-operation alone, men will learn the true art of living. Thus will it be, and thus will men learn to appreciate the beauty of relationship which only co-operation can bestow. Through co-operation the new civilization will be built, the new science revealed, the new understanding manifested. Thus will men grow together in the discovery of their divinity. Thus will they know the joy and happiness of such togetherness.

The Masters, your Elder Brothers, are not strangers to co-operation. In all that They do, co-operation plays a central role. It could not be otherwise in the manifested Brotherhood where the canker of competition is unknown.

It is Our earnest desire that men learn the art of co-operation, and to this end shall We act as mentors, teaching through example. So liberating is co-operation it is surprising, is it not, that men have been so tardy in learning its joys.

The era of competition is fast coming to an end. With its demise, violence and war, starvation amid plenty, greed and separation, will likewise fade from the memory. To replace these sorrows will emerge blessed co-operation, to guarantee to men their essential divinity. Thus will it be and thus will men come to understand another facet in the nature of God.

September 2000

Opportunity and challenge

The problems which assail Mankind are many and difficult to solve; some of them are dangerous and require immediate action. Without help and advice it is unlikely that men would act quickly or adequately enough to avoid catastrophe. For these reasons alone, it is necessary for their Elder Brothers to come forward now as advisers and teachers.

It is thus that We shall take Our places among you and help you to restore your world. Be not afraid that Our coming will reduce your standing as men; We come to aid only, your freedom of will is cherished by Us and will never be infringed.

Many there are now who doubt that We exist. For many Our coming is but a fairy-tale. Soon, however, men will see that fairy-tale come to life and will know that We have ever stood behind you, guarding and protecting you, awaiting patiently the day when We can walk among you, openly, once more.

As We enter, one by one, your life, We see it as Our sacred duty to help you in every possible way. From long experience We know the ways of life. That knowledge, and the gifts so hardly won, We shall place before you for your edification and comfort. We shall show you your past history: events many thousands of years old will rise freshly to your astonished eyes and you will realize the ancient lineage of men. You will realize, too, the glories which have been lost, and strive to recapture the forgotten achievement. Thus will it be and thus will you know a new humility and a new purity.

When you see the heights from which you come you will surely take stock of yourselves and question the reasons for your plunge into anarchy and strife. These, you will find, are inherent in the growing materialism which, age by age, has involved you too deeply for your good, and caused you to forget the Plan. Now, once more, must you recognize this and take the path which leads only to the Light. Much depends on men making the right decisions now for never have men stood in greater danger. We watch and await Our opportunity to extend the hands of friendship and succour, sure in the knowledge that they will be warmly grasped.

We, your Elder Brothers, see this time as one of double blessing: as Hierarchy do We now return openly to the world, the Higher Evolution beckoning Us upwards; and you, Our younger brethren, provide a field of service and a challenge which We take up with Joy. The Plan, and its implementation through men, is Our ever-present concern, and men have much to learn, and to teach, in relation to the lower kingdoms.

Although not openly, We are here in growing numbers. Soon you will see Us and be inspired to emulate Our ways: Our co-operation will replace your competition, Our breadth of view your intolerance, Our love will overcome your violence and hate. Thus will it be, and thus will you turn again to the Plan and make it your own.

October 2000

The people stir

In the coming time, humanity is scheduled to make such progress that a new type of man will find expression. To make this possible, many more advanced souls, who have waited for just such a time, have come into incarnation during the last fifty years. Their gifts are already obvious and they will ensure that the problems of mankind are tackled in the right manner and speed.

Altruism is the keynote of their approach, and a new simplicity and practicality will characterize their thinking. They are not, therefore, to be found in the ranks of the new young millionaires but rather among the practical idealists in every country. They will be quick to recognize the practicality of Maitreya's ideas and seek to implement them without delay. Their youth and enthusiasm will inspire a new approach to the age-old problems which obscure the future for so many, and their unusual maturity of mind will guarantee their success. They represent the best in humanity now, and the best hope for the future.

Whatever aids the well-being of men will gain their support; no stultifying dogma will limit their actions. A new sense of urgency will hasten their feet and a new realism will ensure their wise decisions. Thus will it be. Thus will men rise again from their torpor and set to work to reconstruct their world.

At the moment, a mainly untrue picture of the world is presented by the powerful media outlets. Conditioned as they are by market forces and commercialism, their view is dominated by money and the false values of the 'market'. Thus it is that most people are confused and wracked by stress as they try to understand the happenings of the time.

With the appearance of Maitreya, this sceptical and materialistic view will be replaced by a more sensitive response to the many problems facing humanity. Gradually, the glamour of money will give way to the achievements of service, and millions will acclaim the conquests through service of their brothers and sisters worldwide.

In this way, a new climate of thought will prevail. A new seriousness will enter the public area and all governments and their agencies will find themselves obliged to listen to the people's needs and concerns.

Thus the 'will of the people' will more and more condition the direction of action and little will be done which fails to meet the public need.

The present anarchic and violent assaults, expressing the frustration of millions, show the sense the people have of their strength and need to act. Blind and unco-ordinated as these actions may be, they are, nevertheless, signs of the new times and the first of many such.

Until the world's institutions address themselves to present human need, such demonstrations, more and more daring, will continue. The people are beginning to feel their power and ability to influence events, and to implement their will.

November 2000

A new beginning

When men realize the depths to which they have fallen they will take stock of themselves and begin the journey back to sanity and safety. This will take time, of course, for the fall from Grace into the present corruption and chaos has a long history. For thousands of years, man has made a steady decline from the spiritual base which once ordered his life. He has forgotten his origin and purpose as the Dark Age clouded his memory and waylaid his heart. Lost in the twin glamours of Matter and Time man is only now awakening from his long dream and illusion.

Needless to say, individual men have risen above the herd and fought their way through the fogs of unknowing into a measure of Light. They are the bright stars who have kept faith with their soul's knowledge and purpose and so act as a beacon for the rest. Through these exceptional men and women, the truth of man's eternal journey in ever increasing awareness has been kept alive and fostered in the darkest days.

Now, as we enter the Aquarian Dispensation, a new chapter opens for mankind, and a new beginning is vouchsafed the race of men.

For millennia, mankind has struggled in the dark, unmindful of the group of Elder Brothers Who watch their halting progress and see them safely through the problems and dangers of their own making.

Now, at last, the Brothers may step forward into the light and show Themselves to men.

Now, at last, may They teach openly and guide.

As Brothers, the Masters bring a new understanding of the true relation that exists among men.

As Masters, the Brothers will show men the wisdom and knowledge which one day will be theirs, and so quicken the aspiration of men.

As Friends and Guides They will hold before men a mirror of what they can become and so speed the journey for the race.

They come to teach and to guide and to offer Their succour to all.

Their Great Leader, Maitreya, stands poised to engage on a journey like none other, one which will bring Him openly, in the full light of day, closer to the hearts and minds of men.

His teaching will inspire men to transform and to rebuild their lives for the better, and to shape the future more in the likeness of the Plan.

Thus will mankind rise again, nearer to the high point of the distant past from which it has descended.

Naught there is that can prevent that rise but the will of man itself.

Thus do men stand at the testing time — as never before in their long history— but the vanguard of the Masters is among them and their future is assured.

Maitreya, Himself, stands in the wings, ready to emerge and to face the ignorance of the time. He has gathered around Him helpers from all the continents, men and women of every race and creed. Together they are ready to do battle with ignorance and greed, selfishness and cruelty, and are certain of victory.

December 2000

Overcoming the fear of change

Many await the World Teacher with a growing faith that He can solve the problems which men find so intractable. They sense that they can trust His wise judgement and experience. That this is true cannot be gainsaid. He is indeed a wise counsellor and men should hearken to His advice with confidence. The Law, however, limits the degree to which He may intervene in man's affairs. Men should know that the Law forbids the use of force — man's free will cannot be infringed. Thus it is that men alone must make the decisions for change: as Maitreya has said: "I am the Architect, only, of the Plan. You, My friends and brothers, are the willing builders of the Shining Temple of Truth."

When men see Him, Maitreya will teach the way of peace and love: through the manifestation of sharing and justice alone will both be known. Thus, in the simplest terms does He offer the solution to man's dilemma.

Man, even now, finds his structures failing. He cannot understand how, amidst plenty, crime so burgeons and threatens. He cannot understand how, amidst plenty, not all men know happiness. He cannot see that men live in fear and therefore know no hope.

Caution and fear of change inhibit realism and men are struggling with outworn and crumbling structures. The real and urgent problems elude them and drive men closer to the edge.

Fear pervades man's every action and thought; this alone makes change both difficult and more than ever necessary.

Maitreya, you will find, will counsel change but the desire for change must reside in man himself. Thus will man condition the speed and scope of transformation and thus, too, will the dictates of the Law be obeyed.

Maitreya will address men's fear and help them to slay that many-headed monster. He will show them that they have nothing to fear but fear in the building of the new world.

Many, today, may doubt that this can be accomplished but Maitreya knows that billions are longing for the changes which He advocates, for the world which He envisages. They await only His words, His voice, His call for justice. Into the building of that new world the hopes of men and women everywhere will go. Their age-old desire for peace and justice will, at last, find fulfilment.

These desires and thoughts are already descending, already filling men's hearts and minds and making the future now.

The world is ready, as never before, for the emergence of the Christ. Nothing can prevent this momentous event. Even now, the final preparations are being made. Soon, the Christ, Maitreya, the World Teacher, the Lord of Love Himself, will move openly among us.

January/February 2001

Great things are afoot

Most people would be surprised to know that, with the exception of some important areas of concern, the world is today a safer place in which to live than hitherto. Far from accepting the threat of sudden, catastrophic, warfare consigning humanity to oblivion, most people are now forward-looking, arranging and planning their lives with some measure of assurance and certainly of hope. With the end of the 'cold war' has come the belief and expectancy that mankind will find a way to overcome (or circumvent) its problems, manifold as they are, in time.

So much the more threatening and dangerous to world peace, therefore, is the commitment to the anti-ballistic missile programme announced by the new American administration. It has been presented as a purely defensive weapons-system, defending the United States and Europe (if the peoples agree) from the threat of terrorists and 'rogue' states who have neither the means nor the will to threaten either. In reality, the main concern of those who advocate its installation, despite the upset to the present balance of power and the danger of a new arms-race, is the extension of American hegemony in the world. All that aids its inauguration, therefore, should be opposed by those concerned for peace.

The present American Government is not seeking a new war but is at pains to present itself as impregnable, more than a match for any, or any combination of, enemies. It is the final gesture of the old, decaying order in which competition and confrontation held sway. It is the way of the past and will soon be relegated to the past. Its acceptance would be a major mistake for the world.

Meanwhile, many other issues concern mankind. Global warming is foremost now in the minds of many governments, despite the reluctance of America to commit itself to change.

This commitment, it would appear, will be more difficult to evoke with the new administration but the world is awakening to the dangers although it knows not all the facts. Earth is becoming warmer but half the rise in temperature is inevitable — the direct result of Maitreya's action in bringing the Earth slightly nearer to the Sun. This will prove to have enormous benefits but the temporary disorder in weather patterns is, unfortunately, unavoidable.

People everywhere are more keenly aware of the forward march to power of global corporations, and the dangers they pose to democratic rule. The voices of the people are rising and being heard, none more so than in the USA, the Corporate Giant.

In the Middle East, confrontation is reaching a new extreme. Diehards on both sides prevent all reasonable discussion and the people suffer and die in vain. Maitreya, it would appear, is the sole hope for that sad land.

Maitreya is considering now the steps He might take to help resolve these problems. Humanity's free will may not be infringed but Maitreya is anxious to aid in every way within the law. Thus it is that His appearance before men may be sooner, even, than recently planned. Watch and wait, for great things are afoot.

March 2001

The New Time for men

With every day that passes, mankind is being shown the calamities which occur from the misuse of free will. Divine free will is man's greatest treasure, but only when it is used in accordance with the Plan of the Logos is it lawful and right.

Man has travelled far from that understanding and so reaps the whirlwind of his wrong thought and action. Thus it is that millions suffer needlessly in the midst of plenty, wanting the means that others take for granted as their birthright.

Not for much longer can man support this separation; the Law demands a sustaining balance and, finding it not, acts to adjust and reconcile.

Moreover, the new energies of Synthesis demand expression more and more, and daily ease mankind towards that goal. Men everywhere find the rising tension difficult to bear and flounder wildly in the resulting chaos.

From deep within themselves men sense that the way to the future lies through change but see not yet the outlines of the Path. They await a sign that their needs are known and will be met but trust not the profusion of signs which everywhere announce the presence of that succour. They hope and fear at once and reject the possibility of that for which they yearn. So has it always been.

Meanwhile, sections of mankind press blissfully on, enjoying the easy fortunes which daily astonish their hungry and greedy minds. They are blind to all but their own precarious success and cannot sense the tension or hear the tolling of the bell. The disease of speculation has them in thrall and thoughts of dying ancient Rome's excesses come to mind.

Watching these different and conflicting attitudes stands Hierarchy, seeking to aid in every way it can. Only the free will of men prevents direct intervention but the Law is the Law and must ever be obeyed; nevertheless, much help is extended which mankind never sees.

Maitreya is assessing the situation which exists from day to day, and is looking to emerge before the stock-market collapse already predicted. Steps are now being taken to make this possible. This being so, the time is short indeed until His open mission begins. Watch and be alert that you may not miss the early signs.

Maitreya will seek to galvanize into action the men and women of goodwill everywhere. Many there are who are but waiting for His call. Thus will be set in motion a great debate in which the basic needs of men everywhere will be examined and appraised. In this way men will come to know and test the possibilities that change can guarantee and so find the courage to begin the needed transformation. Thus will it be, and thus will the Great Lord advise and guide and inaugurate the New Time for men.

April 2001

Man's birthright awaits him

Terror still reigns in the hearts of many who face imminent or approaching death. This is a sad fact to contemplate for, assuredly, it need not be so. For most people, the stress involved in coming into the world by far outweighs that of slipping quietly out of the form and gaining, thereby, a new and greater freedom.

A similar state of fear grips many today as they see the crumbling of the old familiar structures. They know not what is coming, only that their world is dying, collapsing before their terrified gaze. On all fronts is this so: economic, religious, social — they awaken daily to the announcement of another loss.

The world is poised between the old and the new; the past and the future, and people hold their breath for an indication of the outcome. The signs are there in abundance for all to see, yet many refuse to see in them the hope they crave, and diminish, thereby, their happiness and calm.

Have no fear of the future for it will be, if man so wills, greater and more beautiful than can be imagined, greater by far than man's highest dreams. The uncertainty and anguish, the pain of loss and change, are but the birthpangs of a new and better world struggling to be born.

This new world, this new civilization, will reflect, more and more, man's essential divinity. Qualities and powers which hitherto have been ascribed exclusively to God will, in true measure, be manifested daily by man. The miracles of today, properly understood, will be seen as normal and consistent with the laws of nature, answering to the control of the enlightened mind and will.

Thus will it be and thus will man grow in knowledge and confidence that he is truly on the Spiritual path once more, that behind him now lie the mistakes of the present time.

When man accepts, in fact and in deed, that humanity is one, that men are brothers, one of another, all things can safely become his. His birthright awaits him.

So must men show that they are ready for peace, ready to enter the future together without bloodshed or competition. They must be glad to share and work in harmony for the good of all. When men, of themselves, come to that awareness, they will call on Maitreya (by whatever name) to show them the way, to guide them out of the morass, and to lead them into the era of peace.

Then will the Great Lord respond. Then will Maitreya call on the army of helpers assembled over the years. From every country this band of willing servers will come, dedicated, and trained in the new procedures.

Thus will man, the disciple under trial, emerge as the Son of God to be, the inheritor of his true function and powers.

May 2001

The Great Mother

More than men think, the world is changing for the better. Despite the ominous clouds drifting across the planet from time to time, the main thrust of events is positive and hopeful. How much more is this the case than is apparent to men only the manifold means at the disposal of Hierarchy can ascertain. However, there are still grave concerns which men ignore at their peril. Chief among these is the environment which, men must know, they daily undermine. This despoliation of nature now threatens the well-being of all and augurs badly for future generations. Pollution of the planet has now reached dangerous, life-threatening levels, thus weakening man's inherent immunity and bringing again to the fore diseases once thought vanquished for ever.

Men must realize their responsibility for the planet on which they live. Stewards, men are, of a strong but sensitive organism and must protect it from harm. Few, today, can claim that this they do. On the contrary, men waste and ride roughshod over nature's generous munificence, unheedful of tomorrow or their children's needs. True it is that many are awakening to this problem, but until it is understood as the concern of all, and tackled globally, little progress will be made in changing direction.

You can be sure that Maitreya is not unmindful of the dangers to mankind if they ignore this pressing difficulty. He will urge men to work — everyone — for the planet's restoration, and point the way to a simpler and happier life.

Once restored again to health the planet will continue to give its bounty to all who approach with care and love. The elementals of the lower kingdoms know well their tasks; free from the influence of men's disordered thoughts, these industrious builders can, in harmony, create a new and better world.

When men understand nature as the Great Mother of all, they will approach Her with reverence. Thus will She reveal to men Her secrets and laws. Armed with this new knowledge, men will in truth manifest as Gods.

Man is a crucible in which is being created a new Being. In the fiery heat of experience man is gradually learning the ways of God. Slow and painful may be the early steps but in time the pace will quicken. Revelation after revelation will expand his consciousness, leading to a crescendo of creativity and knowledge. Man will stand revealed as a Son of God.

The first step is to awaken to the dangers of the present situation. This is already well advanced and many seek to influence worldwide action. Like so much else, that action awaits a change of heart in major nations — the worst offenders in the pollution of the planet.

Maitreya will lend His voice and age-long knowledge to the coming debate — and speak for those who have no voice and suffer in silence.

June 2001

Unity

Whenever men meet together in large groups they adopt a different view of themselves and look at each other in a new way. They are emboldened, strengthened in their desire and gravitate to those who support their viewpoint. This may seem natural but why should it be so?

Essentially, all men inwardly seek unity and find its reflection in conformity of thought and ideas. This instinct is behind the formation of political parties and other groups. The ideological consensus acts as a magnet and strengthens the potency of the whole.

Groups and parties founder when the inner unity is disturbed. Unity is a soul quality and essential for the cohesion of the group. Too great an emphasis on individuals and personality differences thus tends to weaken the unifying ties which hold the group together.

This principle can be seen at work in every branch of human activity. The rise and fall of parties, groups and even of nations are conditioned by this law. Unity is strength, say men, and thus it is, for it is man's essential nature.

Unity is not too difficult to attain in the earlier stages of formation of a group; if the purpose of its inception is magnetic enough, that alone can hold the group together. However, time brings differences and discontent. Strong and varied voices arise and seek to impose their will. If the *desire* for unity is lost the group, at once, is threatened.

The underlying purpose of all life is the creation of unity, thus expressing the interconnectedness of all atoms. For most men, cosmos is a collection of separate material bodies, infinitely large and distant, inertly obeying mechanical laws of matter. In reality, cosmos, Space Itself, is a living entity, the Source of our Being, our Mother and Father. As souls, we know this to be so, and seek to give expression to the fundamental unity of our nature. A group, therefore, loses this unity at its peril. Without such unity it functions not as a group but blindly, without purpose and cohesion, a disparate collection of attitudes and conditioning.

We are entering the Age of the Group; Aquarius, and its energies, can be lived and experienced only in group formation. The major quality of Aquarius, too, is Synthesis. Its fusing and blending rays will impose themselves on the lives of all until, gradually, the higher alchemy achieves its beneficent purpose and the race of men are One. Thus will it be. Thus will men know the truth that Unity *is* strength, the essential nature of our Being, the purpose to which all men strive and to which all activities of men seek to give expression.

When Maitreya, Himself, emerges in the very near future, He will underline the need for unity in all our undertakings. He will show how essential it is that we find an identity of purpose, as men and as nations, in solving human problems, thus putting our potent individualities at the service of the group.

July/August 2001

Detachment

"Sufficient unto the day is the evil thereof." There can be few, especially in the Western world, who are unfamiliar with this ancient Christian maxim. Passed down the generations from adult to child, it has found its way into the moral framework of countless millions. However, despite this long conversance, there are relatively few who appear to understand its meaning, and even fewer who live its wisdom. Essentially, it concerns detachment.

The evil — the criticism, destructive gossip and actions — which abounds in most so-called 'spiritual' groups, succeeds in its intent where there is no detachment. Its bitter and corrosive venom flourishes where it is given the energy of constant thought and defence. Better, by far, it is to leave it to the Karmic Law, than to brood and fret against its source.

This being so, it matters not the nature of the evil, the intended harm. The Law is impartial and works to restore equilibrium. No manner of struggle to right a wrong or defend a reputation can better the Law of Karma in its task.

Save then your energy for better things and let the Law decide the measure and the timing of response.

When evil strikes, the best defence, then, is detachment. When the hunted animal stands, silent and still, the hunter, baffled, goes empty-handed. When a man is detached — free from fear and the need to retaliate — he can calmly leave the Great Law to fight his battle for him. Thus the evil gains not, nor waxes in strength.

This profound teaching of the Christ is usually expressed as an injunction against carrying injury or hurt from day to day — thus prolonging its life and further hurting the victim.

This relates closely to the Christian concept of forgiveness. When a man is truly detached he has already forgiven. He waits patiently for the originator of the evil to realize the harm he does to himself, the victim and the group, and to make amends. Thus is the evil blunted and thus is it "sufficient unto the day".

When Maitreya, the Great Lord, emerges fully and publicly, He will devote much time to the concept of detachment. Not for nothing is it central to His Teaching: He has already given His thoughts on honesty of mind, sincerity of spirit, and detachment. Not all, at first, will be able to follow His thoughts but in time His energy of Love will awaken men to the practicality of His wisdom. Gradually, the old, mechanical reactions of hate and envy will disappear as the social needs are met, as more and more are lifted up by the joy of working for Maitreya's cause. Thus will it be, and thus will the people of all the nations grow in stature as emerging Gods.

September 2001

The reception of Maitreya

As Maitreya's approach comes ever nearer, let us look more closely at the likely reactions to His presence. In the first place, those who have worked to make known that presence may be surprised to find the reactions of many more muted than they envisaged. Initially, this may well be so. In starting His open mission, the Great Lord must tread carefully, not to frighten away those He seeks to help. Therefore, a quiet note, but heartfelt, should be looked for. In time, a greater urgency and force of statement will be appropriate, and trenchant, indeed, will be His call to men. Expect, therefore, a growing emphasis, a sterner warning, from Maitreya's lips. As time proceeds, His thoughts will find response of differing kind. Those more traditionalist will find many of His ideas difficult to embrace, and will denounce them in strident terms. Others, less hidebound, will consider and appraise them, and from this group will He find many who will gladly espouse His cause. In growing numbers, they will gravitate to Him and lend their voice to His counsel.

Proceeding thus, Maitreya's teaching will draw forth from men their highest aspiration, awakening them to the troubles and perils of this time; and also to the simple means of conquering for ever the problems and dangers of today. Thus will it be. Thus will men receive the insight and the leadership they yearn for, and thus will they call for the changes so sorely needed to the fabric of men's lives.

Of course, it is only to be expected that many will oppose the teaching of the Great Lord. Religious groups, deeply embedded in their own doctrines and expectations, will strongly disavow Maitreya's presence and ideas, and many unpleasant accusations will be directed towards Him. Nevertheless, many will be inspired and renewed in faith, and will give of their best for Maitreya's Cause.

The business conglomerate, so highly invested in today's crumbling structures, will react in one of two ways: those who see Maitreya as the enemy of all they stand for will oppose and thwart His counsel to their utmost effort. Those who see Him as the voice of the future, as the only possible way for men, will welcome and espouse His ideas, and lend their expertise to His growing support. Thus will the factions act and take their stand: for or against the future, the only way open to men.

The masses everywhere will follow their leaders. Gradually they will realize that Maitreya speaks for them, their needs, their aspirations for a better, safer life for their families, a future they can dimly feel is theirs by right, waiting to be born. Then will the world's peoples raise their voices in support and praise of the Great Lord, and call on His teaching to enlighten and ennoble them, and to lead them willingly into that beckoning and blessed future.

October 2001

Turn the tide of hate

A period of crisis has descended on the world, one that will bring many nations together in a new way. Mutual fear of terrorism has accomplished what otherwise would have taken years of patient effort to achieve. Even more strikingly, the reasons for terrorism — the hurt, the resentment, the baffled despair of millions in the East — are beginning to dawn on many Americans, enabling them to take a broader view of recent events, and call for caution in response. Above all, a new spirit of co-operation makes itself felt, a new sense of responsibility is dawning in the minds of many, East and West.

Thus this terrible attack, which killed and maimed so many at a stroke, has kindled the fires of change sorely needed in this world, and forced the hands which held it back. Out of this brutal crime may come, therefore, a greater understanding of the needs of men and women everywhere for justice and freedom and the rule of law.

By the standards applied by men, this tragedy has forced the major powers to assemble their military might and strike back in self-defence. Greater, by far, would be the wisdom of opening wide the granaries and the banks, to show an understanding of the problem, and the desire to make amends. Appeasement is not the answer but neither is war.

Only through fair and open trial before the world can the guilt or innocence of men be known. Only by acceptance of some responsibility for the conditions which drive men to these barbarous acts can they be overcome. Men who have nothing to lose put little value on the lives of others or their own.

The advice, therefore, which We, your Elder Brothers, extend to men is thus: call together all parties to the problems which lie behind the acts. Abstain from desperate vengeance and open the door to dialogue. Make sincere effort to understand the grievances of countless millions and help transform their lives and minds.

No longer can the rich impose their will by wealth and weapons alone; sharing of resources is inevitable as the only way to justice and peace.

Take, now, this opportunity to right the wrongs of the past, and remove for ever the canker of terror and outrage.

Maitreya watches from the wings awaiting the moment to emerge. His great heart releases the love which comforts and protects all who can respond; His uplifted hand blesses all who come near.

Take this, His love, and turn the tide of hate.

November 2001

The entry of Maitreya

When, as now, man is at the crossroads, awaiting guidance on which direction to take, he sets up an invocative cry for help. Inevitably, when the cry has reached a certain pitch, We, your Elder Brothers, respond and answer. Thus is it today as men flounder wildly in the chaos of their own making, afraid to take the only steps which will save them from further chaos.

Into this maelstrom Maitreya is about to enter, fully aware of the task which lies ahead. Only a Being of His immeasurable wisdom could accept such a burden. Only someone of His incomparable courage could undertake such a task.

Out of the anarchic conditions of the present must He construct the new and better order. Out of the agony of millions must He fashion a new world.

Who is there to help Him in His work of salvage?

Who would rally to His cause and aid their brothers and sisters?

Now, as never before, is the opportunity to serve a world in labour, a new world waiting to be born.

Maitreya seeks to lift man into his birthright.

He seeks to inspire the creation of a new and happier world.

The Great Lord seeks to invest each individual life with sanctity and worth.

He seeks to rid the world of violence and war.

Where will He find His helpers?

Who are ready to respond?

Who have the courage to aid the Lord of Love?

He knows already those on whom He can depend.

Make ready to see Him.

Burnish bright your resolve.

Be not dismayed by the immensity of the task.

Be simple and heartfelt in all you do.

Maitreya approaches, fast, on a shining white steed.

His mantram is: fear not!

All, in time, will be renewed.

All, in time, will be returned to the Light.

Consider this: "Take your brother's need as the measure for your action, and solve the problems of the world. There is no other course."

Into your unhappy world now steps Maitreya. He knows your agony and suffering better even than you do yourselves, for He knows, too, the joy which is your birthright.

That joy would He restore to you in full and perfect measure. For that is He among you.

Take Him to your hearts and let Him serve you. Know Him as your friend and Brother of Old. Let Him guide you and teach you; thus will you grow in your divinity.

The time has come when you shall see His face. His smile of love will beckon you to His side. You will find your love magnified a thousandfold and, giving it in service to His Cause, enter into the Plan of which you are a part.

December 2001

The missing link

Inch by inch, humanity is nearing its readiness for decision. Events are forcing governments to seek new answers to the vexing problems which, today, defy resolution. More and more, they are hearing new voices with new and varied ideas which advocate an entirely different approach to their dilemma. The thoughtform of the new direction of human thinking and action is gradually taking hold. This being so, despite the present chaos, it augers well for the future.

The nations are finding that the old methods and mechanisms no longer work, that crisis after crisis undoes all forward movement, while the cries and demands of the poor become ever more persistent and loud. Slowly but surely, the necessity to share begins to dawn on the minds of many. Soon this concept will register powerfully on the consciousness of the race and in due course will be established as the 'missing link' in men's thinking.

Of course, not all men will, at first, see the need for this drastic and radical answer to men's troubles. The old competitive instinct dies hard. Gradually, however, the simple good-sense of sharing, the advantages of co-operation, and the renewed feeling of well-being through well-doing will convince all but the few. A new era of light will make itself manifest in the world.

In the glow of this revelation man will begin to realize certain fundamental truths of his existence and Being. He will know, as a palpable fact, that he is one of a great brotherhood who live and suffer and die together, as One. That the divisions and differences, which have meant so much to so many, and have caused so much of the suffering, are only seeming. That behind all outer appearance stands immortal Man, journeying together to perfection and the true expression of his divinity.

405

The world is awakening to the truth of man's existence: Man is divine, the outer expression of his true reality as soul. Through all vicissitudes, his soul has guarded him and shown him the path. Never has the soul been absent from the fray, the high endeavour or the reluctant effort. Man and soul are One.

Such is the truth awaiting man's discovery. The soul awaits this dawning revelation. Man is at the end of his apprenticeship in life.

The soul, from now, directs a higher and a clearer path.

January/February 2002

Warriors of Light

Wherever we may look, today, we see signs of change. Thus has it always been but change now acts at an accelerated pace, is sudden and radical, far from the gradual transformation of the past. The close-knit communications systems, now everywhere available, ensure that all change is instantly known and accepted, more or less, worldwide.

These abrupt variations in the formal structures of men's lives have, of course, profound effects on man's psychological balance. The old certainties seem gone for ever and many are driven to extremes of reaction. Since the political and economic fields are the principal arenas of this upheaval in human thinking and action, they command, too, the involvement of all. All are engaged, willingly or not.

Into this turmoil has come the Christ. His is the task to monitor these changes and, where found wanting and inadequate, excessive and too extreme, to rectify accordingly. This is done by the distribution of energies until a temporary balance is achieved.

Thus the Great Lord works to control the rate of change and to minimize the cleavages which this process brings into being. His aim at each step is the maintenance of equilibrium. To aid Him in His delicate endeavour, the Spirit of Peace or Equilibrium through Him pours His mighty cosmic Law.

Thus the world is changing for the better. Thus the New Time is slowly taking shape. Despite all evidence to the contrary, the New Age struggles to be born.

Quietly, and almost imperceptibly, the broad outlines of the new dispensation are beginning to take hold of men's minds. The needed new relationships are making themselves felt in an ever more urgent way, and men are more ready than ever before to contemplate far-reaching alterations in the pattern of their lives.

To Us, the Watchers behind the scenes, this is an indication that humanity's response to the new and higher energies is sensitive and correct, and augurs well for the future. This is a time of crisis, and in crisis men are often bolder, more creative, in their thinking.

Maitreya is preparing Himself for His imminent appearance before the world. All preliminaries are ready and in place. His army, as He calls it, is assembled and braced for action. Each knows his place and his work.

Never before has a spiritual force of this magnitude been gathered together on Earth.

Never before has an Avatar of Maitreya's stature been present to lead them. Together these Warriors of Light will prove invincible.

March 2002

Humanity's choice

Many are the ways in which humanity is advancing, knowingly or not. From Our viewpoint, these forward steps are clearly to be seen. Notwithstanding the present chaos and crisis, the amelioration of the worst conditions of human life, in many places, goes on apace. It is true that there are areas of the deepest deprivation and neglect; that millions still starve and die without cause or need; that half the world cries out for justice while the others bask in the sunshine of their complacency and ignorance. Nevertheless, real and far-reaching changes are taking place and augur well for the future. This gives Us hope that humanity's response to Maitreya will be eager and swift.

When Maitreya appears before the world He will outline the programme for its renewal. He will show that the present methods of coping with our many problems are deeply flawed, relying as they do on rivalry and self-interest; that the present tensions and dangers are a direct result of the imbalances created by complacency and greed; that by co-operation alone will the problems of the world be solved, the poor and starving fed, the health of the planet secured, war a forgotten nightmare of the past.

The peoples will listen and debate and take their stand: for the creation of a new and better way of living based on accepted brotherhood and sharing, or a descent into further degradation and violence and final self-destruction.

Humanity must make its choice. Men and women everywhere should understand that this is a choice for life, unimaginable in its newness and grandeur, or ignominious death by their own hand. Better by far it is to face boldly the future and build together the new, than to creep, defeated, to the abyss.

How will you choose, then, reader? How will you cast your life? Will you stand with Maitreya and His call for justice and freedom? For a world remade by sharing and love? Will you come to know your divinity and that of your brothers? Your path to the stars a reality before you?

Will this decision, your soul's choice, fill you with gladness? And take you to the Source of Love Itself?

Maitreya knows already those on whom He can depend. He knows that the hearts of men are sound and strong, on them He can rely. He knows that His army is ready for the good fight for the Common Good. That the men and women of Goodwill everywhere are sensing His presence and responding to the world's need.

He has no fear that the men and women of today will miss their destined opportunity to cast their vote and their choice for the General Good. Fearless, they are ready for the future and longing to serve.

April 2002

A time of decision

The world is in a severe state of crisis, engendered, in the main, by the US President's response to the terrorist attack of 11 September last year. The war in Afghanistan and the recent upsurge of Israeli brutality are linked, as is the proposed attack on Iraq. Basic to each is the settlement of old scores. Such behaviour of childhood is an ignoble and irresponsible method of dealing with events which threaten the well-being of the world. The Masters do not advocate appeasement of terrorism, but the manner of response in Afghanistan and the Middle East is not to Our taste. It takes no account of the *causes* of terrorism — the poverty, frustration, humiliation and despair — and merely perpetuates the violence and brutality. Lost in the glamours of self-pity and injured pride, America has lost also wisdom, caution and a sense of proportion.

Israel, meanwhile, stung into action by suicide bombings, as always over-reacts, using as excuse "a war against terrorism" to impose its will. In the shameless persecution and humiliation of Mr Arafat, Israel's leaders and army should take no pride. The people of Israel, more than most, should understand the agony of the oppressed.

When will these men learn that the world belongs to all? They are neither rulers nor policemen whose wealth and might confer control of others. When they share that wealth for the General Good they will see the end of terrorism, and sleep at night more soundly. The men of power, who seek to run the world for the benefit of the few, are drunk on the power which they wield, unearned.

More and more, it becomes evident that a wiser voice is needed in the world, one that will be listened to from many points of view. Such a voice, the voice of Maitreya, will soon be heard above the cries for revenge and hate. Soon, the world will awaken to His presence in our midst and the Great Choice will be offered to men. Thus is this a great testing time for humanity. Thus is this the time of decision, a time without precedent.

When men understand this, they will rally to the banner of Maitreya and make known their demands for justice and freedom. They will show their willingness to share and to serve, and thus remake this world.

Thus will it be, and thus will men renew their ancient pledge, and retrace their footsteps to divinity.

May 2002

A new day

When men take stock of the world situation they see only the difficulties and traumas, the dangers and crises, and, paralysed by fear, do little to overcome the inertia their despair engenders. Thus it is that men miss the progress of their best efforts and seldom understand the sequence of events. They understand little of the laws which underlie all happenings, and cannot, therefore, control their outcome. Were they to live according to these unseen laws, their lives would develop in harmony and order.

Despite such ignorance and fear, men today have reached a point of new sensitivity to the forces which drive them ever forward on their path. They sense, albeit fleetingly, that there is much that they do not understand, much less control, but that slowly they can begin to visualize a greater meaning and purpose, a greater unity and beauty, in and around them.

As We, the Watchers, from Our vantage point, consider man's efforts to control his changing world, We welcome the signs of greater sensitivity to the higher forces impinging on men's lives. We await, gladly, an intensification of this response and a more beneficial use of these forces.

True it is that We see, also, an escalation of hatred and cruelty, brutality and war, but these, the reactions of fear, are nearing their end and will subside.

This, a period of transition, is indeed a difficult time. Many men are reaching for the future, longing for change and fresh answers to the problems. Others hold grimly to the old ways and seek to stem the onslaught of the new. We watch and wait, confident that men will find the way.

Maitreya, the Master of the Masters, is poised to begin His emergence, to work openly before men. This cannot mean that His work behind the scenes will cease entirely. Much that He does even now supports the efforts of some who otherwise would fail. His help and guidance directs the hand of more than one wise leader and protects them from harm.

Those who would assault the world to prove their strength attack Maitreya too. Behind all people of goodwill stand Maitreya and His Group; They form a shield on which all arrows beat in vain. Come quickly to His side when He emerges. Rally to His Banner of Peace, Justice and Freedom and aid Him in His mighty work. A new day in the lives of men is dawning, a day unlike ought known before.

June 2002

Maitreya at the door

Under the impact of the new incoming energies, great changes are taking place in the world. For some, these changes are benevolent and useful, leading to a better-ordered and safer world. To others, however, they signify only breakdown and disorder, chaos and mayhem, the work of desperate and evil men.

Of course, if your primary objective is the upholding of the 'status quo', all change, however needed and overdue, is suspect and undesirable, the work of 'militants' and 'mischief makers'.

Thus it is that much of the many changes now occurring is seen as threatening the fabric of society and is a source of constant worry, fret and fear.

Did men but see the true nature of the transformation now being wrought by these beneficent energies, they would more calmly understand, and co-operate with, their action.

Needless to say, the 'status quo' can never be upheld for long; change and evolution are the very nature of life, and, for good or ill, impose the pattern of the new. The form and quality of the new structure are conditioned by men themselves. Thus useless it is to resist the Great Magnet that drives all life forward on its perfecting course.

When Maitreya and His Group walk freely among men, much will be revealed of the laws which govern life. Men's bafflement will give way to a dawning understanding and a wiser response to the phenomenon of change. The old diehards, of course, will remain, but their influence will ebb as the new takes hold. Thus will it be, and thus will men realize better the nature of the adventure we call life.

Maitreya, Himself, stands at the door, His hand uplifted to knock. His signs increase apace as He awaits recognition. Welcome Him to your heart and ease His entry; let Him work through you. Remember that your brothers, also, deserve to know the Great News; leave them, and your sisters, not in the dark.

We have reached the eleventh hour. The destined time is upon us. The long wait is all but over. Harness now your strength for the great work ahead. The times are as never before. The angelic myriads tremble in expectation. Maitreya's warriors for Truth tighten Their girths and assemble behind Him.

In the midst of chaos and war, and threat of war, the Great Lord lifts His hand. His arrows of Light will pierce the darkness of the time and bring respite to men. His Great Heart glows with love for all peoples. The starving and the oppressed are His especial care. Aid Him in His momentous task.

July/August 2002

Maitreya hastens to emerge

Many today would be amazed by the prospect which We, your Elder Brothers, see for man. Despite the hazards and tensions, the crises and alarms, We know that men will rise above them and create the New Time. We know that the time of testing is all but over, that a watershed has been surmounted, and that man stands at the threshold of discoveries beyond his imagining.

We see, indeed, the problems which men face. We know the apprehension which kills the joy in many human hearts. We share the pain and agony of countless millions living and dying in despair.

We know that despite the dangers and injustice, the spirit of hope is ever ready to rise and inspire the loftiest deeds, for it is the divine in man and is unquenchable.

"The deepest dark is just before the dawn" goes the old adage, and thus it is today for men. Amid the chaos and fear, the perplexity and pain, We see the resolution and the end of conflict, the glow of the light which will awaken men to the promise of the future.

All works under Law and a new state of equilibrium is being created by Us. Appearances notwithstanding, a new rhythm asserts itself and will bring into balance this discordant world.

Maitreya Himself wields this mighty Law and brings its cosmic origin to the affairs of men. Thus will new hope arise in men and thus will they take the steps to reshape their future in accordance with the Plan.

Maitreya's foot is at the threshold. His hand prepares to knock. Listen carefully that you miss Him not. He comes to fulfil the Law; to serve the Plan; to teach mankind; to lead His Brothers into Their destined future. He comes to see enacted His promise to men made long ago: to redeem them by His love and awaken them to their divinity.

When you see Maitreya do not be confused by His initial reticence; He must earn the trust of those whom He would aid. In due course, He will speak as speak He must to awaken the conscience of men. Then will He inspire the action to remove the barriers now separating men so condemning millions to starve and die in misery. Thus will it be, and thus will men awaken at last to the plight of their brothers and sisters who, too, have called Maitreya to their side. Maitreya hastens to emerge.

September 2002

The family

The family unit is the basis of all social life. Its importance cannot be over-emphasized. Today, this pre-eminence is being eroded by neglect, experiment and a misunderstanding of the essential needs of children.

All children need a stable background in which to grow and the exemplars of that process, a mother and father. That not all parents provide that stability or offer worthy examples is, sadly, all too true, and many factors are involved in this unfortunate condition: lack of education, poverty, inadequate housing, illness, and irresponsible and feckless adults, immature and unfit for the rigours of family life.

Let it also be said that millions in every country, poverty-stricken and deprived of every amenity, strive valiantly, and mostly succeed against all the odds, to hold their families together and provide a stable and loving example to their young. They are the unsung heroes of the race who, through tenacity of purpose and endless self-sacrifice, represent the best that humanity can show.

The new education must address this fundamental problem and institute the training and requirements for family life. It is odd, is it not, that this most basic aspect of social life should receive such scant attention, and be left to the vagaries of chance to such a large extent?

In most countries, the right to drive a car is regulated and controlled by age and tests, more or less severe. Doctors and nurses, pilots and drivers of trains, all of them, may carry out their useful service only after due training and careful preparation. And rightly so. Yet millions of young people are allowed to enter this field of service — the most difficult in the world — for the most part devoid of training of any kind. The simple biological urge to reproduce, and the domination of the woman's 'time-clock', are considered sufficient to grant the right to multiply and add to a congested world.

The young couples commence the subtle and difficult art of upbringing and nourishing of souls in incarnation with little more than their conditioning to guide them. That conditioning they duly pass to their children and so the follies and ignorance perpetuate. Thus the need for the light of a new approach to this sacred service.

Today, there is an added and growing twist to the problem. Mounting sexual experimentation in the field of family life is leading to a distortion and misunderstanding of the true nature of the parent-child relation. The child is a soul in a family of souls. This provides the family unit with the opportunities for resolving karma developed over many incarnations together, in varying relationships.

Hierarchy is not the enemy of homosexuals, but the growing demand of homosexual men and women for the right to raise children is mistaken and unhelpful to the child.

All people, of whatever sexual persuasion, should think deeply about the nature and purpose of incarnation: the nurturing of souls who need a mother and a father to provide the examples, guidance and karmic opportunity to grow and evolve according to the Plan. If, for whatever reason, people feel inadequate to the task, a wise self-sacrifice for this life may be the wisest course.

October 2002

The glamour of power

At the beginning of every year, mankind, almost universally, celebrates the opportunity to begin afresh and to make resolutions towards betterment of one kind or another. As this year of tension and crisis draws to a close, men may look for new and more constructive policies and actions which will change the lives of all for the better.

This period of crisis is soon ending, to be followed by one of experiment in every branch of human life. Vast new vistas await man's exploration as he grapples with and solves the problems which beset the world today.

The minds of most are focused on the political crisis which threatens to destabilize the world. This is natural and inevitable. The hysteria engendered in the United States by the events of 11 September 2001 has swept across much of the world. The fighting talk and tone of the American President has fanned the flames of fear, making it all but impossible to take a balanced view. That such a balanced view is to be desired is obvious if correct assessments and responses are to be made. Speculation and rumour hold sway in the present situation and drain the vitality of the watching world.

The first priority is true knowledge of the facts. This, however, is hard to find. So many voices chant or scream their various conflicting information, so many opinions are elevated to the status of facts, that few can be believed or listened to with respect. Under such conditions caution and restraint are wisely counselled.

Comprehensive actions are under way and planned, and few can see whereto they lead. Our view is that they will be both positive and negative in effect: the destruction of a bleak and punitive tyranny at the cost of many innocent lives, and the further destabilization of an area already in crisis.

There are voices in America and elsewhere which call for caution but, it would seem, they are not strong enough to stem the passion of the group of zealots around the President. They are lost in the glamour of power and will take much to bring to reason. The oil-rich sands of Iraq are too tempting a target for their unconstrained greed and urge to dominate.

Nevertheless, those who oppose the launching of a dangerous war on Iraq must continue to make their opposition known. They must strengthen their will to march and demonstrate, to make their voices heard. These reckless men must realize that the world does not belong to them; that if they rule they must do so within the law; that many past and greater empires have fallen from the same cause.

This indifference to world opinion can be maintained for a time only. World events, events of a different nature, are moving now so fast that they will outstrip these men of the past, locked in the outworn methods of the past, and consign them, silently, to that vanishing yesterday.

Maitreya, the Great Lord, is emerging and will show the way. Be not discouraged for all will be well.

November 2002

The destined path

It is becoming increasingly clear that man is ready for a great leap forward. Despite the many tensions and dangers which still exist, and which to many seem increasing, the human kingdom is moving forward and upwards in line with the Plan which guides the actions of us all. The Cosmic Magnet draws everything towards a planned destination; the energies of the magnet wax in power and cannot be withstood. Man must learn and understand the power and benefice of Cosmos. Thus will he grow correctly with the minimum of suffering.

The Light of Cosmos shines on man as never before, inspiring him to simplify his life and so regain the connection with the Source which, sadly, he has lost.

Were men to heed these words, they would soon enter into a state of Being altogether new in their long journey to perfection.

Time, for the old ways, is fast running out. The old thinking and acting, which cause men so much distress, is nearing its end. A new Light sheds its beauty over humanity and brings to a conclusion the aberrations of the past.

Thus do We see the future for man as one bathed in the light of the new understanding. Thus do We rejoice at the nearness of the time.

Man's long struggle to build the structures which will serve his rightful purposes is almost over. The required forms are already dimly sensed and soon will break upon his understanding as revelation.

From that moment alone, his progress will astonish all but the watching Brothers. We have for long worked towards this end and wait patiently for its enactment. We know that men's hearts are ready to give form to their loftiest aspirations, to enter willingly into a future as yet unknown, to rectify the mistakes of the past and to begin again on the long ladder of ascent. We know this to be so and have confidence in man's capacity to change when needs he must.

This is such a time. Conditions on Earth are deteriorating rapidly: the divisions which have dogged men for centuries raise, as ever, their perennial problems. The planet groans under the impact of man's wanton destruction. Men await a sign, an assurance of leadership and guidance, and an opportunity to hope.

The signs, for men, are everywhere to be seen. The guidance is assured. The reasons for hope are long and constantly offered.

That men heed them not results from fear. Blind, men are, because they are afraid to see. When, soon, Maitreya steps into the centre of man's affairs, making known the reasons for, and the solutions to, man's problems, they will see that the leadership they yearn for has long been theirs to enjoy, that the time has come to abandon the destructive ways of the past, and that all unknown, they have within themselves the hope and capacity which will remake this world and set it, once again, balanced and safe, bravely on its destined path.

December 2002

A saner view of life

At first sight, it would appear that the world is now in deeper crisis than ever before. War and terrorism have quickened the pace of events and filled the hearts of millions with fear. Were this the true reading of the present situation there would indeed be cause for fear and lamentation. Happily, this view is superficial and hides the many changes for the better which, quietly, with little attention, are likewise taking place. War and terror are sensational and make potent news. Far-reaching actions which enhance the lives of millions seldom make headlines, and are lost amid the tumult of imperious governments and uneasy dictators.

The world is deeply indebted to the many United Nations agencies whose careful, selfless work goes steadily on amid the rhetoric and bravado of the power-drunk politicians. The time is fast coming when men will realize that the needs of the world are the needs of men and women everywhere: for food and work, for health-care and education. These are the priorities which should guide men's actions and engage their energy and resource. These are the perennial needs of all; humanity neglects them at its peril.

Specialist non-governmental groups likewise add their insights and researches, awakening men to the dangers in the headlong rush to further abuse this already ailing planet.

Many see who erstwhile did not. Many walk who formerly sat and watched their brothers run and play. For the first time in their lives, the world is full of hope for many who suffered in silence.

To these quiet and patient ones, life is opening its windows, letting in the sunshine and fresh air. Through the work of the many agencies new, invigorating energy now flows, and the people respond and rejoice. These, the servers, are the true heroes of this time. Not those who drop the bombs from the high clouds but those who sense the needs of their brothers and sisters, and act, no matter the cost.

When Maitreya makes His appearance, openly, to all, He will inspire the creation of a saner attitude to life grounded in serving the needs of men and women everywhere. He will show that the conflicts of the present are not inevitable. That leaders of nations have a responsibility to humanity at large, and not alone to their subjective feelings or ideology. He will call for caution and wisdom with regard to today's weapons of terrible power, and warn of the fruitlessness of war 'for the sake of peace'.

Peace, He will show, is not difficult to find if honestly sought. Peace, He will say, will be achieved only with justice and freedom for all. Thus will Maitreya set the target for change. Thus will men be inspired to take the simple step into the unknown and to see the fulfilment of the dreams and longings for peace which men have for long held in their hearts.

January/February 2003

The rise of people power

When all is said and done, there is but one way to describe the present international situation: chaotic. Power-hungry warmongers, reluctant 'agnostics' and self-appointed heroes, eager to save the world, struggle to win the support of the people for their various points of view. The voice of the people struggles to be heard amid the tumult but, more and more, is a factor to be reckoned with.

In many countries, vast throngs demonstrate their opposition to a forced and unfair confrontation, and express their fears of a terrible aftermath.

Throughout history, similar situations have arisen again and again, but only very seldom has the will of the people, even when directly involved, been an important factor in the deliberations and decisions made. In recent centuries, only in the great transforming actions of revolution has the people's voice been central to the action, and made its mark on the time.

Today, once again, the moment has come for the people's voice to be heard. Today, once more, it is essential that the needs of people everywhere for justice, freedom and peace are heard and recognized by the wielders of reckless power.

These dangerous men, caught up in the glamour of their power, must realize that the time for war is past, that humanity longs for peace and a security quickly vanishing. The little 'Napoleons' must be told that their days of power are over; that the times have robbed them of all relevance; and that the power now lies with those who serve the true needs of the people.

When Maitreya enters the fray, He may at first go unheeded in the hectic events which daily drain men of serenity and calm. Soon, however, men will find that their thoughts and needs are being heard and given voice by a mind more thoughtful and persuasive than their own. In this way they will feel emboldened and join together the better to be heard.

Maitreya will address their most urgent needs, their deepest hopes and fears. He will speak for all men, for people everywhere, and will thus make known the quality of the new society which inwardly satisfies the dreams and expectations of all.

Soon, indeed, will Maitreya enter, openly, the lives of men. He is well prepared and eager for the challenge which lies before Him, and His courage will strengthen those who can respond. From His great heart will flow the love which it is His nature to bestow, and when men are ready He will declare His name and office. Thus will the Great Lord manifest His close relation to men and women everywhere, and thus, too, will He fulfil the trust which men, for ever, have placed in Him.

March 2003

The ending of bondage

As the simple snowdrop breaks through the snow and heralds the coming spring, so do the people everywhere make known their demands for justice and peace, and an end to a long winter of thraldom and tyranny. The people's voice is rising, imperious to be heard. It is the harbinger of the new time, the new dispensation, struggling to be born. Despite, nay, because of the plans and actions of dangerous men, the people are throwing off their ancient yoke and claiming their right to be heard. A new urgency and a new confidence invests their claim with power. The power of the people's voice breaks through the age-old bondage and points the way to the future. More and more, the people are realizing that the role of government is to dispense the needs of the people, that there is no problem or difficulty in which war is the only solution. The sour voices of power-hungry leaders may, for the moment, seduce the fearful or unwary, but their time is limited, is drawing to a close.

A new time is in the making — of justice, freedom and peace. In this coming time the peoples of all the nations will see fulfilled their dreams and hopes of a better life: of meaning and purpose, of beauty and understanding, of right relationship and love. Each day will bring a new discovery, inner and outer, each hour an opportunity to serve. Thus will it be, and thus will each man, woman and child glorify the divine in all of us, and show in all its variety the many-sided beauty of God.

When Maitreya emerges, He will seek to canalize the aspiration of countless millions who sense these truths but cannot give them voice. In Him will they find a spokesman, eloquent and severe as circumstances require; through Him will they find their needs made known, the needs of all for a just and peaceful world.

This process is already under way. At marches and demonstrations, where the people call for justice, peace and sanity, Maitreya may be found in one or other guise, playing the part of the people and speaking in their name. His energy of love pervades these gatherings of the just and inspires them to further effort. His strength becomes theirs and they feel undaunted and sure. In this way, the Lord of Love is turning the tide of hate, is potentizing the ardour of millions, and is finding that the people everywhere are aware of their destiny and are seeking the means to implement their heart-felt desires.

April 2003

The waiting world

The world is reeling from the impact of the recent invasion of Iraq by American and British forces. Seldom has a war of such seemingly limited scope and duration had such momentous repercussions, or caused so much heartache and heart-searching. Seldom, indeed, has such reckless folly been recognized and denounced by the majority of the peoples of the world.

The tragic events of 11 September 2001 have opened a direful door of opportunity for this US Administration, on the pretext of fighting terrorism, to usurp the 'moral high ground' and carry out cruel acts of piracy on its selected victims.

The war is on, perhaps almost over, but the people of sanity and heart have found their voice and a means of being heard. At last, at long, long last, the people are beginning to sense their power and their right to speak, to influence, and to shape their destiny.

Out of the chaos and misery of this contrived and unnecessary war will come such changes that its perpetrators could never have imagined.

They have overridden the united will of the assembly of nations, mistaking its wisdom for fear, its caution for cowardice. They have used the ways of the past and will find them unavailing in the times which lie ahead. In their arrogance and lust for power they have overreached, and set the peoples of the world against them. Their wicked folly has awakened humanity to rise and defend itself against this usurpation of its rights.

When men come to measure the damage done to international relationships by this foolish, unilateral act, they will find much to cause dismay. Many years of careful nurturing, the slow building of trust, have been set at nought. A deep sense of suspicion, distrust and fear now stalks the diplomatic corridors of the world. Many leaders among the nations sense that one of them — the most powerful — is now out of control, that old accords are broken and that they must look elsewhere to rebuild their past security and alliance. America's pre-emptive stance, its thinly-disguised imperialism, has isolated that great nation from the truth and from the community of nations whose leaders shake, sadly, their heads and ponder gravely on the future.

The world awaits the emergence of the American soul, that which gave birth to the beauty of the Marshall Plan so long ago. The world, too, awaits the emergence of Maitreya to show men the way. The teachings of Maitreya will awaken and invoke the idealistic soul of the United States, and turn its best citizens to the light which they have always held in their hearts. They will make accord with their brothers and sisters throughout the world, and in unison, inspired by Maitreya, they will bring justice, and therefore peace, to the waiting world.

May 2003

The creation of trust

If men would know peace they have the simple duty to establish the way of peace. There is but one way to peace as all men know in their hearts: the creation of justice. When men at last acknowledge the necessity of justice, for themselves and for others, the blessed day of peace will dawn on this earth. The path, too, of justice is not difficult to find; it requires only the acceptance of sharing.

The divine principle of sharing is central to life; it underlies all harmony and balance. Without sharing, each effort to attain equilibrium comes to naught.

For centuries men have known this to be true. These ideas have permeated the great movements which have held aloft for men the concept of Liberty. They are ingrained in the Constitutions of many countries. Why then do men find them so difficult to implement? Why, and for so long, do they suffer their non-realization?

The answers to these questions are manifold but one, above all, is basic and persisting: men live in fear. The fear of change, of loss, of still greater insecurity, fills the minds of countless millions, creating, as a result, the inertia which ties them to the ways of the past. These ways may be onerous and difficult to bear but they are the known ways, the ways of the forefathers. This conditioning saturates and holds sway in the world, manipulated and fed by the actions of greedy and powerful men.

Fear arises where there is a lack of trust; few there are who trust their fellow men. Thus men have for long lost the sense that they are One, brothers and sisters all, engaged in the tasks of life together, sharing these tasks for the Common Good, and sharing, too, the wherewithal for each one's needs.

The rediscovery of this common heritage will galvanize humanity and awaken it to its destiny: the creation of a way of life in which men become co-creators with God.

It is Maitreya's task to remind men of their heroic destiny, and to persuade them that the act of sharing will engender the trust they seek. He will show that sharing is no longer an option, a choice, but the inevitable consequence of their realization that humanity is One.

Thus will Maitreya and His Group guide humanity away from the abyss which, many believe, threatens to engulf it. And thus, too, will He set men firmly on the course to realize their divine destiny.

June 2003

Aiding the cause of peace

It is frequently the case that, in acting for what is seen by them as the good of the world, countries wreak havoc on a world scale. So dense are the fogs of glamour which surround their actions, so illusionary is their thinking, that great harm may be done, and much pain and suffering caused, for the best of reasons.

Thus it is today. In recent times, the USA, under the banner of 'the war against terrorism', has invaded Afghanistan and Iraq, causing thousands of civilian deaths and great physical damage to their infrastructures. The Taliban, fanatical and rigid but, in the main, uninvolved in terrorism, are dispersed but are now regrouping, training in the skills of terror. In Iraq, Saddam Hussein is no more, but a terrible legacy of deprivation and suffering, lawlessness and chaos, has replaced his baleful regime.

Now the attention of the US administration has turned to Syria, Iran and North Korea; they are warned to change or face the wrath and might of the upholders of 'peace', and the champions of 'liberty' in the world.

Thus does America plunge the world into the atmosphere of stress and fear, and thus do these give fruit to epidemics and natural disasters, which, in turn, serve to increase the fear and stress.

What can be done to stabilize this dangerous situation? How can the nations keep America in check? By what means can ordinary people bring their weight to bear? These are large questions and have, indeed, no simple answers. They require wisdom of an exceptional order and a co-ordinated approach.

Firstly, the world must realize the true nature of the problem: the USA today is led by men responsive to a nefarious energy which prompts their actions and puts peace in jeopardy. It

435

stimulates their glamour for power of an international extent, and threatens the peace of the world. It has outposts in Israel and Eastern Europe, Israel being the major focus. This destructive energy derives, though in diminished potency, from that which plunged the world into chaotic war during the twentieth century and which, men thought, was safely put to rest.

It can be seen, therefore, how necessary it is that there be peace in the Middle East; how necessary it is that the Palestinians have true justice and a viable homeland. This is the most important problem facing men today. Failure to solve it would be disastrous for the world.

It will take the combined resources of wisdom and will of both Hierarchy and men to overcome, finally, this malignant force. A clear understanding by men of the true nature of the threat is thus imperative. Men must organize and act in unison. They must call for an end of oppression of the Palestinian people and so end the fear which haunts the people of Israel. The United Nations must bring all possible pressure to bear on both America and Israel, standing up to the superpower and aid the cause of peace. The peoples of the world are already on the march. They must raise their voices and demand that peace be theirs. They are the inheritors of the future and must fashion it in peace.

We, the Masters, your Elder Brothers, will do Our part but We are hampered by your lack of understanding and will. Hence these words.

Act without fear. Be wise and diligent in your actions and all will be well.

July/August 2003

The brightest future

From where, one may ask, is the vision to come which will inspire men to relinquish the ways of the past — war, competition and destruction of the planet — and so lead to the creation of a path to sharing, justice and peace? For how long must men wait for a sign that this is even feasible? Where should men look for a glimmer, even, of hope? Without doubt, there is much happening in the world to strain the credence of all but the most convinced that this much to be desired event is not only possible but assured.

From what basis can such a statement be made? From what superior knowledge does it issue? How in this uncertain world can such confidence be maintained? The answers to these legitimate questions lie in the fact known to all Hierarchy (but not yet to all men) that Their Head and Leader, Maitreya Himself, is, for many years now, present in the everyday world; that many of Their illustrious Brothers, likewise, walk once more with men. This fact alone is quite without precedent. It betokens something wonderful and new for men. For the first time in countless thousands of years these 'men without fault' will teach men how to live, simply and well, in peace and right relationship.

Thus it may be said that the future for man is assured. Men, however, must accept and put in place the mechanism for peace: the recognition that all men are equal and one, each an expression of the divinity which permeates all Being. When this is clearly understood, men will have little difficulty in creating the path to peace. The divine aspects of justice and freedom will gain new meaning and importance, and hasten the day when sharing of resourses assumes its natural, logical place as the answer to man's present dilemma and strife.

Until now, all such ideas and demonstrations of spiritual living were made by men alone. Slow indeed has been the response to their heroic example. Nevertheless, circumstances are now exerting on men unusual and insupportable pressures — men must adapt and change, or perish.

As they search for answers to their problems they will find Maitreya and His Group ready to respond, ready to guide men away from danger and further folly. They have the answers which thus far have eluded men, the answers which alone will assure the future, the brightest possible future, for the race of men.

September 2003

Aquarius, the giver of Unity

Each age confers on humanity a specific quality of achievement. Pisces, the age now at an end, has given to men the divine achievement of Individuality, together with the qualities of Devotion and Idealism. These are mighty advances in the long journey of evolution and have prepared mankind for the blessings of Aquarius.

The new age, Aquarius, has, too, its intrinsic quality — Synthesis — and in this coming time will, indeed, cause this divine attribute to manifest its beneficent Unity throughout the world. This present time of turmoil, division and separation will gradually give way to an era in which the ever-increasing forces of Aquarius will perform their magic, blending and knitting together the disparate, unruly, parts. Thus will men undergo an extraordinary transformation, greater and faster than ever before in their long history.

For this to happen, men must respond correctly to the incoming energies, recreating the world's structures in such a way that they present no barrier to the synthesising forces of Aquarius.

Hierarchy, physically present among men, will lend all Their experience and knowledge to this end. Thus will it be, and thus will men renew their ascent towards their God-given destiny, demonstrating in all its glory their unity with God and with all men.

Soon, Maitreya will emerge, and after Him the vanguard of the Masters. They will advise and guide the direction of the needed changes, adding Their wisdom to the deliberations of men. All that men now hold dear will be held in question; all that has brought the world to its present sorry and dangerous state.

Soon, the weakness of the present structures will begin to show itself to even the most blinkered viewer. The cracks and rifts will become apparent for what they are: the signs of breakdown of an outworn and decaying order ready for renewal. The speed of that renewal lies in the hands of men; they alone must give full welcome to the new, and enter gladly into the tasks of reconstruction.

Guided and helped by Hierarchy, men will soon realize the benefit of change, and trust the wisdom of their Elder Brothers to see them safely through the period of transition.

Thus will it be. And thus will men re-find the divinity now, seemingly, lost. They will put aside, at last, the talent for war and confrontation. Learning to share, they will inaugurate the era of trust. Trusting, they will co-operate in solving the many problems which now face them, and in grateful imitation of the Masters will awaken to the love which has been ever present but unknown.

October 2003

The secret of living

It is little known today that in ancient times, when man was younger and wiser, the word to 'steal' was unknown in any language. The Masters of Wisdom then lived openly among men and encouraged them to live without crime. No door was locked and sharing was the norm. For long ages, in many areas, this blessed state pertained.

How far from that simple splendour has man fallen. How far from his purpose has he strayed. Man today is standing at the crossroads: one path, the path of separation and cleavage, on which man now stands, leads unerringly to perdition. The other beckons man towards the fulfilment of his destiny, the wonder of which today cannot be described, a path on which man will find within himself the means of becoming a God.

To help men choose, to aid their judgement, the Masters are, once again, returning to a world in which They, too, struggled and suffered as do men today, uncertain of the path and the needed action. From Their vast knowledge and experience They will offer Their advice, and guide men safely back from the abyss. Thus will it be, and thus will men begin again the upward climb to the mountain top, sure in the knowledge that their Mentors, their Elder Brothers, will not desert nor mislead them.

When men take the decision to share together the produce of this bountiful world, an extraordinary and mysterious happening will take place: at a stroke, men will realize that the need for war is past, the menace of terrorism will quickly disappear, the trust engendered by sharing will make the problems facing men, environmental and territorial, resolvable in blossoming goodwill.

Through sharing, men will realize that they are brothers, and acting as brothers in close co-operation, will begin the process of transforming this world.

Thus will God's plan for men and planet Earth regain its momentum, and thus will men grow apace in wisdom and love. They will rediscover the secret of living in all its simple grandeur and dignity, respecting each man's right to be and live in harmony. They will come together in veneration of God's plan and purpose, and add their insight and longing for truth to the annals of men.

Maitreya and His group of Masters stand ready to help men in their hour of need. Patiently, They await the moment when They may enter the affairs of men and, with discretion, within the Law, give of Their bounty and aid. That moment is not far off.

November 2003

A time without precedent

Little though it may seem to be the case mankind is moving steadily towards its destiny. Despite the tensions and anxieties of the present situation, We, your Elder Brothers, have full faith that men will awaken to the dangers and take timely action to meet them. That faith stems, in large measure, from knowledge of the fact that men are not alone, but are, indeed, the recipients of care and succour from Us. We see men not as separate but as younger brothers on the path of evolution, facing and resolving, with Our help, the many difficulties and dangers which that path presents to the ignorant and the wise alike.

Men should understand that this is no ordinary or usual time; it is, indeed, a time climactic in scope and character, a time without precedent. For this reason alone, the problems and dangers are magnified and entail the most careful handling by men and Us. Our physical presence among men, albeit in relatively limited numbers as yet, ensures that Our help is forthcoming in larger measure than ever before, and will be equal to the task.

Our confidence is bolstered by the fact that Our Great Leader, Maitreya, Himself, is among men. His resources are vast. Behind the scenes as yet, He works ceaselessly to bring peace and progress to the affairs of men, seeking, within the Law, to disentangle the many warring interests, and so create the conditions on which true peace depends. Justice, alone, will bring the peace which men desire, and only when justice reigns will war become a fading memory. In almost every country is Maitreya to be found, creating a network of helpers in every field. Thus does He stitch together the fabric of the new.

These selected workers know well their task. They will soon emerge and bring new thinking to the world, showing how imperative it is to make justice the primary goal for men. They will show that this alone will end for ever the scourge of war, the pestilence of terror; that only a rational reconstruction of our economic structures will make justice possible and bring mankind together on a basis of trust. Thus will it be, and thus will the wisdom and precepts of Maitreya penetrate and influence the thinking of men.

Many now are responding to this teaching. In every country, groups are forming and demonstrating for a better life for men, calling for an end to war; justice and freedom for all; sharing as the natural and only way to guarantee the future of the race. Have no fear, men are awakening to the call, and will assuredly triumph.

December 2003

TRANSMISSION MEDITATION

As the energies of the incoming age of Aquarius stimulate our hearts and minds, and as we begin to make contact with that higher aspect of ourselves, the Soul, we experience an inner prompting to be of service to others. Inevitably this brings us into contact with people and circumstances where this Soul stimulus can be put to practical use.

Service is most potent when performed in group formation. As this relates to meditation, it is known that far greater energy can be handled by groups than by individuals meditating alone. Thus, Transmission Meditation offers a unique opportunity to serve humanity, working with others, right where you are.

Transmission Meditation is a group service activity which 'steps down' great spiritual energies that continually stream into our planetary sphere. The process makes these energies more useful to humanity, much like electrical transformers step down the power emanating from generators so it can be used in household outlets. These transformed spiritual energies are gradually uplifting all life forms, changing our world for the better.

During Transmission Meditation, humanity's 'elder brothers', known in the East as the Masters of Wisdom, direct energies from the highest spiritual planes through the energy centers (chakras) of the group members. This creates a pool of energy that is more accessible to humanity and other kingdoms in nature. Based upon their greater understanding of our world situation, the Masters then re-direct the transformed energies to wherever they may be most needed at the moment.

Transmission Meditation is a safe, scientific, non-denominational, and extremely potent form of service and personal growth. There is never any fee to participate. It will not interfere with any other spiritual or religious practice. To the contrary, it will enhance your existing meditations and any other service activities in which you may be engaged. Many people find that they can demonstrate love more easily after regular Transmission Meditation. Others report that their minds become more stimulated and creative, or that their will power and overall strength of character improve.

There are hundreds of transmission groups around the world meeting on a regular basis. You may join an existing group in your local area or form your own. To form a group, all you need is the intention and desire to serve. A group may begin with as few as three people. Simply invite a few friends of like interest to meet with you regularly. These can then be encouraged to invite others.

No special expertise in meditation is required in order to transmit energy. All that is needed is the ability to maintain an alignment between the physical brain and the Soul, or Higher Self. The Masters do the rest. *Simplicity is the keynote.*

Share International is happy to provide you with a list of groups in your area or the names of other individuals who have expressed an interest in joining a group. If there is no local group, we encourage you to start one. It is very simple, requiring a minimum of time and preparation.

For more information or to request a referral, write to one of the three Share International offices listed at the end of this book or visit our website:

Share-International.org/transmission

FURTHER READING

(Books listed in order of publication.)

The Reappearance of the Christ and the Masters of Wisdom
by Benjamin Creme

In his first book, Benjamin Creme makes the startling announcement that Maitreya (the Christ), as World Teacher for the coming age, is already among us — gradually emerging into full public recognition. Expected by various religions under different names, He is here to promote co-operation among the many ideological factions, galvanize world goodwill and sharing, and inspire sweeping political, social, economic and environmental reforms. Creme puts the most profound event of the last 2,000 years into its correct historical and esoteric context and describes what effect the World Teacher's presence will have on both the world's institutions and the average person. Through his telepathic contact with a Master of Wisdom, Creme offers insights on such subjects as the soul and reincarnation, telepathy, nuclear energy, ancient civilizations, problems of the developing world, a new economic order, the anti-Christ and the 'last judgement'.

ISBN 0-936604-00-X, 254 pages

Messages from Maitreya the Christ

In preparation for His emergence into the modern world, Maitreya — the Christ and World Teacher for the age of Aquarius — gave 140 messages through British artist and esotericist Benjamin Creme. They were communicated telepathically during Creme's public lectures in London, beginning on 6 September 1977. Through these messages, Maitreya releases fragments of His teaching, to prepare the climate of hope which will allow Him and His group — the Masters of Wisdom — to step forward without infringing human free will. He suggests the lines that social change must take and urges us to work urgently for the rescue of millions suffering from poverty and starvation in a world of plenty. He describes His mission and relationship to us, giving hints on how we will recognise Him. He reveals our true nature as spiritual beings, destined to return to that high Source. He assures us that Sharing and Justice, Brotherhood and Freedom *will prevail*.

2nd Edition. ISBN 90-71484-22-X, 286 pages

Transmission: A Meditation for the New Age
by Benjamin Creme

Help the world... and yourself! Benjamin Creme explains that the next step in today's 'spiritual revolution' is putting the gains of personal development to work for the world. Transmission Meditation is a group service activity which 'steps down' the great spiritual energies that continually stream into our planet, focused by the Masters of Wisdom — our 'Elder Brothers'. This process, which makes the energies more useful to humanity, is like that of electrical transformers that step down the power between generators and ordinary outlets. These transformed spiritual energies are gradually uplifting *all life forms* and changing our world for the better. A perfect vehicle for the aspirations of very busy people, the meditation is safe, highly scientific, non-denominational, free of any charge, and unbelievably potent. Creme answers hundreds of questions about this unique form of service which also leads to accelerated spiritual growth.

4th Edition. ISBN 90-71484-17-3, 204 pages

Maitreya's Mission, Volume One by Benjamin Creme

Creme continues the extraordinary story he began in *The Reappearance of the Christ and the Masters of Wisdom*. He recounts further events in a story beyond comparison — the return to our world of the Christ, known as Maitreya, and His group of Spiritual Masters. As human consciousness steadily matures, many of the ancient 'mysteries' of the evolutionary journey are now being revealed. This volume can be seen as a guidebook for humanity as it takes its first steps into the spiritual life. Its canvas is vast: from the new teachings of the Christ to meditation and karma; from life after death and reincarnation to healing and social transformation; from initiation and the role of service to the Seven Rays; from Leonardo da Vinci and Mozart to Sathya Sai Baba. It sets the scene and prepares the way for the work of Maitreya, as World Teacher, and the creation of a new and better life for all. It is a powerful message of hope.

ISBN 90-71484-08-4, 419 pages

Maitreya's Mission, Volume Two by Benjamin Creme

This inspiring and heart-warming book offers new hope and guidance to a suffering world on the threshold of a golden age. It presents the teachings of Maitreya — the Christ and World Teacher for this age — on both outer (worldly) and inner (spiritual) levels, His uniquely accurate forecasts of world events, and His miraculous appearances to people throughout the world. It also contains a series of interviews with the Master of Wisdom whom author Benjamin Creme has been associated with for more than 40 years. These interviews throw new light on some of the greatest problems facing humanity. More insightful information is offered on such diverse topics as the growth of consciousness, psychology, nuclear weapons, the environment, AIDS, the stock market, and science and technology in the New Age. Transcripts of Creme's lectures on 'The Overcoming of Fear' and 'The Call to Service' offer valuable guidance for those who tread the spiritual path.

ISBN 90-71484-11-4, 753 pages

The Ageless Wisdom Teaching by Benjamin Creme

In every age, or in times of exceptional crisis, great spiritual teachers have come into the world to enable humanity to take its next evolutionary step. Each has given a body of teaching, emanating from a common wellspring of ancient knowledge known as the Ageless Wisdom. As an esoteric *science* — meaning simply that it lies beyond the understanding or comprehension of the average person — it presents a systematic and comprehensive account of the evolutionary process, in man and nature, from an energetic standpoint: how the universe came to exist, how it operates, and humanity's place within it. Esotericism, as it is sometimes called, is also the *art* of working with those energies, which emanate from the highest spiritual sources. From behind the scenes, these teachings have guided and shaped civilization after civilization, leading to all the great advances in human endeavour, be they in the sciences, politics, the arts or religion.

ISBN 90-71484-13-0, 62 pages

Maitreya's Mission, Volume Three by Benjamin Creme

Benjamin Creme is one of today's most powerful voices challenging the millennial 'prophets of doom' with his compelling and detailed vision of the future — what he calls a "brilliant new civilization in the making". This sweeping transformation is now possible, Creme says, because a group of fully enlightened teachers known as the Masters of Wisdom are returning to public roles in the world and offering their counsel. At their head is Maitreya, the World Teacher for this Age. In this volume Creme covers topics both profound and practical, ranging from mankind's origin to the principle of sharing as the first step toward global peace; from meditation and service to the technology of light; from reincarnation and karma to a pollution-free environment. A section on miracles explains the source and purpose of weeping Madonnas, crosses of light, healing waters, 'milk-drinking' statues, crop circles and more.

ISBN 90-71484-15-7, 704 pages

The Great Approach by Benjamin Creme

"This information is about the total transformation of every aspect of our lives ..." begins Creme's ninth book. In this volume he addresses the problems of our chaotic world and its gradual change under the influence of a group of perfected men, the Masters of Wisdom, who are returning openly to the world for the first time in 98,000 years. With their leader, Maitreya, the World Teacher, they will guide humanity out of the present morass, and inspire the building of an entirely new kind of civilization where justice and freedom are the norm. In a most original way the book moves from idealism to the practical means of bringing the new structures into being. It throws a searchlight on the future, predicting our highest achievements and revealing some of the amazing scientific discoveries which lie ahead. It shows us a world in which war is a thing of the past, and the needs of all are met.

ISBN 90-71484-23-8, 320 pages

The Art of Co-operation by Benjamin Creme

Why is the world perpetually in crisis, on the brink of self-destruction? Essentially, it is because we do not yet realize that we are one global family sharing a common planetary home. Upon that recognition, and the new approach to living it will engender, rests the destiny of the world. Benjamin Creme examines a world locked in ancient *competition*, trying to solve increasingly dangerous problems with ineffective, outworn methods, while the answer — *co-operation* — is perennially ignored. Part One discusses these opposing ways of approaching life and their impact on society. Part Two tackles the ever-present problem of illusion — the 'fog' that hides reality, causing endless pain and suffering in the world. Part Three presents the idea of unity as the fundamental state that all of us, knowingly or not, are seeking. Ancient wisdom and practical solutions are skillfully interwoven with the help of Creme's spiritual teacher — a Master of Wisdom.

ISBN 90-71484-26-2, 235 pages